"We Are Who We Say We Are"

"We Are Who We Say We Are"

....

A Black Family's Search for Home Across the Atlantic World

MARY FRANCES BERRY

New York   Oxford

OXFORD UNIVERSITY PRESS

Oxford University Press is a department of the University of Oxford.
It furthers the University's objective of excellence in research,
scholarship, and education by publishing worldwide.

Oxford   New York
Auckland   Cape Town   Dar es Salaam   Hong Kong   Karachi
Kuala Lumpur   Madrid   Melbourne   Mexico City   Nairobi
New Delhi   Shanghai   Taipei   Toronto

With offices in
Argentina   Austria   Brazil   Chile   Czech Republic   France   Greece
Guatemala   Hungary   Italy   Japan   Poland   Portugal   Singapore
South Korea   Switzerland   Thailand   Turkey   Ukraine   Vietnam

For titles covered by Section 112 of the US Higher Education
Opportunity Act, please visit www.oup.com/us/he for the
latest information about pricing and alternate formats.

Published by Oxford University Press
198 Madison Avenue, New York, New York 10016
http://www.oup.com

Oxford is a registered trademark of Oxford University Press

Library of Congress Cataloging-in-Publication Data
Berry, Mary Frances.
   "We are who we say we are" : a Black family's search for home across
the Atlantic world / Mary Frances Berry.
      pages cm
      Summary: "Supplement text for courses in African-American History and History
of Immigration. The Afro-Creole story offers a unique historical lens through which to
understand the issues of migration, immigration, passing, identity and color - forces
that still shape American society today"--Provided by publisher.
      Includes bibliographical references and index.
      ISBN 978-0-19-997833-5 (paperback : acid-free paper)   1. Snaer, Louis Antoine,
1842-1917--Family.   2. African American families--Biography.   3. Free African Americans--
Biography.   4. Creoles--America--Biography.   5. African Americans--Genealogy.   6. African
Americans--Race identity.   7. Blacks--America--Migrations--History.   8. Passing (Identity)--
America--History.   9. New Orleans (La.)--Biography.   10. California--Biography.   I. Title.
      E185.96.B47 2015
      973'.0496073--dc23
                                                                                        2014029007

Printing number: 9 8 7 6 5 4 3 2 1

Printed in the United States of America
on acid-free paper

To Elsie M. Lewis:
Mentor and friend

CONTENTS

....

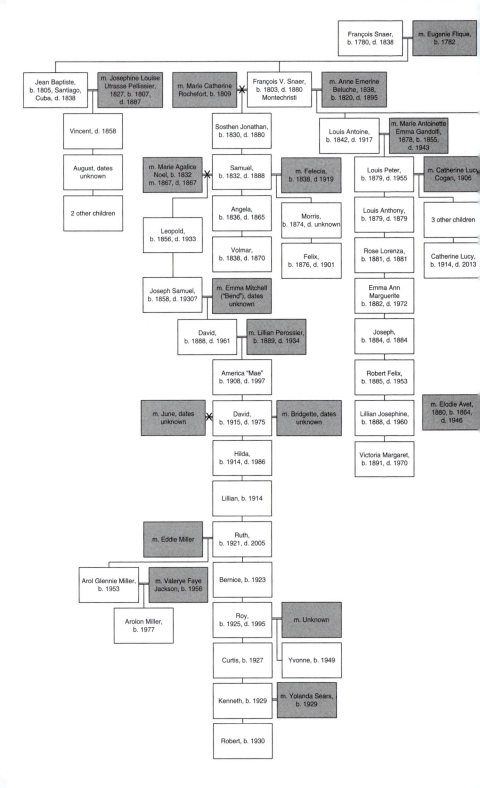

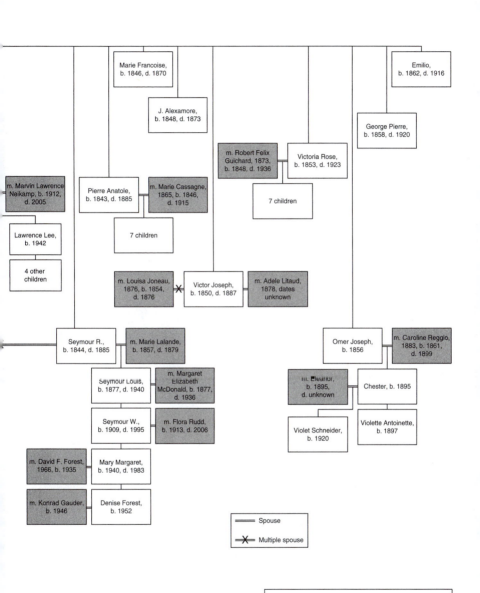

SNAER FAMILY TREE

Marie Francoise, b. 1846, d. 1870

J. Alexamore, b. 1848, d. 1873

Emilio, b. 1862, d. 1916

George Pierre, b. 1858, d. 1920

m. Robert Felix Guichard, 1873, b. 1848, d. 1936

Victoria Rose, b. 1853, d. 1923

7 children

m. Marvin Lawrence Neikamp, b. 1912, d. 2005

Pierre Anatole, b. 1843, d. 1885

m. Marie Cassagne, 1865, b. 1846, d. 1915

Lawrence Lee, b. 1942

7 children

4 other children

m. Louisa Joneau, 1876, b. 1854, d. 1876

Victor Joseph, b. 1850, d. 1887

m. Adele Litaud, 1878, dates unknown

Seymour R., b. 1844, d. 1885

m. Marie Lalande, b. 1857, d. 1879

Omer Joseph, b. 1856

m. Caroline Reggio, 1883, b. 1861, d. 1899

Seymour Louis, b. 1877, d. 1940

m. Margaret Elizabeth McDonald, b. 1877, d. 1936

m. Eleanor, b. 1895, d. unknown

Chester, b. 1895

Seymour W., b. 1909, d. 1995

m. Flora Rudd, b. 1913, d. 2006

Violet Schneider, b. 1920

Violette Antoinette, b. 1897

m. David F. Forest, 1966, b. 1935

Mary Margaret, b. 1940, d. 1983

m. Konrad Gauder, b. 1946

Denise Forest, b. 1952

===== Spouse

=X= Multiple spouse

PREFACE

Years ago, I was researching a history of the "Negro" regiments known as the Native Guards, men who served in the Union Army during the Civil War. Among their members, I discovered a young free man of color, Louis Antoine Snaer, a Union officer who served valiantly throughout the war. Snaer was one of many New Orleans free men of color who joined the army, but the only one to remain an officer after the Union capture of Port Hudson in 1863. The other free men of color were ejected when Union commanders decided African Americans were unfit for leadership and could not expect white officers to respect them. But Snaer remained in the service, became a Union military hero who led troops in battle, and retired as a decorated officer.

I began to research his life, eventually getting in touch with his great-great-grandson Larry Niekamp, who lives in California. We shared what we knew. His mother had commissioned a search for her roots, but did not acknowledge that people designated as colored or mulatto in occasional Census listings were her ancestors; perhaps she concluded, they were slaves of their white family. I went on to other projects, but Larry continued to research his family and created a website about Louis Antoine's military career. Now Snaer is mentioned occasionally in websites devoted to black military history but remains mostly ignored in histories of African Americans in the Civil War and histories of New Orleans and Louisiana.

When I returned to the subject of Louis Antoine, I became even more puzzled. He moved his family to northern California after 1896 when the U.S. Supreme Court endorsed segregation in the *Plessy v. Ferguson* decision. They left behind their identities and their histories as Colored Creoles, as members of a community deeply embedded in the social, cultural, and economic life of New Orleans. I asked myself: How did he first straddle and then cross the color line, leaving his heritage, his community, and a part of himself and his family behind?

When the California grandchildren of Louis Antoine Snaer asked him about their roots, he told them, "We're just Americans." Of course, the story was not that simple: Snaer was a Colored Creole hiding his identity. Like many Americans he was an amalgam of forbears whose lives took them across the Atlantic world. Snaer's family could be traced to a European immigrant who traveled to Saint Domingue in the eighteenth century, where he married a woman with African and white ancestry before the Haitian Revolution, to Cuba, and then to New Orleans.

I began to understand that the whole Snaer family needed exploring. Some did not tell their children they were "just Americans" but stayed "colored." A few were like NAACP leader Walter White, who used his absence of skin color to spy on white supremacists in the early twentieth century. The Snaers' story is first of all an important American story. Some Snaers held slaves while embracing an equality-of-human-rights ideology; others fought for abolition. Some supported the Confederacy; others fought for the Union, like Louis Antoine. One was a successful lawyer who faced down a mob intent on lynching the murderer of his brother, and another was one of the first African American classical musicians. Some held political office during Reconstruction, elected by votes from newly enfranchised freedmen. Some served in the military during the world wars, insisting on being classified as "Negro" although they appeared white, while others enrolled as white. Some stayed in New Orleans; others left. Some returned, coming home to struggle against racial repression. Some participated in the post-1945 civil rights revolution. They reflect a range of the experiences of African Americans in the United States.

This book is about the history of citizenship, identity, and economic opportunities across the Atlantic world, using the angle of vision provided by the Snaers' history. It is also about racial passing. Those Snaers who passed were not "tragic mulattoes," longing for their blackness. Having abandoned the contradictions and exclusions of Colored Creole identity, they did not believe the tragedies they experienced were tied to their racial heritage. Some did not even know of their colored ancestry.[1]

Some Snaer descendants lived as blacks, some as whites, some as both, and some as neither. Some became "Filipinos" or "Pacific Islanders" along the way; some became white Mississippians. Most of the women were housewives, but a few worked outside the home. Among the women, one white Snaer was a secretary, another a landscape architect; a colored Snaer became a business manager. Those who lived white masked their real and marginalized selves, to be sure, but their descendants did not live their lives. They may have lost their boundaries, but in fact they created new ones.

Racial passing is not just a matter of pretending to not be of African descent. It requires a complex self-invention. Some Snaers covered, moving in and out of racial categories, discontinuously passing, from a needed job to home to school to a social club to segregated public places. Others had to pretend continuously every day and hour all in the same day, as did Louis Antoine while he was an officer in the Union Army. Successful racial passing meant not just possessing the correct skin color, but also the language, body grammar, and demeanor. The Snaers' migratory patterns made their passing easier in an age before massive government documentation and the Internet. When the adults spoke Creole French to each other or they cooked a mess of shellfish flavored with Creole spices, such idiosyncrasies were simply considered markers of their Louisiana heritage, rather than as, perhaps, part of a "racial" culture.[2]

The story of the Snaers and the Colored Creoles of New Orleans is also about identity and agency. This is true about those who passed and those who stayed "colored." Men and women are to be sure culturally constructed. However, they have different degrees of agency, the power to alter the times. Through their own self-determination, the Snaers tried to remain what they thought they were and not what whites permitted them to be. This was true whether they went north and west and passed or at home in New Orleans.

The Snaers' story tells us how we are defined in the reality of daily existence. The state enforces the definitions of place through legislation and court decisions and selective enforcement; social and economic interactions reinforce them. The story of Colored Creoles like the Snaers is a complicated one, as is the entire script of race and hierarchy in America. It is about the exercise of self-determination contained by law and social reality.

The children and grandchildren of the Snaers and other Colored Creoles who passed are examples of race detached from biological essence. Their fathers and mothers took advantage of their lack of color to benefit from the privileges accorded to whites. They became creatures of mobility and subversion. As such, acknowledging African blood became a social and political obligation. But when they did pass, that act became an undetected crime. They were outlaws, border crossers. If New Orleans is regarded as a colony, as Saint Domingue once removed, the Snaers were the triangular trade; Colored Creoles experienced colonialism and racial subordination from both sides of a crumbling divide. In both places subordination was contested and unstable and the racial hierarchy was upended by violence.[3]

This book is also about New Orleans and the Snaers' experiences living among Colored Creoles, slaves, slave descendants, and other African Americans there. Virginia Dominguez describes how "Two types of Louisianans consequently identify themselves today as Creole. One is socially and legally white; the other, socially and legally colored. The white side by definition cannot accept the existence of colored Creoles; the colored side, by definition, cannot accept the white conception of Creole." The irony, of course, is that both are mixed-race people divided by a nebulous, arbitrary color line.[4]

African American descendants of slaves also insisted on identity differences. Oretha Castle, a student civil rights leader in New Orleans, described the difficulties in consolidating a movement in 1964: "We're split in so many different ways, we don't just have Negroes. We have our Catholic Negroes and our Protestant Negroes, our downtown Negroes and our uptown Negroes, our light Negroes and our dark Negroes. And we have too many Negroes who don't think they're

Negroes." The Snaers lived these differences, which receded somewhat during Reconstruction after the Civil War but had always been
a barrier to collective action. In September 1963, when Castle Haley
and the other protest leaders arrived at the largest march and de-
monstration in New Orleans, it marked the eroding of the differences among "Negroes." Ernest "Dutch" Morial, the most eminent
young Colored Creole lawyer in town, marched alongside her. He
told his fellow Creoles to forget the divisions and join the movement
because they were all "black" now. Some of the Snaer descendants
who, like Morial, could have passed but did not became civil rights
protestors.

The historical divisions among people of African descent in New
Orleans are perhaps more complicated than the experiences of those
African Americans elsewhere. However, the coming together of the
community to demand equal citizenship reinforces awareness that all
over the South the civil rights movement was largely made by South-
erners, by local people, and mostly by African Americans. Dutch
Morial and others were Southerners, like Martin Luther King and
Coretta Scott King and others who, even when they left the South for
educational opportunity or military service, returned home. Oretha
Castle's family had migrated to New Orleans from Tennessee. The
New Orleans Snaers were part of the movement.

Their experiences are a different migration story. For generations, the story of African Americans has focused on their migration
out of the South since the end of Reconstruction, in the late 1890s
and the early twentieth century. The migrants, pushed by racial violence and suppression, sought economic opportunity and less racial
segregation in the North and the West. Some came home to visit, or
sent money home, or sent their children to the South for the summer,
but African American migration changed the North and America.
When those who led the civil rights movements of the 1950s and
1960s were growing up, this was the African American story. It is a
true story but largely remains the only story.[5]

But the standard migration story overlooks the importance of
those African Americans and their children who stayed at home, or
returned after brief sojourns away. While they were away, they learned
lessons and gained education and experiences that they employed in

the struggle. They became inside agitators, who were the leaders of the civil rights movement and constituted most of the protesters who were jailed, abused, and killed. Colored Creoles like the Snaers had a history of mobility across the Atlantic world, and some migrated to the North and West, but those who came to rest in New Orleans became inside agitators. In 1982, Colored Creole Dutch Morial, one of those inside agitators, won the mayor's race to become the first African American mayor of the city. Inside agitators made the south into a place that today welcomes back the descendants of those blacks who had left for the north and the west, changing southern politics and society.[6]

In 2003, Arolon Miller, a direct descendant of Samuel Snaer, the African American composer, decided to make a change in the family reunion. On the Internet she found some of the white Snaers her family had not known previously and invited them to come. Larry Niekamp was one of them. The interaction was cordial but problematic; long-ago abandonment and such different life experiences made conversation difficult. The African American Snaers did not blame the white Snaers; they blamed whites generally for foreclosing equal citizenship, thus leading some ancestors to escape by passing. They understood that their family members, whether passing or not, represented the heterogeneous collectivity of people of African descent.

ACKNOWLEDGMENTS

....

This book started many years ago in Elsie M. Lewis's graduate seminar on the Civil War, in which John W. Blassingame was a fellow student. Ten books later, as I finish it, I hope I have remembered those who helped along the way. I would like to thank Arolon Miller, Larry Niekamp, Yvonne Snaer-Smedley, and Denise Snaer-Gauder for sending me information and photographs of their ancestors. I also greatly appreciate discussions with Kenneth and Yolanda Sears Snaer, Arol "Glennie" Miller, and other Snaers over the past few years. Conversations with his son, Marc, and his widow, Sybil, enlarged my understanding of the late New Orleans Mayor Ernest "Dutch" Morial, whom I had the pleasure of knowing. Also thanks to Rachel Emmanuel for information about lawyers in Louisiana, including A. P. Tureaud.

The following people, libraries, and archives provided essential material: Irene Wainwright and Greg Osborne at the Louisiana Division of the New Orleans Public Library; Christopher Harter at the Amistad Research Center at Tulane University; the Office of Archives and Records, Archdiocese of New Orleans; the New Orleans Notarial Archives Division, New Orleans Parish; and, at the National Archives, Sarah Jackson and the staff in Records of the Adjutant's General Office, Civil War, Record Group 94.

John Garrigus helped me to negotiate French digital archives for information on immigration to Saint Domingue. Carroll Smith-Rosenberg was especially helpful on questions of identity and citizenship.

Rebecca Scott, Mary Niall Mitchell, James Hollandsworth, Jack Beerman, Arthé A. Anthony, and Sharlene Sinegal DeCuir graciously exchanged information. Camille Charles and Thadious Davis raised important questions concerning the passing phenomenon. T. J. Davis, Barbara Savage, V. P. Franklin, and Melinda Chateauvert read all or portions of the manuscript at different stages of development and provided insightful commentary, as did Robert Cassanello, Christy Clark-Pujara, Minkah Makalani, A. J. Williams-Myers, Pero G. Dagbovie, John Hartigan, Maida Odom and Rose Brewer.

My editor, Brian Wheel, recognized the importance of this book to the history of the United States. Thanks to Gina Bocchetta and Brianna Provenzano, who kept us on track.

CHAPTER 1

....

Becoming Colored Creole

Stepping ashore in Saint Domingue in the late 1700s, Francois Snaer arrived in the most prosperous of all European colonies in the New World. Located on the western third of the Caribbean island of Hispaniola, the French colony had grown significantly from a coastal stronghold. The creolization of this island represents the complicated legacy of race mixing and colonization: It was Indian, Spanish, French, and finally Haitian. In 1639 a motley French crew of buccaneers took over Tortuga, off the northwest coast, and then moved onto the larger island. Although the French came as interlopers, France recognized and encouraged their presence, appointing a governor for the area in 1641. Recognizing the superb natural harbor on the northwest coast, a government-paid buccaneer, Bertrand d'Ogeron, founded Cap-Français (later called Cap-Haïtien) in 1670, giving the French presence its first big boost. France claimed ownership of the area as war booty while Spain kept control of the eastern two thirds of the island, where Spanish settlers had concentrated since the early 1600s. But France had what it desired: rich coastal plains for sugar production, served by numerous excellent harbors. Cap-Français, where Francois Snaer disembarked, became the hub of a booming plantation, merchant economy.

Over the next hundred years Saint Domingue experienced continuous growth and prosperity. Tobacco, indigo, and cocoa sustained early French settlement, but the shift to coffee, cotton, and sugar created fortunes and immense demands for labor. That labor was performed by enslaved Africans. By 1750, an average of 700 ships a year

1

plied a triangular trade centered in Saint Domingue's Le Cap. The ships imported Africans and exported sugar, coffee, and cotton to Marseilles, France's leading port. It was the second largest slave colony after Brazil in the 1700s. About 800,000 blacks landed in Le Cap. Europeans compared it favorably with the French city of Lyons, calling it "the Paris of the Indies," although neither Paris nor Lyons had slave labor. A French fleet commander, noting its culture and growth, observed that "all go there to know fashions, for its size and commerce."[1]

Le Cap had a dynamic cultural life. Print shops opened and a bookstore with a library opened in 1765 and another in 1775. The city had a museum, botanical gardens, and a number of newspapers. A 1,500-seat playhouse had performances three times a week; seats were reserved for whites, free people of color, and slaves. By 1789, at the beginning of the French Revolution, Le Cap had six theaters and staged the latest plays performed in Paris. The cultural elite formed the Société Royal des Sciences et Arts, which by 1789 had twelve permanent members, forty resident associates, and forty nonresident associates, including Benjamin Franklin.[2]

Le Cap flourished as a commercial center and port serving the surrounding plain even after the founding of the western city of Port-au-Prince, which became the new capital of the colony in 1760. Not only did more slaves arrive at Le Cap, but as the economy grew so too did Saint Domingue's white population, numbering about 30,000 by 1780. Merchants such as Snaer helped to meet the consumption demands of a growing economy.[3]

Not much is certain about the ancestry of Francois Snaer except that he was European and his native language was French. Some of his descendants believe he was of Dutch origin. In fact, many Dutch buccaneers, merchants, artisans, and farmers came to Saint Domingue from the Dutch island of Curaçao, which lay within easy sailing distance of Saint Domingue on the southern Port-au-Prince side. Further, Belgium and the Netherlands were French at various times and the French language was spoken. We do know of his migration to Saint Domingue and the conditions in which he lived before fleeing the Haitian Revolution to Cuba. We know little explicitly about his attitudes toward race and slavery, but he married a mixed-race woman, Eugenie Flique, about whom little is known. Because of the marriage, he was subjected to the political and social strictures imposed on free men of color. Therefore, his border crossing gave him an important sense of the identity of a colored man. The social and political context of his experiences in Saint Domingue influenced his future in Cuba and New Orleans and his ideological preferences.[4]

Médéric-Louis-Elie Moreau de Saint-Méry, who lived in Cap-Français beginning in 1772, provides detailed information concerning Le Cap at the time in his *Description topographique, physique, civile, politique et historique de la partie française de l'isle Saint-Domingue.* However, with a very successful law practice, and as a member of the Superior Council of Saint Domingue, where he became a spokesman for the colony's planter elite, his experiences were probably not the same as Francois Snaer's. Snaer was probably a small merchant of uncertain heritage—French perhaps, Dutch perhaps—but he was certainly not a well-connected Parisian.

We know that Francois was in Saint Domingue during the Haitian Revolution and left with numerous white and mixed-race French refugees for Montecristi, Santo Domingo (later the Dominican Republic), with the declaration of Haitian independence in 1804. During his time in prerevolutionary Saint Domingue, he lived in a multiracial society and eventually became the head of a mixed-race family that splintered but endured for generations.

In Saint Domingue, Francois Snaer found European emigrant men routinely establishing intimate relationships with free and slave women of African descent, resulting in a sizeable mixed-race population of people. Known as free people of color, they would later become identified as Colored Creoles. The Code Noir dating from 1685 permitted interracial marriages in Saint Domingue, unlike the Code Noir of 1724 for Louisiana, which prohibited such marriages. The 1685 Code prohibited concubinage (living together out of wedlock), but such relationships accounted for most of the increase in the mixed-race population. Moreau opined: "This illegitimate commerce [concubinage] which offends the customs and the religious morals, is nevertheless regarded as a necessary evil, in the colonies where white women are in small number, and above all in Saint Domingue, where this disproportion is even more greater."[5] By 1789 slaves and free people of color, both black and of mixed race, outnumbered the white population by a ratio of about 16:1. Moreover, mixed-race free people of color controlled one third of the wealth in the colony.[6] Most of Saint Domingue's free people of color, two thirds of whom were of mixed racial descent, became midsized coffee or indigo planters. Only 15 percent lived in towns, where they made up 11 percent of the urban population. Light color correlated with wealth and legitimacy. Dark-skinned freed women had usually been the nurses or mistresses of their owners.

Moreau, representing the view of elite white males, described the large urban female mixed-race population as exotic and sensual mulatresses. He claimed they were usually the children of slave concubines, or mistresses or prostitutes, and although living in one or two rooms, had fortunes to spend on luxurious living, jewelry, and dress. The most prosperous and glamorous reportedly lived in Cap-Français. These mixed-race women might treat their own slaves harshly, but they were generally on good terms with slave women and prided themselves on their charitable giving to the poor and sick.[7]

Moreau found, consistent with elite assertions about sumptuous displays by women and other second-class citizens, that their "desire for costly attire is so insatiable that one sees plenty of mulatto women in Saint Domingue who could change their clothes completely, day by day, for a year." According to him, they wastefully refused to wear their expensive clothes and jewelry more than a few times. But notary records of legal transactions contradict his observations: They show free women of color buying and selling real estate and slaves for profit and trading luxury goods they bought when they needed capital.[8]

These mixed-race women became part of a sizeable number of Colored Creole families of quite respectable merchants and artisans, with the women owning real estate they inherited from their fathers. Between 1782 and 1784 free people of color appear in 315 contracts and other business-related transactions in the notarial records, and 56 percent were free women of color, a total of 178. Perhaps Eugenie was one of the exotic mulatresses who engaged in extravagant habits or one of these respectable women. Whatever the case, Francois married her and their relationship endured.[9]

Through the African culture of the slaves, the absence of religious constraints, and suspicion of authority, the immigrants and colored population in Saint Domingue created a whole new borderless culture and a Creole language. In fact, several different Creole cultures developed in the south and west among agriculturalists and in Cap-Français.[10]

Successful white planters living in mixed-race families had the luxury of doing mostly as they pleased in rural areas. Most whites, like slaveholders in the United States, were not planters. Like Francois Snaer, they were artisans, shopkeepers, merchants, and teachers, and often had only a few slaves. These whites were committed to slavery and saw free persons of color who engaged in the same enterprises as serious economic and social competitors. They also saw themselves as a group occupying a status between plantation slaves and wealthy white planters and resented the mulattoes who constituted a third estate.[11]

In rural areas, gender and property ownership counted as much as physical appearance in determining race, but race and color mattered more in the more populated areas. Free people of color wore European dress. Well educated in the French manner, they knew French and the Creole language and were more scrupulous Catholics, trying in every way to separate themselves from the status of the slaves.[12]

As the population and economic importance of Saint Domingue developed under the French monarchy, tensions between whites and the free people of color mounted. Anticolonial radicals seeking to end French control of the colony sought ways to create a united front among well-off planters and merchants and the poorer whites, who resented economic competition from free people of color. Despite recognition in the Code Noir of 1685 of their full French citizenship, including the right to own property, French officials responded by hardening racial distinctions, limiting the rights of free people of color.

In the 1770s, during the American Revolution, increasingly free people of color were segregated in churches, theaters, dining establishments, and public conveyances. They also were forbidden from practicing law, medicine, pharmacy, or any learned profession and could not vote or hold public office. In addition, to address the complaints of disaffected whites, a philosophical anti-free people of color discourse emerged. The campaign for white solidarity embraced the use of racial stereotypes, condemning free people of color as weak and immoral. Public discussion in the coffeehouses and elsewhere openly included jokes and rumors focused on the lack of virtue and sexual promiscuity in the colonies. It featured white women producing illegitimate children and white men lusting after colored women.[13]

White colonists and French officials started denouncing mixed-race people as impure and recording their status based on appearance. Colonial notaries began designating individuals as "mulatto" or "person of color" in the official records. Economically successful mixed-race people, formerly known just as "colonists," became "mulattoes." Class no longer insulated free people of color. People became "raced" in that race mattered.[14]

In 1773, French officials ordered mixed-race persons, Colored Creoles, to adopt African names and to eradicate their French or European names. They also required them to affix the African name to all manumission requests. Some simply changed the letters in their European name into something different, saying it was African. "Fabre" became, for example, spelled backwards, "Erbaf."[15]

In 1779, colonial officials ordered free people of color in Cap-Français to carry a certificate from a militia captain to move from parish to parish. Officials also forbade them to wear finery or clothing unbefitting to their inferior status. In 1779, for fear they might join slaves in revolt, the government subjected them to a curfew. By demonizing actions and propaganda, the colonial leadership sought to isolate free people of color and their families from even their white relatives. By 1785 mixed-race families saw that race had replaced economic class as the primary dividing line in society.

Despite the legal strictures in the 1770s and after, European immigrants and free people of color continued to establish relationships. Although most mixed-race relationships did not result in marriage, those between white men and women of color meant a loss of social status and privileges for the husbands. As early as 1733, the governor general of the colony expressed the view that anyone who "would marry a negresse or a mulatto cannot be an officer" or hold any other political post. In 1762, a churchwarden was forced to retire from his post because he married a mixed-race woman. The Minister of Marine forced a captain of a legion to retire when he married a mixed-race woman in 1777.[16]

Given the social and political stigma, there were few such marriages compared to the concubinage that existed. Thus, Francois

Snaer's marriage to Eugenie Flique, a mixed-race free woman of color, subjected him to the restrictions applied to free men of color. Her sister also married a European immigrant, Francois Pascal, who was subject to the same restrictions. Many free people of color, however, continued to thrive economically despite their legal inequality. On the frontier and the southern provinces, with increased fervor they protested the tightening racial restrictions.[17]

Amid this mix of people, Saint Domingue and Le Cap society pulsated with tensions and insecurity. Political contestation thrived in an atmosphere where the Crown permitted a great deal of autonomy, and this led to demands for even more local control. Upheavals began with French parliamentary battles against the absolute monarchical power, dating from the reign of Louis XII in the mid-seventeenth century, that led to the French Revolution. These tumultuous events, including the rise of Napoleon and the end of the Revolution in 1802, had repercussions affecting the opportunities and legal existence of free people of color in Saint Domingue. A heated public debate proceeded in France and in the colony about citizens' rights, identity, and status.[18]

Parallel to the Revolution and political changes in France, a struggle for power between planters; landless white shop owners, artisans, and workers; free persons of color; and slaves took place in the colony from 1791 to 1804. The events resulted from the various interpretations that whites, slaves, and free people of color had of the values of the French Revolution, which each tried to achieve in reality. Matters became even more complex because of shifting alliances among the three groups and the colonial government's efforts to maintain authority.

After the Declaration of the Rights of Man in August 1789, Julien Raimond and Vincent Oge, two wealthy free men of color, led an effort to have the Declaration applied to give political rights to free men of color. Some mulattoes had for years moved to France to get an education or to avoid the color line in the colonies. Oge, Raimond, and other *Colons Americains* succeeded in making the question of equal rights for free people of color into the leading colonial question before the National Assembly in 1790 and 1791. The Society of the Friends of the Blacks, a French offshoot of the British abolitionist movement, established in 1788, encouraged their efforts. The National Assembly passed a new voting provision that did not mention race, but this neutral language gave no explicit endorsement for the claims of the free people of color. The colonial assembly in Saint Domingue, using its discretion, continued to deny them the right to vote.

Oge then mounted an armed rebellion demanding the nonracial basis for free male suffrage, as was seemingly permitted by the National Assembly. He and his fellow insurgents were captured, tortured, and charged with sedition and inciting slaves to rebel, even though ending slavery was not part of his program. Oge was executed in the public square in Cap-Français in February 1791.

Mounting protests in France concerning Oge's rebellion and martyrdom led the National Assembly to pass compromise legislation explicitly giving voting rights to free people of color descended from free parents. Although only about 400 individuals would benefit, whites in Saint Domingue reacted strongly against the whole idea, insisting that other decrees since the Revolution began gave them local autonomy to rule. Whites, regardless of class, opposed more voting rights for anyone other than white males. In August and September 1791, free people of color responded by open revolt in the west province. At the same time, in the north, black slave leaders, including some Maroons, instigated a rebellion starting on August 22, 1791. The free men of color in the west were not available to help the whites because they were engaged in their own rebellion to gain political rights at the same time.

After four days, one third of the northern plain was ashes and all the plantations were destroyed. By late September more than 1,000 people had been killed and 161 sugar plantations and 1,200 coffee plantations were laid waste. Whites decided to offer an alliance and support of voting rights to free people of color for fear they would become allies with the slaves. They signed a Concordat to that effect. Whites and free people of color were then supposedly united to suppress the slave rebellion, but it smoldered instead of dying. Whites disavowed their promises, thinking order had prevailed, and the National Assembly revoked the earlier decree giving voting rights to a few at their behest. By November 1791, hearing formally of this repeal, free people of color joined slaves in rebellion. While these events triggered the departure of many refugees, Francois Snaer remained in Saint Domingue.[19]

The French National Assembly decided that the Declaration of the Rights of Man, although ambiguous, seemed to offer free men of color the right of citizenship. Emphasizing this interpretation, the king signed the Assembly decree of April 4, 1792, providing citizenship for property-owning free men of color. Some free people of color then turned against the slaves and joined the whites at this point. But Colored Creoles knew that the citizenship decree required enforcement to take effect. On June 2, 1792, the French National Assembly appointed a three-man Civil Commission to go to Saint Domingue and oversee enforcement of the decree.

Commissioner Léger-Félicité Sonthonax arrived on September 18, 1792, and began developing an alliance with the free men of color. He promised to ensure their citizenship. They accepted his promise and joined loyal French troops to fight the radical independence-minded whites and to pacify the slaves. Within four months the slave rebellion had been contained and the white resistance defeated, and the still-slave colony remained loyal to France, with mixed-race property owners enjoying full French citizenship. But things quickly fell apart. In February 1793, France declared war on Britain and the white planters thought they had an opportunity to regain power.

In the ensuing conflict Republican French forces, with the aid of slaves, who were later freed, defeated the white royalist forces at Cap-Français. The Republican commissioners promised freedom to the slaves who would fight on their behalf. Free men of color joined the Republican forces. Thousands of whites, including Moreau, fled Le Cap. This incident marked the end of white domination of the island and the beginning of overall slave emancipation. In August 1793 the Republican French administrator of Haiti abolished slavery. The National Convention formally abolished slavery throughout France's colonial empire on February 4, 1794, a ban that stayed in effect until Napoleon reinstated slavery in 1802.[20]

When the French extended abolition to all, this accelerated the flight of refugees and marked the beginning of the era of Toussaint Louverture. He rallied the French revolutionaries who wanted autonomy in April 1794, and accepted allegiance to France.

In 1802, after confirming Louverture's command of the colony, Napoleon sent the Leclerc expedition to suppress the rebellion, instead of using Louverture and attempting indirect rule as the monarchy had. The expedition won easily at first against Louverture's black army, and a captured Louverture died in prison in France. But within a few months more than 20,000 of the 41,000 men sent to the island had died of yellow fever, including Leclerc. By October 1803, Louverture's lieutenant, Henri Dessalines, had regained control. The French conceded failure in 1803 and evacuated. Dessalines announced an absolute anti-white policy: All the plantations were burned, and whites who did not leave and those associated with them would be killed. On January 1, 1804, Haiti declared itself an independent nation. The free people of color had allied with the slaves at crucial points in the Revolution, but they had continuously distinguished themselves from slaves and owned slaves. They even had disputes in their own ranks based on color. Historian Cyril R. L. James, writing about class disparity and racism among people of color in Saint Domingue, noted that "Black slaves and Mulattoes hated each other . . . the man of colour who was nearly white despised the man of colour who was only half-white, who in turn despised the man of colour who was only quarter white, and so on through all the shades."[21]

During ten years of crisis and revolution, slaves, whites, and free people of color had been trying to create or preserve their own versions of the future. Over that time, several waves of migration had ensued. Haitian independence provided for the time being a definitive answer for the Snaers, Eugenie's sister and her husband, and others in mixed-race families. In ideological terms, like other free people of color they wanted political rights for themselves but did not oppose slavery. The French were ousted and could not protect them in Saint Domingue. As a mixed-race family they cast their lot with French and colored refugees. It was not easy finding transport because of the stiff competition for spaces. Francois and Eugenie, perhaps pregnant with her first child, ended up at the closest refuge possible, just on the other side of the island in Santo Domingo.[22]

When Francois and Eugenie fled Saint Domingue in 1803, they landed first in Spanish Montecristi, Santo Domingo, on the western side of Hispaniola. Like the earlier Saint Domingue refugees in the 1790s, they left their homes in various states of preparedness. Some had time to gather and transport their goods with them; others simply left with what they were able to put their hands on at the last minute before their sudden departure. Historical circumstances forced their status upon them and made Spanish Montecristi a satisfactory shelter for Saint Domingue refugees.

Montecristi had long been a neutral port, established by Spain in 1749 to prevent encroachments on their trade. During the Seven Years' War it became an important post for interimperial trade and smuggling. New York merchants, for example, traded with non-British sellers there. Open to flags of all nations, Montecristi had no customs officials: Anyone could come and go as they pleased.[23]

Conflicts leading to Haitian independence changed Montecristi's status. Louverture in 1793 joined with Spanish insurgents to fight against the French. Spain was at war with France, and the colonists of Spanish Santo Domingo accepted the blacks as allies to their own forces. But with the abolition of slavery in France by the Republic in 1794, Louverture and his black troops turned against the Spanish and won. They subdued the territory, and in 1795 Spain ceded Santo Domingo to France. However, the Spanish continued to exercise power locally and even kidnaped slaves from Saint Domingue. In 1800 Louverture invaded and by 1801, with the entire island under his control, he freed the slaves.[24]

When Leclerc arrived to retake Haiti in 1802, his appointees reestablished slavery by the time of his death in July 1802. In December 1803, although the French had been routed from Saint Domingue, the French troops in Montecristi, Santo Domingo, were still stationed there, and the peace made no provision for their removal. With other refugees, the Snaers fled to Montecristi, residing temporarily at least under French protection. Francois and Eugenie's eldest son, Francois V., was born while they were there in 1803 or 1804.[25]

Montecristi did not become a new home for the Snaers: With other refugees, they soon continued their journey. Dessalines issued two proclamation of threat to Santo Domingo in 1804 and 1805, denouncing the French commander in Montecristi, who continued to issue decrees and in general acted as if France were still at war with Haiti. His behavior complicated international trade, slave ownership, and other issues. For example, some in the United States wanted to trade with Haiti and others wanted to undermine it because it was a nation created by slaves, in contradiction to pro-slavery orthodoxy. The commander's behavior basically jeopardized Haiti's postcolonial sovereignty. In 1808, he shot himself rather than accept the final defeat of the French.[26]

In late 1804, as the conflict worsened, Snaer and his family, along with other refugees, decamped to the Spanish colony of Cuba on whatever vessels would take them. France and Spain were temporary allies. In Montecristi, with the French garrison, they were still French, their identity situated through French culture. Now they had been unmoored and cast adrift from their identity, but there were already earlier immigrants from Saint Domingue in Cuba. They landed in the rural area of Santiago de Cuba, later Oriente, on the other end of the island from Havana.[27]

The group included merchants like Francois, artisans, tailors, sugar mill technicians, and coffee plantation managers, a majority of whom were free people of color or Europeans married to colored women with mixed-race children, like Francois.[28]

In Paris in January 1805, the Spanish *chargé d'affaires* estimated that 18,213 Saint Domingue deportees, white and colored, had taken refuge in Cuba. Francois and Eugenie's second son, Jean Baptiste, was born in Santiago around 1805.[29]

The Snaers and other early refugees joined other earlier-arriving *Francesas* from Saint Domingue in Santiago, dating from the slave uprising of August 1791 and the burning of Cap-Français. With each successive military campaign during the conflicts in Saint Domingue, more immigrants fled Hispaniola. Some refugees went to other Caribbean islands. Some who could find and pay for passage went to New York or Philadelphia. Others sought refuge in the area closest to their abandoned homeland, either because they could make it no further or they hoped to be able to return.[30]

We do not know how Francois and Eugenie regarded their family's future, whether they expected to put down roots or to move on. Upon their arrival, they found the French refugees of 1803 and 1804 had established themselves to some extent. Some had been officers, or from military families, who chose to take refuge in Cuba as a matter of honor and joined the military service of the Spaniards of Santo Domingo.[31]

The immigrants who came in successive migrations had different degrees of difficulty adjusting and surviving, depending on their skills and financial resources. Santiago de Cuba and the whole mountainous Oriente region adjusted to the difficult challenge of incorporating so many new arrivals.[32] Altogether about 25,000 to 30,000 refugees, about one third of whom were free people of color, went to

Cuba between 1791 and 1810. Upon their arrival, refugees grouped together and the families that could reconnected, which at least temporarily eased social and economic differences. At least Eugenie's sister and her husband Francois had migrated with them.[33]

Shortly after the first waves of immigrants began to arrive in the early 1790s, Santiago de Cuba felt the strain of the rapid population increase. Such basics as fresh drinking water and places for the sudden mass of arrivals to sleep caused local official Sebastián Kindelán to write to Cuba's Governor General Someruelos, begging for assistance. He suggested that the governor general could ease the pressure on the city by redistributing the French arrivals to other areas, even overseas. His pleas were ignored. Kindelán and Santiago de Cuba's other municipal officials were not only overtaxed in providing basic sustenance for the refugees; they were also, during the period of fighting in Saint Domingue, concerned about the defense of their own city. Kindelán kept a constant watch for the appearance of foreign ships in the harbor that could represent military threats.[34]

But once the fighting ended, overall the Haitian Revolution and the migrations helped the Cuban economy: The population of Santiago de Cuba, which had been less than 1,000 in the seventeenth century, grew to about 21,000 in 1792 and 33,000 by 1808. A 1789 royal order permitted foreigners and Spaniards to sell an unrestricted number of slaves to the island. In 1792 the Crown approved bringing slaves directly from Africa to Cuba. Free trade in slaves and then the disruption of sugar production in Haiti meant prosperity for Cuba. The Haitian Revolution and the abolition of slavery had destroyed the greatest sugar and coffee producer. Cuba had four times the land area and now would have enough slaves to produce more than Saint Domingue had at the height of its glory.[35]

The refugees from Saint Domingue, with their skills, slaves, and some capital, started coffee production in the eastern sections of Cuba. They were joined by French émigrés who decided to leave Louisiana after the Louisiana Purchase of 1803. In addition, prices of sugar and other products increased because of the market disruption caused by the Revolution. Soon blacks outnumbered whites, and planters fearful of a slave revolt similar to what occurred in Saint Domingue needed Spanish protection and stopped talk of possible independence from Spain.[36]

The Snaers did not stay in Cuba for long, but they found benefits to holding on to French identity. They experienced a well-developing culture influenced by the *Francesas* in Santiago de Cuba. Since 1799, Calle Gallo ("Rooster Street" in Spanish), one of Santiago's main streets, had been renamed Grande Rue ("Grand Street" in French). The Snaers lived among many others who shared their history. By the end of the first decade of the nineteenth century, one out of every four people in Santiago had come from what became the Republic of Haiti.[37]

Francois Snaer, although he was European, by virtue of his marriage, mixed-race family, and economic status had been subjected in Saint Domingue to legal restrictions imposed on free men of color. In Cuba free people of color had a long history of service in the militia, and the new arrivals were expected to serve. They had been treated equally with whites and given human rights protection. So whether as a white or mixed-race male Francois was subject to militia service.

With long unguarded shorelines and a sparse population, Cuba invited attacks not only by veteran troops of established nations, but also by a constant succession of independent privateers, pirates, and freebooters of all kinds, who infested its shores almost from the first days of Spanish colonization. To provide the needed forces for defense, the Crown from the beginning of its volunteer civilian companies turned to both its free white colonists and to its growing Negro and mulatto free male population for support.

Recognizing its dependence on the free colored population in Cuba, the Royal Government went out of its way to guarantee to these free men the right to bear arms and encouraged their volunteering by maintaining their equal rights with the white militia companies, including, after their organization into separate colored military units, the right to select their own officers. Not only did the Crown grant these militiamen the right to the *fuero militar*, which protected them from criminal prosecution by civil courts, but by 1770 they were needed and respected.

Far from being ceremonial groups with bright uniforms who performed at parades and other social gatherings, these colonial militia companies served almost exclusively as active military units. Observing strict military discipline when in service, from the beginning, usually with no pay except when on full campaign, they provided guard duty, military construction, and assistance to local police.

They saw use in military actions against the continuously invading buccaneers, privateers, and other irregular forces and also faced veteran European troops in battle. After the British captured Havana during the imperial wars in 1762, the city was returned to Spain the next year, and the Spanish reorganized the militia. Scattered white and colored companies were organized into battalions with permanent staff and training officers. As a result there were three battalions, each comprising 800 colored soldiers, in addition to local companies. In 1769, when Alexander O'Reilly gathered a military force to take possession of Louisiana from the French, 160 of the 240 militiamen he took along with 1,847 royal troops were colored militiamen from Cuba. By 1770, there were over 3,000 colored militiamen out of a total army of 11,667. On several occasions colored militiamen joined major military expeditions beyond the confines of Cuba.[38]

But liberty was precarious for some Saint Domingue colored refugees in Cuba. Before being accorded equal rights they had to fend off enslavement: Due to the needs of sugar production some free people of color found themselves captured and enslaved. Other newly freed individuals tenaciously secured and maintained documentation to substantiate their free status in Cuba.[39]

Over the next decades, the former members of Saint Domingue's colonial elite helped to establish a very favorable perspective toward the Haitian refugees. They established coffee plantations in the hills and mountains surrounding Santiago. These planters of Saint Domingue had experience growing coffee, a crop new to Cuba. Sugar cane production and the French taste for coffee, its spreading popularity in Europe, and the business acumen of the Saint Domingue plantocracy—once scions of the world's most profitable colony—combined to inaugurate a new political economy in eastern Cuba.[40]

In Oriente, *Francesas negros* dressed, danced, and performed according to French Creole traditions they had practiced in Saint Domingue. They used drum rhythms, creating their own *tumba francesa* ("French drum"). While the original ballroom dances of the white plantocracy faded from custom over the years, black *Francesas* preserved their own versions of these dances.[41]

The planter class held elegant parties, cultural activities in Parisian style. These *Francesas blancos*, as these white immigrants were called, brought to the eastern provinces a repertoire of ballroom dances, known as *contredanse* in French (*contradanza* in Creole), but "The musicians who played for the Cuban contradanzas were black."[42]

The language, song, and dance of blacks and mixed-race people who came from Saint Domingue and stayed over time also became part of Cuban culture itself. Some blacks and mixed-race persons integrated into the population via marriage or Spanish citizenship.

Both enslaved and free blacks gathered for mutual aid and cultural expression in cabildos, social organizations active in Cuba since the early colonial period. Cabildos functioned as support networks—for example, organizing funerals and taking up collections for members in need. They also held dances and sponsored processions on holidays. The black *Francesas* from Saint Domingue began to form their own cabildos.[43]

The immigrants who stayed in Cuba emphasized rather than downplayed their French culture. Elite Cubans had long regarded French culture as the standard for civilization, and by the early years of the nineteenth century their appetite for French style was firmly established. Geographer Joseph Scarpaci highlights this attitude by noting that "In the early nineteenth century, Havana's elite drew on French culture for ideas and models to emulate. Habaneros danced and dressed like the French elite before the immigration of French and Spanish residents who had resided in Haiti and Louisiana." Reinforcing this attraction to French ways were the enthusiasms of the wealthier Saint Domingue immigrants themselves, who lost no time in creating a cultural environment in Santiago de Cuba that enabled them to continue many of the social activities they had practiced in Saint Domingue.

The *Francesas* of color may have held on to dance and song styles that recalled their French Creole traditions as a way of highlighting their affiliation with France and therefore with a culture that Cuban Criollos held in high regard. In Santiago, the immigrants appear to have been aware of the Cuban attraction to French culture and often played up their French backgrounds to better position themselves to earn a living. Capitalizing on this Cuban attraction to French ways, many immigrants opened schools where they taught dances and offered music classes.[44]

Essentially, *Francesas negros* used music and dance to project their identity in public spaces. They used their performance traditions also to identify themselves as separate from the black Cubans, avoiding consignment to their inferior class. Even when *Francesas negros* became assimilated, they held on to the French identity through their performance. This approach seemed to have a positive impact. The Frenchness trumped race, and *Francesas* as a positive label became applied to the whole Saint Domingue refugee population and not just those with African descent.[45]

The Snaers and many of the migrants appreciated the respect for French culture and the receptivity to their arrival, but Cuba turned out to be only a way station to New Orleans. There they would find the same cultural bias toward French culture that existed in Cuba. A trickle of immigration to New Orleans from Saint Domingue had begun with the slave uprisings in 1791. There were fewer than 100 refugees between 1791 and 1798, many of whom are believed to have been whites. A minor migration ensued in 1803 and 1804 following the disbanding of Leclerc's army in Saint Domingue, when some of these refugees went to Louisiana.[46]

Not until 1809, six years after Napoleon sold the colony to the United States, did the arrival of Saint Domingue refugees in Louisiana begin in earnest. In reaction to Napoleon's placing his brother Joseph on the Spanish throne in 1808, authorities in Cuba and Puerto Rico expelled all French men who had not married Spanish women or taken Spanish citizenship. The Snaers and the Pascals and other refugees from Saint Domingue were forced to leave and were sent to Louisiana.[47]

CHAPTER 2

Becoming Americans

With their expulsion from Cuba, the Snaers were stateless again, heading for yet another nation to try to find a home. Improvised flotillas of merchant ships flying various flags with Cuban documents took them and other refugees from Cuba to the Gulf waters off New Orleans. The U.S. Customs officials asked the huge array of vessels to slow at Plaquemines to enter in an orderly fashion, but some just hid among pirates and privateers so as not to disturb American officials. There they unloaded and from time to time refugees slipped into the city. Francois and Eugenie Snaer and their two sons, Francois and Jean Baptiste, and the Pascals were among these.

The Snaers, along with the other refugees in the migration from Cuba to Louisiana, doubled the number of French speakers in New Orleans by 1810 and allowed the city to expand its role as an exotic locale. There were about 10,000 arrivals from Cuba from May 1809 through the first part of 1810. Only about 2,700 were white; the remainder was almost evenly divided between free people of color and slaves. A majority of the whites were males; the slaves and free people of color came in families like the Snaers or included slave women and their children. From 1805 to 1810, the population of New Orleans grew from 8,475 to 17,242, due in large part to the Cuban immigration. The population of Louisiana rose from between 36,000 and 50,000 in 1803 to 153,000 in the 1820 Census.[1]

When the refugee influx began, the entry of slaves and free men of color over the age of fifteen had been prohibited since 1808. After the prohibition in the U.S. Constitution against abolishing the slave trade before 1808 expired, Congress outlawed the international slave trade, although the ban was largely unenforced. Also, Louisiana planters expressed concern about "French Negroes" importing revolutionary ideas. At first, Governor Claiborne ordered the detention of slaves accompanying the refugees on the ships and the impoundment of the vessels. But, in May, he began petitioning Washington, on behalf of white passenger slave owners, for discretion to allow slaves brought from Cuba to enter New Orleans, asserting that it was justified on humanitarian grounds.[2]

In addition, with the ships impounded, refugees who were permitted to dock had to leave their possessions on the ships. Soon, rules would be bent and the entry of slaves was later legalized by a special act of Congress. White passengers identified some blacks as their slaves with no proof and managed to retain possession as they landed.[3]

Free people of color found some receptivity from government officials. On May 18, 1809, New Orleans Mayor James Mather told Governor Claiborne "a few characters among free people of colour have been represented to me as dangerous for the peace of this territory," but he had not found any problems with them. The men, he said, "possess property and have useful trades to live upon." He had not received "one single complaint" about them.[4]

Governor Claiborne wanted to keep track of single men among the colored refugees. He asked Mayor Mather if any were also allowed to enter and whether some above age fifteen left after arriving in the city. He also wanted an update generally on new refugee arrivals and whether they were "sickly" or "what kind of talents" they have.

The mayor replied that two thirds of the men had trades. He had given sixty-four bonds for free people to travel but he didn't have records of any who actually left. He explained that "when [the men] they come to commissary of police and are given time to find documents they don't show up again," and perhaps they sailed away some place or went back to Saint Domingue.[5]

Some white Creole families planned to seek refuge eventually in France. Others, upon arriving in Louisiana, as they had done in Cuba, looked at their move as nothing more than a stopover before the time when they could regain control of Saint Domingue or broker a peace agreement. Soon, such an outcome was obviously impossible. They found the lifestyle and even the colonial architecture in New Orleans similar enough to that of Saint Domingue that they felt comfortable and became reconciled to staying. The mixed-race families, including the Snaers, kept an eye on Haitian developments. Some went back and forth between Louisiana and Haiti, but after some time, like the whites, most settled in Louisiana.

The Snaers made landfall in the United States at Barataria Bay. On the Gulf of Mexico about fifty miles south of New Orleans, the inlet with its maze of waterways and marshlands served as an ideal base for French-speaking smugglers, pirates, and other brigands in southeastern Louisiana. The notorious pirate and privateer Jean Laffite and his older brother, Pierre, operated from the bay in the early 1800s. So did Rene Beluche, a New Orleans-born pilot who thrived on transporting refugees from Santo Domingo and Cuba to New Orleans. Beluche became a friend, and in time an in-law, of the Snaers. He or someone like him delivered the family to U.S. shores about 1805 in a wave of thousands of Saint Domingue refugees defying U.S. efforts to block the illegal immigration.[6]

The Snaers made Barataria Bay's French community their home for almost ten years. The place became something of a new French colony as the Saint Domingue refugee influx deepened and spread ties of culture and common interests. All manner of men, women, and children came to live there. The refugees included slaveholders and their slaves, former slaveholders who had lost or divested their slaves, former slaves who had snatched their freedom, emancipated slaves, and longstanding free persons of color. As many as 800 free men of color who had served in France's Republican Army, routed in the Haitian Revolution, were among the lot, and fighting for the U.S. side against Great Britain in the War of 1812, many of them proved their attachment to their republican ideals and to the United States as their home.[7]

Francois Snaer, who was about thirty-two at the time, did not appear among the list of those fighting in the Battle of New Orleans during the War of 1812. He had been subject to militia service in Saint Domingue, but service had not brought equality of rights. However, he and his family, among other refugees living in Barataria, made their way to New Orleans for the first time after the war. What they saw when they entered the city resembled Cap-Français. For the refugees, the stuccoed houses with airy galleries, the brick pavements, the overall architecture of homes and public buildings, the weather, the vegetation, and even the river and the lake evoked memories of Le Cap.[8]

But beyond the architecture, the Snaers became a part of a New Orleans that had grown from a colonial supply depot into the second largest port in the country, and soon became the fourth largest in the world. Even before the introduction of steamboats in 1812, New Orleans was destined to become a major shipping center of the United States. Flatboats from throughout the Mississippi Valley brought the agricultural bounty of the land for trans-shipment to ports on the East Coast, Europe, and Latin America. Into the port came manufactured items, tropical fruits, and coffee from foreign lands. Cotton, the main export, drove the city's development as a major *entrepôt* into and out of the United States. New Orleans had an interracial, multicultural population when the United States acquired it in the Louisiana Purchase. The Snaers' arrival, along with other refugees, ensured that it stayed that way. Whites of foreign origin, migrants from other states, including slave traders, slaves, freed people, and free people of color trafficked the river and docks. New Orleans became a wide-open town, an entertainment mecca, the Las Vegas of its day: What happened there stayed there. High and low culture included not just the architecture from the Spanish and French periods, but theater and opera. River rats, lumberjacks, workers on holiday from up and down the Mississippi, and tourists from all over came, attracted by its freely available pleasures, including prostitution and gambling.[9]

The Snaers and the other free people of color, fully one third of the approximately 10,000 Saint Domingue refugees, expanded the diversity of the local population. Their numbers included Francois Germain Plessy, born in France, married to a free woman of color who had emigrated to Saint Domingue. A carpenter, he was the grandfather of Homer Plessy of the 1896 *Plessy v. Ferguson* case upholding segregation.[10]

Once in New Orleans, the Snaers easily became part of the colored Creole population concentrated in an area adjacent to the French Quarter, in Tremé between North Rampart and North Broad and from Canal Street to St. Bernard Avenue, and the Marigny, downtown below Canal Street but away from the waterfront. The Marigny, a suburb of the Quarter, is bounded by Esplanade Avenue;

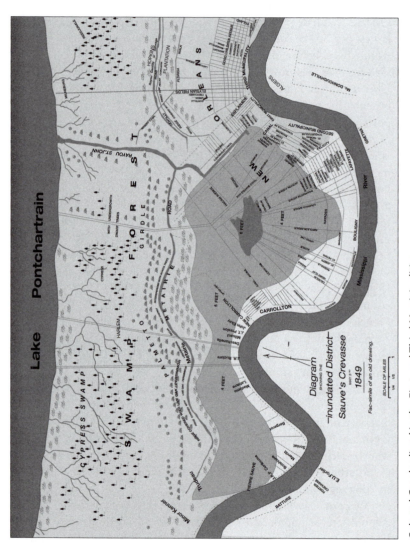

Colored Creoles lived in the First and Third Municipalities.

St. Claude Avenue, which becomes Rampart on the other side of Esplanade; Press Street; and the Mississippi River.

Tremé developed from plantation land owned by Claude Tremé, a native Frenchman, which he parceled out for sale at prices the refugees could afford. The Marigny was laid out in the first decade of the nineteenth century by eccentric Creole millionaire developer Bernard Xavier Philippe de Marigny de Mandeville on land that had been his family plantation just downriver from the old city limits of New Orleans. He established the portion of Marigny closer to the river first. The area on the side of St. Claude Avenue away from the river became alternatively the "New Marigny." In the Marigny in the early nineteenth century, white Creole gentlemen maintained households for their mistresses of color and their offspring. Supposedly, while such liaisons were hypocritically denounced elsewhere in the United States, Bernard Marigny referenced these interracial liaisons (known as *plaçage*) when naming streets in the Marigny, such as Rue d'Amour (now Burgundy) and Rue des bon en Enfants (Good Children).[11]

In 1818, father Francois apprenticed his younger son, Jean Baptiste, age thirteen, to live with another free person of color, master tinsmith Marin Broh. The apprenticeship lasted from four to six years. At first the apprentice would produce cookie cutters and other simple items. Then came items such as cake and pie pans, and with mastery the apprentice produced elegant chandeliers and crooked-spout coffeepots. He then became a journeyman before becoming a master and employing others. Some tinsmiths took to the road as peddlers or tinkers in an effort to save enough money to open a shop in town.[12]

The free people of color and slave refugees included a variety of artisans who constructed and adorned New Orleans. There were house builders, furniture makers, carpenters, masons, and bricklayers. They dominated the fields of cabinet making and iron work, constructing much of the city's iron grillwork, balconies, fences, and gates. They dominated iron work until the 1830s, when foundries began casting iron for local and national markets. Their work is still visible in residences dating from the period and in cemeteries.[13]

Perhaps with savings he had accumulated in Saint Domingue, in 1820 Francois Snaer bought property and established a successful grocery store that he operated along with his elder son, Francois. Grocery stores sold alcoholic beverages by the glass, operating more like a bar. Although they were both classified as free people of color, Eugenie was a housewife; she did not work alongside her husband in the store.[14]

The property Francois bought was located in the Tremé on St. Claude Street, between Dumaine and St. Philip Streets. It was apparently one of two lots owned by Augustin Macarty, the son of Augustin Guillaume de Macarty and Jeanne Chauvin de Lery, members of a prestigious white family, allied by marriage to one of the last Spanish governors, Don Estevan Rodriguez Miro. Macarty had served as mayor from 1815 to 1820. He and his cousin Eugene had long-term relations each with a mixed-race woman. Each mistress inherited, along with their respective children after the father's death. Eugene and his mistress, Eulalie Mandeville, lived for some years in a house at the corner of Barracks and Dauphine streets across from the beginning of the Tremé, just off Rampart in the French Quarter. During the years before the Civil War about three fourths of the property in the Marigny and 80 percent in Tremé belonged to Colored Creoles like the Snaers.[15]

Francois built two "Creole cottages" for their residence and the store. Oriented toward the back of the property, such cottages consisted of four main rooms downstairs with an interior chimney, and two rear small rooms upstairs called "cabinets" flanking a recessed gallery. The front of the house abutted the banquette or sidewalk and the back included a yard. To maximize air flow and cool the house, cottages had no hallways or high ceilings. Such houses also usually had a wooden fence, a detached kitchen, an outhouse, and a cistern in the back yard and backyard patios. The Snaer property lay in an area now encompassed by Louis Armstrong Park, but examples can still be seen in New Orleans today. Although colored Creoles dominated the Tremé and Marigny, some, including tailors, cigar makers, and at least one wealthy undertaker, had white clients. Owners of real estate rented to whites, and the census of the area included interracial households and large numbers of white immigrants.[16]

Free colored Louisianans were the most literate and prosperous free people of color in the United States; the Snaers owned an extensive amount of property. Possessing at least $2,000 in in land and moveable goods throughout his adult life, Francois Snaer was considered wealthy in the antebellum period. In 1836, in New Orleans, 855 free people of color paid taxes and owned about $2.5 million in real property, including 620 slaves. Most, however (75 percent), worked as skilled laborers or artisans such as cigar makers, cabinetmakers, or carpenters. Professionals made up only 2 percent of the population, and businessmen (mainly shopkeepers, like the Snaers) constituted only 5 to 7 percent. New Orleans free people of color proudly embraced their reputation for working hard, saving, and acquiring real estate. They numbered about 20,000 persons, almost 20 percent of the local population. Charleston had only around 1,500 free people of color, about 5.4 percent of the population. In the North, Philadelphia had a slightly larger population of free people of color but experienced a period of decline attributed to race riots and fires; the number of institutions, such as schools and churches, and the population fell.[17]

As the population of New Orleans continued to grow, the Snaers, along with other Colored Creoles, had to negotiate the harsh official efforts enacted by the U.S. territorial government to limit interracial contact and to maintain the tripartite racial system. The restrictions were reminiscent of the colonial efforts to regulate free people of color that they experienced in Saint Domingue. In 1806, the new American territory adopted a Black Code for the regulation and punishment of slaves. The Black Code reenacted many of the provisions of the Code Noir and added a provision that "free people of colour ought never to insult or strike white people, nor presume to conceive themselves equal to the white; but on the contrary that they ought to yield to them in every occasion, and never speak or answer to them but with respect, under the penalty of imprisonment."[18]

The Colored Creoles faced numerous restrictions. Starting in 1840, they had to designate themselves as free men or women of color in French or English after their names in all legal transactions. The New Orleans mayor's office required them to register each year, providing proof of their free status if they were "black" rather than "mulatto." Registration also required an affirmation of their status by a white person.[19] Only those born in Louisiana were exempted from this requirement.

Ordinances also prohibited the congregating of free people of color in public spaces, including one, dating from 1816, that segregated theaters and public exhibitions. Another ordinance forbade opening establishments or cafés that served liquor. Beginning in the

1820s the public streetcar lines either excluded persons with African ancestry or operated separate cars for them. Segregation or exclusion became the rule. Although public schools began opening in 1842, only whites were permitted to attend.[20]

Some Colored Creoles ignored some of these legal prohibitions and other rules that simply went unenforced. For example, children who appeared to be white attended schools designated for whites. The Saint Domingue refugees living in New Orleans seemed to have ignored the registration requirements; the Snaers do not appear in the lists of registrants at the mayor's office. They may have believed the requirement should not apply to them, since Francois was white and his mixed-race wife and children were not black. The laws and regulations did acknowledge that free mixed-race families like the Snaers had a distinctly higher status than slaves. They could not vote or hold public office, but they could serve in the military. Until around 1830, a few Colored Creoles served on the city police force. In the eyes of the Louisiana law, there was (with the exception of political rights, of certain social privileges, and of the obligations of jury and militia service) all the difference between a free man of color and a slave that there was between a white man and a slave. In addition they, along with the slave population, were used to apportion the Louisiana General Assembly, which gave the southern parishes more representation because of the large slave population.[21]

Also, free people of color who entered the state lawfully, established permanent residency, and carried on a useful trade could enter and leave the state on business. They could own property, including slaves; make contracts; acquire by inheritance; and transmit by will. When charged with a crime they, in theory, received the same procedural due process as whites; they could also bring suit and could appeal. Also, unlike slaves, they could also serve as witnesses and parties to suits that involved the rights of white persons. Free people of color could petition the government for redress of grievances and could receive all of the sacraments of the Catholic Church, including baptism, marriage, and burial.[22]

Also, the legal system made overt manipulation of the rules possible when whites desired it. On occasion, whites even permitted free people of color to vote in order to win closely contested elections. They apparently voted on several occasions after 1830.[23]

Unusual among those of mixed race, the Snaer sons, Francois and Jean Baptiste, were legitimate. As late as 1820, only 10 percent of free colored infants in the baptismal registers of St. Louis Cathedral and St. Mary's Chapel at the Ursulines convent listed parents who were legally married. The infants usually had a white father with a white wife, but their mother was a colored woman. A recent study suggests, based on marriage records, that free people of color from Saint Domingue were less likely than long-established ones to make legitimate marriages and were more likely to place their daughters as white men's concubines. However, because the number of free colored women exceeded that of men, a large number of marriages could not take place. The gender ratio, little better by 1850, meant that free women of color, generally, remained more likely to become a white man's concubine.[24]

The large-scale immigration of Saint Domingue refugees not only doubled the population of New Orleans in one year, but it also had an important social and cultural influence on Creole Louisiana. The very fact that New Orleans remained at least partially a Francophone city well into the nineteenth century can be traced to this massive influx of Creoles from Saint Domingue. Not only did the refugees speak the same language, but they also shared a similar colonial history, religious and cultural institutions, and a three-tiered racial hierarchy. The white Francophone population of New Orleans and the new immigrants from France who flowed into the city, threatened by economic and cultural competition from the recent wave of American migrants into Louisiana, at first welcomed these Creole newcomers, with whom they found much in common, and some intermarried. In this environment French cultural institutions, including poetry societies, coffeehouses, millineries, and literary and commercial society, grew exponentially.[25]

In this social and cultural environment, the Colored Creoles maintained the commitment to the liberty, equality, and human rights ideals of the French Revolution, which they brought with them. But still supporting slavery, they used human rights language to oppose their relegation to a subordinate caste even while they possessed slaves. Some Creoles of color maintained ties to Haiti as the Haitian government vacillated, depending on shifts in power from mulattoes to blacks and attitudes toward mulatto exiles. The antebellum New Orleans white press did not often voice the views of the city's Colored Creoles, but the press in Haiti covered their sympathy for Haitians. For example, in August 1831, a hurricane struck the towns of Les Cayes and Jérémie on Haiti's southern peninsula. When news of this disaster reached New Orleans, the city's Colored Creoles organized a committee, "Les jeunes gens de la Nouvelle-Orléans," to collect money for a relief effort. In March 1832, the poet and educator Numa Lanusse, president of the committee, sent a letter to Haitian authorities with the equivalent of about $2,000 and a list of 180 donors. The Snaers appeared in the list along, with almost all of Louisiana's prominent Colored Creole families, including the Macarty, Lambert, Rillieux, Dubreuil, and Toussaint families.[26]

Some New Orleans Colored Creoles frequently went back and forth to Haiti, and some always had relatives remaining there. Even after the l'Institution des Catholique pour l'instruction des Orphelins (school for colored orphans) was founded in 1848, the schoolchildren wrote to fictional and real pen pals in Haiti.[27]

Refugees from France's political upheavals in the 1830s and 1840s further reinforced New Orleans' French culture and community. Congregating in the growing districts of Marigny and Tremé and in what came to be known as the French Quarter or Vieux Carré, the fresh arrivals slowed the city's "Americanization," stemming from the U.S. takeover of the former French and Spanish colony in the Louisiana Purchase of 1803. They increased interracial contacts, too, joining integrated Masonic lodges and spiritualist societies, and they contributed significantly to cultural enterprises such as the 1845 Creole poetry collection edited by Numa Lanusse's brother Armand titled *Les Cenelles*.[28]

Other interracial cooperation led to the founding of the Sisters of the Holy Family by a free woman of color, Henriette DeLille. She gave credit to French immigrant Jeanne d'Aliquot for her religious education and sense of social responsibility. The story of d'Aliquot's rescue upon her arrival after falling into the Mississippi River, by a colored person, became part of local lore. She committed herself to help people of color. This story is an unusual part of the history of Colored Creoles, which usually (as did history generally) focused only on men, as in Rodolphe Desdunes' *Our People and Our History*.[29]

Once Jean Baptiste Snaer finished his tinsmithing apprentice-ship, he married Josephine Louise Utrasse Pellissier, a free woman of color, on September 17, 1827. The two lived in New Orleans, not far from the Snaer family home. After about ten years of marriage Jean Baptiste died, perhaps of yellow fever; one of the recurring epidemics ravaged the population in 1837. In 1841, his widow, Josephine, lived a few blocks away from her Snaer relatives along with four of their children. Francois and Eugenie had successfully established them-selves in New Orleans as a well-off Colored Creole family becoming Americans.[30]

CHAPTER 3

Family Troubles

All seemed well in the Snaer family as the younger Francois joined his father in the prospering grocery business. Francois married Marie Catherine Rochefort in 1829. She was another immigrant, born in about 1809 in Baracoa, near the northeastern tip of Cuba, beyond a high mountain range from Santiago de Cuba, where the first European settlements took place. Typically for the times, Marie's illegitimate birth resulted from a liaison between a white planter, Pierre Rochefort, and Marie Louise Beauchamp, a woman of color born of Saint Domingue refugee parents. She and Francois had four children, Louis Sosthene Jonathan (born 1828), Francois Michel Samuel (born 1832), Ameline Adelaide Angela (born 1836), and Francois Volmar (born 1838). They resided with the other Snaers at 237 St. Claude Street. The 1830 Census reported six family members living in the household: the elder Francois and his wife; Francois and his wife, Marie; their son, Louis Sosthene Jonathan, and their old slave, Thereze. Francois purchased a younger slave woman, Rachel, in 1826 to do the housework for Mrs. Snaer.[1]

Francois and Marie Catherine had a stormy relationship. They traded accusations of domestic violence throughout their marriage. In 1830, Marie Catherine filed a suit for separation in the New Orleans Parish court. She claimed that since their marriage in 1825, he had repeatedly subjected her to "excesses, cruel treatment and outrages," which "made it insupportable" for them to live together. He even "went so far as to beat her in a cruel manner" late in the evening and in a "manner so scandalous as to disturb the whole vicinity and to cause her neighbors to come to her assistance." She alleged that the mistreatment resulted from her refusal to agree to his disposal of some of their community property to friends or relatives. She asked for permission to sue for separation and to have their property assessed and divided and for Francois to pay the costs of the suit. She wanted permission to reside at her mother's residence with their two children, Sosthene Jonathan, age two, and Samuel, an infant. She also asked to receive fifty dollars per month in alimony and maintenance.[2]

However, Marie Catherine apparently abandoned the suit. There were no further proceedings filed and no decision was ever reached. She remained in the marriage and had sexual relations, whether voluntary or not, with Francois because by 1834 she was pregnant again. However, the conflict continued and she filed again for a separation, after having already left the household to seek refuge with her mother because of his behavior. This time, she claimed that in addition to his "cruel treatment," he had "publicly defamed her." After the earlier episodes, "believing that her husband would come to a better understanding of his duty as a married man, she had consented to reconciliation." But, yet again, his behavior grew so aggravated that she feared for her life and "that of the child now in her bosom" and so she moved in with her mother, Madam Pascal.

After the death of Marie Catherine's father, her mother had married Francois Pascal, a tinsmith by trade. In the 1850 Census, Francois Pascal reported considerable wealth, placing him among the well-off Creoles like the Snaers. Showing the close kinship networks and intermarrying among colored Creoles, the younger Francois Snaer and Francois Pascal were cousins. They were both born in Santo Domingue and their mothers were sisters born of Saint Domingue refugee parents. Pascal, upon marrying Marie Catherine's mother Marie Beauchamp, became her stepfather.[3]

Marie Catherine asked the court's permission to take some furniture and clothing from the household. She also wanted forty dollars per month in maintenance and asked to keep her children because of their "tender age."

She wanted the property inventoried and an order restraining Francois from disposing of it until a separation suit was settled. She had to post a $1,000 bond with a surety. Judge Charles Muriam issued the order for the sheriff to keep Francois from disposing of assets until further orders of the court.

Although he was among the wealthy Colored Creoles, worth well over $10,000 in 1850, Francois Snaer countered with a demand for a reduction in alimony and the custody of the two children. His response characterized her charges as "false and malicious." He wanted a divorce, claiming she had threatened his life; she had already left home without his authorization. He also insisted on custody of the children. He stood on good legal grounds because at that time, fathers generally received custody, no matter how they abused their wives. In a patriarchal system, they supported the family and had responsibility for order and discipline.

Francois also claimed that he owned a great deal of property before their marriage, which was not part of their community property; therefore, she could make no claim. Beyond his real estate, he acknowledged possessing tinware worth $2,500 and groceries and dry goods worth $5,000. He also insisted he had made loans of about $3,726.25 in notes, including money owed to him by the Pascal in-laws.

He claimed he could not pay $40 per month in alimony because his income amounted to only $22. He wanted any property awarded to her reduced by the amount of the debts, child custody, a reduction in alimony, and a divorce or separation. The court required Marie Catherine to answer in a few weeks.[4]

Unable to obtain custody of the children, Marie Catherine did not proceed with the suit and remained in the marriage with Francois. She also bore at least two more children, Angela and Volmar. Francois continued to acquire property. In 1837, he bought three more lots north of the Tremé.[5] Although she failed in her legal claims, Marie Catherine's resort to legal action led to an airing of the nature of their relationship and the disclosure of Francois' finances, which continued to have lingering effects after her death. Marie Catherine died mysteriously on May 2, 1838, at age twenty, according to the Recorder of Births and Deaths, before which Francois V appeared in October 1838. Buried in St. Louis Cemetery No. 2, her tombstone bears the inscription *La Vertu guidait ses actions* (Virtue guided her actions). The deaths of Francois the elder and Jean Baptiste were recorded in the same year. In this period, yellow fever epidemics may have complicated recording of the burials of the dead.[6]

In 1840, following the death of Marie, his father Francois, and his mother Eugenie Felique, Francois and three Snaer males lived at the St. Claude residence: Samuel, Volmar, and Sosthene Jonathan; one female, Angela; and an additional unnamed male slave and Thereze. But the children never reconciled with their father, frequently complained of mistreatment, and ran away repeatedly to stay with their Pascal grandparents.[7]

Around 1841, Anne Emerine Beluche, a free woman of color twenty years his junior, became Francois' new wife. Pirate Rene Beluche, the famed privateer and fighter with Jean Lafitte, and Marguerite Despian were her parents. Sosthene Jonathan, Francois Samuel, Angela, and Volmar technically still lived in their father's household, but they spent most of their time at the Pascals'. When Sosthene Jonathan, Samuel, and Angela reached their early twenties and Volmar was nineteen they sought to break all ties. Understanding the depths to which their relationship with their father had sunk and also still resenting his treatment of their late mother, they asked for an apportionment of whatever estate they could inherit. This required a new inventory of their father's property.

Francois offered witnesses to prove he had cared for the children and that he did not "beat" them but treated them mildly and saw to it that they received reading, writing, and music lessons. He attested to still possessing "an old Negro called Thereze." Mrs. Snaer and a younger slave did the housework together. The children worked about the shop, but Snaer employed an adult male clerk, Valsin Weitz, who also lived in the household.[8]

Sosthene Jonathan had lived in and out of the city. He worked as a dry goods clerk in Baton Rouge and La Fourche. He and Francois Samuel had supported themselves for at least five years. Francois Samuel, "crippled" according to the testimony, gave music lessons and had several paying pupils. Volmar stayed with his father for a time while attending school but returned to the Pascals', where the census taker counted him as residing in 1850. He became a coopersmith by trade. The inventory described property worth about $20,000. The estate consisted of the St. Claude Street property and several lots worth $4,000, and Thereze, the eighty-year-old slave, worth $25. After subtracting costs provided by Snaer, each child received $279. After the final accounting of the estate, Marie Catherine's children left the household permanently.[9]

Sosthene Jonathan settled in St. Tammany Parish on the north shore across Lake Pontchartrain from New Orleans. Volmar stayed with the Pascals. Angela, who according to the testimony did not want to live with her father, went to stay with Francois Samuel and remained with his family when the Civil War began.[10]

Francois Samuel became a very important composer and music teacher. He and other musicians played his compositions in theaters and concert halls. In 1850, at just age eighteen, he wrote his first known piece, "*Sous la Fenêtre*" (Under the Window). He played several instruments, including the violin and violoncello, and was regarded as a brilliant pianist. He produced many orchestral pieces, overtures, waltzes, polkas, mazurkas, and quadrilles. Nevertheless, Rodolphe Desdunes, in *Our People and Our History*, said that he was "too timid to seek publicity and too indolent to break loose the shackles that bound him from birth." As a result he was not remembered "as the artist he really was."[11]

For many years Francois Samuel's livelihood depended mainly on his post as organist at St. Mary's Church on Chartres Street and his works, include a number of liturgical pieces. He married Marie Noel Agalice, who had inherited property from her mother. They had two children, Leopold, born in 1856, and Joseph Samuel, born in 1858.[12]

In his second marriage Francois and Emerine remained well-off financially and seemed to have a happier, calmer relationship. They had ten children, eight boys and two girls. Among them, Louis Antoine, their first child, born on June 13, 1842, Rene Seymour, named after Rene Beluche, born in 1844, and Alexamore, born in 1848, gained more prominence as adults. Seymour later decided to use "Rene" as a middle name, perhaps not wanting to remind people of the pirate. The Snaer children, like the majority of persons of school age in their neighborhood, spoke French as a first language.[13]

Francois and Anne Emerine's children were christened at St. Augustine Church in the Tremé. The church played an important role for the free people of color, as it was another expression of their desire for solidarity. By the early 1800s well-off free Colored Creole leaders and philanthropists such as Louis Charles Roudanez and Marie C. Couvent lived in the Tremé. In the Faubourg, free people of color organized various community self-help institutions, including mutual aid societies and nursing homes for the aged and ill.

Free Colored Creole families also assiduously contributed funds to the diocese to establish their own church. Most were Catholic. Since the colonial period all persons in the territory had to be baptized, married, and interred in accordance with the Catholic religion. Free people of color complained of discrimination in the city's churches, including the requirement that they stand or kneel at the rear so as not to offend whites. Their petitions succeeded. The Ursulines, in 1838, donated to the diocese the property at the corner of St. Claude and Bayou Road to build the church.

On November 14, 1841, Monsignor Antoine Blanc laid the building cornerstone. A few months before the October 9, 1842, dedication of St. Augustine Church, the people of color began to purchase pews for their families. Upon hearing of this, white people in the area started a campaign to buy more pews, beginning the War of the Pews. The free people of color ultimately won: They bought three pews to every one purchased by whites. In an unprecedented social, political, and religious move, they bought all of the pews on both sides of the aisles. They gave those pews to the slaves as their exclusive place of worship.

When the church opened, it was interracial but segregated. Slaves sat in the outer aisles and free persons of color and whites sat separately in the center aisles. This practice continued until the end of slavery. The Snaers regularly attended St. Augustine. Other churches became the preferred place of worship for New Orleans people of color over the years, but St. Augustine retained its historic status.[14]

Although some Colored Creoles were well-off, they shared with everyone else in New Orleans the perils of living in a city in a swamp, rife with disease and without indoor plumbing. Yellow fever epidemics occurred several times in the 1820s and 1830s, one of which led to the deaths of Jean Baptiste and the elder Francois Snaer. There was a cholera epidemic in 1848, and another yellow fever epidemic in 1853, one year after the legislature abolished the three separate municipalities and consolidated the city government.[15] The 1853 yellow fever epidemic slowly swamped the city, creeping into the news even though all through June and July the coroner's reports avoided identifying the fever as the cause of so many deaths. In the summer families who could afford it typically left for the beach resorts on the Gulf or to visit relatives away from the heat and the mosquitoes. But that summer, even many grocery stores and bars closed. Traffic in the streets consisted almost entirely of the sick, physicians attending to their patients, and hearses carrying the dead to the cemeteries. Although the connection between mosquitoes and the disease was not scientifically made until the 1890s, the crisis brought more attention to gutters, sewers, and other public sanitation measures. The accepted lore of locals that Creoles were acclimated to the weather and that only newcomers contracted the disease significantly decreased. The Snaers, including Louis Antoine (at 11 their oldest child), their four younger children, and newborn Victoria, remained in the city but remained unaffected by the epidemic.[16]

Population changes as a result of European immigration meant that antebellum New Orleans was increasingly becoming a white city, limiting prospects for persons of African descent, whether slave or free. Between 1820 and 1860 over a half-million immigrants disembarked in the city. The Irish potato famine, beginning in 1845, and the revolutions of 1848 and surrounding events pushed them from their homes. Most were Irish, German, French, or Italian. In Louisiana in 1830, the free colored population numbered 16,710, among 89,441 whites and 109,588 slaves, or 15 percent of the state's free population. In 1860, they numbered 18,647, among 357,456 whites and 331,726 slaves, or 5 percent of the free population. The changes in New Orleans were even more dramatic, as the free black population in the city declined from about 37 percent in 1830, to 6.7 percent in 1860. There were 25,423 Negroes, including almost 10,000 free people of color, and 144,601 whites.[17] The neighborhood populations changed also. The Irish congregated across Canal Street from the French Quarter and Tremé between the Garden District and the Mississippi River in what became called the Irish Channel. Italians moved into the Marigny and the French Quarter, which by 1900 was 80 percent Italian. Germans lived in the Marigny and across Canal Street in the central business district. After 1845 Irish and German immigrants took jobs as domestic servants, waiters, and hotel workers, jobs formerly held by Negroes (including free people of color, free Negroes, migrants from the North, and slaves). Cabs and wagons, usually driven by non-whites in the 1830s, became almost exclusively handled by whites two decades later. Non-whites remained market sellers, but whites replaced the peddlers in the group. The docks, once crowded with black and colored stevedores and steamboat roustabouts, became, by the 1850s, an Irish preserve. Whites held jobs increasingly in printing, baking, sail making, glazing, lithography, engraving, and piloting. In 1850 most free Negroes, including largely Colored Creoles, in New Orleans were skilled workers and artisans, including carpenters (like Adolphe Plessy, the father of Homer Plessy of *Plessy v. Ferguson* fame), masons, cigar makers, shoemakers, clerks, mechanics, coopers, barbers, draymen, painters, blacksmiths, butchers, cabinetmakers, cooks, stewards, and upholsters. Some were brokers, doctors, jewelers, merchants, and musicians.[18]

White workers began to dominate jobs as screwmen, loading cotton ships, and also as yard men in cotton presses. The printers, pilots, and screwmen formed unions and then, as craft unions, excluded non-white workers. By the 1850s half of the white population consisted of immigrants, who fueled the nativist Know-Nothing Party.[19]

As bilingual Catholics, white Creoles shared a common ground with the immigrants. Creoles downtown aligned themselves with immigrant groups under the banner of the Democratic Party to add to their numbers in trying to maintain some influence against the Americans. But elite white Creoles allied politically with elite Americans. This alliance foundered because the Whig Party, the only alternative to the pro-immigrant rhetoric of the Democrats, hewed too close to the nativism of the Know-Nothing Party. Some Creoles joined the Know-Nothings, arguing against immigrants, and some tied yellow fever to the vessels and the immigrants they brought.[20] The Colored Creoles also related to new immigrants, and some established mixed-race marriages. Among the immigrants, Juan Presas of Catalonia married a woman from Saint Domingue. Their daughter Elizabeth married an immigrant from Sardinia, a druggist named Joseph Gandolfi. The Presas were a mixed-race family like the Snaers, and after the war, one of their children would marry Louis Antoine, the eldest of Anne and Francois' children.[21]

The tightening racial restrictions of 1850s affected all free people of African descent. In addition to the Colored Creoles, New Orleans had a sizeable free Negro population, which had migrated from other Southern states after the Louisiana Purchase. An area above Canal Street in the Second Municipality became known as the American free Negro section. Protestant and English-speaking free Negroes established churches, lodges, and other institutions. While racial discrimination affected both groups. The Snaers, like other Colored Creoles, did not interact or socialize with English-speaking free Negroes. However, they mingled freely with French speakers, whether slave or free.[22]

Whatever language they spoke, free people of color tried mightily to keep their status separate from that of the enslaved people of color. Legally, the first civil code permitted slaves only one type of legal action, a claim to freedom. The law presumed, as elsewhere in the United States, that anyone who was "black" was a slave. This presumption constrained the liberty of dark-skinned people of African descent and, as the decades passed, had consequences for any person with even a "drop" of African blood. In 1810, as a result of *Adele v. Beauregard*, the Louisiana Superior Court in New Orleans decided that people of color enjoyed a "presumption arising from colour." Their status as mixed-race free people of color differentiated their legal status from that of "full-blooded" blacks. Light-skinned and white-appearing Creoles, including some of the Snaers, benefitted from this decision.[23]

In this case, Beauregard had brought Adele as a girl from the West Indies, sent her to a New York boarding school, and then brought her to New Orleans to serve as his slave. She fled his household. The court decided that "Persons of Color may have descended from Indians on both sides, from a white parent, or mulatto parents in possession of their freedom." Slave status attached automatically to black people, but not to those of mixed heritage; when a person was of mixed race, her or his slave status had to be documented, "Considering how much probability there is in favor of the liberty of these persons," the court said, "they ought not be deprived of it upon mere presumption." As a result, the whiter a person appeared to be, the greater likelihood that he or she could avoid being regarded as a slave. In New Orleans, Judge Francois Xavier-Martin heard a number of these early suits and usually decided that the man or woman in question was a free person. But the result also depended on whether the plaintiff had support from an influential person. The presumption changed in 1836 in *Berard v. Berard*, when the court decided that mixed-race and non-black people could not be presumed to be free people of color. In the twisted logic of racial justice, the Louisiana Supreme Court asserted that when a person filed a freedom suit, claiming he or she was in fact free, that person must therefore be a slave, unless he or she could prove otherwise.[24] Earlier restrictions on their activities and movements, including the requirement to register at the mayor's office, remained in place, although they were sometimes ignored. But in the 1850s, restrictions on the rights and opportunities of free people of color in New Orleans grew tighter. Suspicious whites harassed and kept them under surveillance. Other restrictions forbade the incorporation of any new societies for their benefit; the keeping of coffeehouses, billiard halls, or retail stores where liquor was sold; and socializing or worshiping with slaves. Some legislators even sought to re-enslave free persons of color.

In 1858 the city enacted a law declaring all non-white religious bodies illegal. Officials closed and took the property of the largest denomination, the African Methodist Episcopal Church, for violating the law. Founded by free people of color in Philadelphia when officials at St. George's Methodist Episcopal Church pulled blacks off their knees while praying, the denomination spread throughout the states. The church lost a case attacking the ordinance in the state Supreme Court. It was not until the end of the Civil War that African Methodist Episcopal churches reopened in New Orleans.[25]

After Louisiana's legislature outlawed manumissions in 1857, the increase in the population of free people of color slowed; many left for France, Liberia, Haiti, or Mexico. Desdunes noted that in 1855 "Mr. [Lolo] Mansion generously donated a part of his fortune for the relief of our people, and a number of them profited by his generosity, escaping the hardships of prejudice. Mexico and Haiti opened their doors to them." Haiti, suffering at this point, wanted to attract wealthy mulattoes. There is some evidence of migrations to Mexico in this period, and research has identified descendants still there.[26]

Some Colored Creoles passed for white on occasion or tried to pass completely. In an 1859 case, a tenant refused to pay his rent, asserting that the woman who claimed she had made the transaction could not be the landlady because he had been renting from a woman of color of the same name. To collect the rent she had to prove that first she was white as she claimed and that he was mistaken about her race and in fact owed her the rent. After she lost the case, she moved to Cuba, leaving her son behind, disclaiming her marriage, and leaving the man formerly known as her husband to care for the child.[27]

As the Colored Creoles saw harder times in the 1850s, the Snaers remained relatively solvent because Francois inherited the grocery business from his father. The 1870 Census listed Francois as one of six colored grocers who owned more than $5,000 worth of property. He reported $10,000 in real property and $400 in personal property.[28]

The Snaers belonged to the small upper tier of Colored Creoles: the always free, merchant and professional classes. But some in the family, like Volmar and Sosthene, belonged to the middle group of artisans, who only with difficulty avoided poverty in hard times. Among the three classes of people of color, the lowest economic class consisted of those who had recently gained their freedom. Whatever their economic circumstances, Francois and his relatives, friends, and other Colored Creoles maintained a sense of community—a common Roman Catholic religion, language, and culture.

Francois Snaer (1803–1880).

Despite instances of attempts at passing to avoid the restrictions, color was not an absolute dividing line among New Orleans Colored Creoles in this period, as it apparently was among Southern free people of color in Charleston, for example. Background, language, culture, and financial resources mattered more. In 1860, in Louisiana, 3,489 of the 18,467 free persons of color reported full African blood. About 70 percent at that time consisted of octoroons, quadroons, or mulattoes, displaying a range of colors. Francois and his children generally appeared light enough to pass for white, although some white Snaers' family lore is that his children with Marie were somewhat darker.

The closeness and kinship of the Snaers and Pascals reflected the pattern of relationships generally found among Colored Creoles. They formed small, tightly knit communities devoted to their own advancement and protection. They lived on the same streets or nearby plantations, socialized with one another, attended church together, provided an education for one another's children, and married each other. For example, Antoine DeCuir and Antoine Dubuclet, the richest Colored Creoles in Pointe Coupee Parish, agreed to the marriage of DeCuir Jr. and Josephine Dubuclet. They had owned a plantation of more than a thousand acres in Pointe Coupee, with at least 112 slaves. Seymour handled some of Josephine Dubuclet's legal affairs.[29]

The Snaers and many other free people of color had difficult choices concerning education for their children. The very wealthy could send them to France. The Catholic Church not only owned slaves but abided by the state law distinguishing the races; however, as early as 1724, French-speaking Ursuline nuns opened their schools to colored children. By 1841 the second teaching order of African descent in the United States, the Sisters of the Holy Family, founded by Henriette DeLille, took up the task.

The Snaer children apparently attended Catholic schools or public schools after they were established, passing as white in order to attend. Other Colored Creoles and free Negroes sent their children to secular schools. About a thousand free people of color attended private schools in Orleans Parish in 1850 and 336 attended such schools in 1860. The l'Institution des Catholique pour l'instruction des Orphelins was the best known. It opened in 1848 in the Faubourg Marigny, adjacent to the Quarter, growing out of a bequest by a native

African woman, Marie Justin Camaire, a free woman of color and widow of a prosperous free Colored Creole, Bernard Couvent. Founded for orphans, children of artisans, tradesmen, and other free people of color attended. The umbrella of the Catholic Church protected it from state hostility to schooling for non-whites. In 1852, the school moved permanently to the third district on St. Antoine Street between Bons Enfants and Morales Streets. It taught boys and girls separately in English and French in a six-year course of instruction.

The children paid according to their parents' means. Francois Samuel Snaer, among other Creole artists, artisans, and educators, taught there. By 1860 the patronage of the Catholic Church was not as much of a shield: Legislation designed to suppress free non-white institutions had reduced enrollment of children of color in the city from 1,008 to 275.[30]

The Colored Creoles in New Orleans had a clearly established identity in 1860, although a few would pass or attempt to pass to gain an advantage; they were soundly denounced by the group. They also had a history of using their own resources individually and collectively to advance the group. The limits the law placed on their status and activities affected their opportunities, but they manipulated the rules as much as possible. For a few that meant passing or attempting to pass for white.

Their insistence on the importance of shared cultural identity protected and expanded the space available within the limits of the Colored Creole community. The coming of the Civil War would rend asunder their identity and assumptions.

....

CHAPTER 4

Fighting for Democracy

A disconsolate Native Guards lieutenant, Louis Antoine Snaer, at age twenty-one pondered his own future in July 1863 at the funeral of his fallen brother-in-arms Andre Cailloux, killed on May 27, 1863, at the Battle of Port Hudson. Cailloux died a hero in the Union's frontal assault against the Confederate stronghold straddling Louisiana's East Baton Rouge and East Feliciana Parishes on the Mississippi River, about eighty miles northwest of New Orleans. The battle turned into a forty-eight-day siege. The Union prevailed eventually and, with the fall of Vicksburg 160 miles north on July 4, 1863, won full control of the Mississippi River. Mulling his options, Louis Antoine decided he wanted a future as an Army officer, and that required hiding his identity as a Colored Creole and passing for white.

The fighting relieved the colored troops from their customary drudgery. White Army commanders invariably assigned colored troops to dirty, menial details. The government paid colored troops less than white troops, worked them harder, and equipped them poorly. When the army command deigned to send colored troops into battle, it commonly used them as cannon fodder. So it was at Port Hudson: The Native Guards were ordered into the front ranks of an impossible assault. They went with courage and daring, with officers like Cailloux and Snaer leading, embracing their self-sacrifice to show their mettle as men in the hope of winning recognition of their human equality.[1]

Louis Antoine Snaer in uniform.

Snaer's decision arose from his questioning of the value of the death and the blood, sweat, and tears he had witnessed. Cailloux's death and the sacrifices of his other fallen and wounded Native Guards comrades appeared to make little dent in the disdain and discrimination whites heaped on them. The racial animosity was palpable, but it was not simply about color; a deeper divide loomed. Color lay in the mind's eye, not in actual appearance. They shunned Cailloux, who proudly described himself as the "blackest man in New Orleans." But the Colored Creole officers ran the gamut from Cailloux's blackness to Edgard Davis's light blue eyes, ruddy complexion, silky hair, and a mustache so sandy as to appear almost red. Louis Antoine's fair complexion, gray, eyes and light hair did not distinguish him among the colored officers with whom he joined the Union Army in 1862 or the whites.

For Snaer and his fellow young Colored Creole officers, the Union's reaction to their continued military service presented their first racial identity crisis. Their responses reflected the conflict between the human rights ideology that applied to themselves as Colored Creole citizens and their long record of military service; they did not view ex-slaves as their equals. This tension would persist throughout the Civil War, during Reconstruction, and afterwards.[2]

Confederate sharpshooters showed the degree to which they despised the Native Guards, as they did other colored troops, by firing to prevent Union details from retrieving the Native Guards wounded and killed in the assault that felled Cailloux. Because the Union Command then refused to call a truce, their sniping forced his corpse to lay rotting in Louisiana's humid heat for forty-one days, from May 27 to July 9, when Confederate surrender allowed its retrieval. Decomposing and riddled with rifle shot, Cailloux's remains included only his gold ring bearing the insignia of the Society of Friends of the Order and Mutual Assistance.

Louis Antoine and the other mourners found little solace in what the *Daily Picayune* called the "unprecedentedly large" funeral. The *New York Times* described it as "The most remarkable affair of the kind that ever took place in New-Orleans or in the South." Thousands of people lined the streets for a mile; many of them wore crepe rosettes and held tiny American flags. The Society of Friends of the Order and Mutual Assistance ushered Cailloux's remains in a horse-drawn caisson, draped in the flag, displaying his sword, belt, uniform coat, and cap and surrounded by flowers.[3]

Colored Creoles, of all colors dark and light and often in the same family, organized such Orders, despite the legislative prohibition against such mutual aid and burial societies, part of the restrictions limiting the rights of free people of color. Colored Creoles saw the societies as too important to their collective progress to allow their closure, and in ignoring the ban, forced a continuing confrontation with the authorities.

Among the thirty-seven societies in attendance at the funeral on Wednesday, July 29, 1863, some dated from long before the Civil War, while others were more recent. The societies served as an extended family devoted to mutual uplift. Also, for the mainly Catholic Colored Creoles, the societies, like Protestant churches led by African

Americans, provided arenas where these subjugated populations could exercise authority. The Friends of the Order had purchased a lot at Urquhart Street in the Marigny. On the lot not far from Cailloux's cigar-making shop, they built the hall in which they held his funeral. He was the secretary of the Society.

The band of the all-white Forty-Second Regiment Massachusetts Volunteer Militia (Infantry) played during the services. Claude de Maistre, a dissident priest who was in trouble with the diocese for his racial liberalism, among other alleged failings, administered the full rites of the Catholic Church at the request of Cailloux's widow, Felicie, who showed her regard for the priest who married them and the Creole community's respect for de Maistre's views.

Eight soldiers, escorted by six black captains and six members of the Friends of Order, bore the casket from the hall. Two companies of the just-organized Sixth Louisiana (Colored) Regiment, in which Louis Antoine's younger brother Pierre served, escorted the funeral cortege along Esplanade Avenue toward the burial place. Members of the male and female colored societies lined the crowded street. In apparent disdain whites, who still supported the Confederacy, heckled the grieving family and mocked the mourners along the route.[4]

Along with the Friends of the Order, some of the Native Guards officers, including Louis Antoine, along with their sick and wounded soldiers, and dignitaries, served as pallbearers. All joined the family in following the cortege to the Bienville Street cemetery, St. Louis Cemetery No. 2, for the burial.

Louis Antoine, like other Colored Creoles, loved and admired Cailloux. Charismatic, with polished manners, bilingual, athletic, a good horsemen and boxer, he was a fine figure of a man with a manner and air of command that even attracted the gaze of white supremacists. Marion Southwood, a Confederate sympathizer who lived in New Orleans during the war, described him as "a large, good looking Negro, dressed to death, a *la Militaire*" astride "his fine horse, caparisoned ditto, who rode up and down the streets quietly, showing off, making the vulgar stare, and enticing the Negroes to go to war. He and his horse were in danger of melting in the hot summer sun, when the perspiration would roll off both of them."[5]

The funeral and the Battle of Port Hudson received widespread media coverage at the time. The *New York Times* and other press saw the battle as proving the mettle of black soldiers, whom Lincoln had decided were important to victory in the war. The ex-slaves, runaways, and freedman had faced questions about their fitness and ability to fight. The Cailloux story provided a perfect answer to the critics. Louis Antoine and other Colored Creoles lifted Cailloux high as the symbol of their quest for freedom and equality of rights. In his short life he had gone from slavery to freedom to military command to the vindication of African American manhood. He lost his life, but his memory served as a powerful incentive.[6]

Historians and Civil War military history buffs have told the riveting Cailloux story repeatedly. However, missing pieces of the narrative are important to understanding the issues that continued to resonate in New Orleans during and after the Civil War and Reconstruction. The "blackest man in New Orleans," the fallen hero, became one symbol of the solidarity between persons of African descent no matter what their physical appearance. The Union reaction to the colored officers elicited responses from Snaer and others that reflected their view of their history of a continuous search for self-determination. It also led to one Colored Creole officer, Louis Antoine Snaer, becoming the only Negro to lead troops in battle throughout the war and in the process becoming a military hero.

Everyone's life changed as a result of the Civil War. Cailloux's funeral was only the latest and worst reminder for Louis Antoine and other Colored Creoles that their very status as citizens and their personal identity had changed. First, given their paradoxical support for slavery, they had to react to the Confederate call for the immediate mobilization of troops in May 1861 after the firing on Fort Sumter that started the war. Military participation had always given Colored Creoles an opportunity to reinforce their privileged status above that of the slaves. They had helped to save the city in the War of 1812, at the Battle of New Orleans. Every year in the celebrations of the victory they eagerly joined in the recognition ceremonies.

They had formed an association of colored veterans of 1814 and 1815 to provide "mutual support in the event of death or incapacity to work" and celebrated their martial past. Although Louisiana authorities eventually stripped them of their arms, the state paid free colored soldiers pensions and the federal government granted them bounties. They honored the tradition of celebrating their service and did not let it die.[7]

While not as disadvantaged as colored middle-tier families such as the Caillouxs, the Snaers and all Colored Creoles had suffered as a result of the economic dislocations and tightened restrictions on people of color in the 1850s. Like others in the top tier among New Orleans free people of color, however, the Snaers were still well-off financially. They considered how to respond to the calls for military participation from the perspective of their community's traditions and the prospects for their families.

Despite recent scholarly criticism of the view that some free people of color actually supported the Confederacy, some did so and for their own reasons. In all more than 740 Colored Creole men enlisted in the colored militia. The Confederacy called it the Native Guards, separate from the regular military. In view of their conflicted ideology of supporting both human rights and slavery and a tradition of military service among the free people of color who had served since 1799 under three flags (Spanish, French, and American), it should not be surprising that young Colored Creole men answered the call to serve. Among the general regional support for the Confederacy, the increased restrictions on their status as people of color, and their inability to predict the war's outcome, it was a community faced with few options other than to appear patriotic.

In addition, some owed a great deal to their close ties to slave owners. Cailloux, for example, who served originally for the Confederates, had owners who let him learn cigar making and then hire his own time before supporting his successful manumission petition in 1846.[8]

Any excuses made after the fact for joining the Confederacy should be evaluated carefully. Charles Gibbons, a free colored house painter, told a Union inquiry commission that he had feared for his life if he did not join the Confederate militia. Certainly others felt that way, but some among the professional and propertied classes might have joined the Confederacy as a result of enlightened self-interest. Some wealthy Colored Creole plantation owners saw their livelihood as dependent as that of whites on the labor of their slaves. Some might have joined because of their perception of self-identity: They were free and more than 80 percent of the free population had white European blood, while fewer than 10 percent of the slaves had white ancestry. Ideology was offered as a reason by Colored Creole

Captain Louis Rey in a toast before the Native Guards during the Christmas season of 1861 when he equated the Confederate rebellion with the American Revolution and saluted the present "revolution and all revolutions—for they give birth to the progress of man and lead him on the way to true fraternity."[9]

The free colored Confederate regiment organized in New Orleans consisted of eleven Native Guards companies of about forty men each. From the Snaers, Auguste, probably the son of Jean Baptiste and Josephine, carried the family banner as a private in the Young Creole Guards. Andre Cailloux, then age thirty-seven, enrolled as a First Lieutenant in the Order Company, named for the Friends Society to which he belonged. Colonel Felix Labatut, a leading white businessman and politician about sixty years of age, who owned about $10,000 worth of property in the city, commanded the troops. The free colored officers and 731 enlisted men marched with white troops on November 23, 1861, in a parade of the Confederate forces in the city. In many families one or two males of military age volunteered to carry the family name.[10]

The free people of color soon discovered that the Confederates saw them only as symbols to tout their group's support for slavery and secession. There was no sign of the spirit of true fraternity the Colored Creoles sought. The Confederates had no intention of using them militarily. They drilled mostly without arms or uniforms. Similarly, free women of color offered their services as nurses but were not called upon for duty.[11]

The Colored Creole community enthusiastically supported the regiment. Military service, whatever the issues, had always been a way to support Colored Creoles' claim to citizenship status. Students at l'Institution des Catholique described their activities in compositions and tagged along at the grand reviews as the regiment marched and trained on Sundays. Women presented flags blessed by priests to the men, and the churches held celebrations.[12]

In the meantime, the economy worsened because of the Union blockade of the port. Some free colored artisans suffered severe economic reverses. The Snaers were able to hold on to what they had, but some free people of color who had greater resources invested in urban real estate and increased their wealth. Thomy Lafon, who became a large contributor to charities, increased his wealth from $10,000 to $50,000 by speculating in swamplands during the Union occupation.[13]

On February 15, 1862, the Confederates reorganized the militia and restricted it to white males only. However, they reinstated the colored militia on March 24, 1862, when David Farragut entered the Mississippi River. When forced to flee, the Confederates advised the Native Guards to hide the weapons they had before they were discovered by the Union forces. They disposed of their uniforms and hid their old muskets in Economy Hall, Claiborne Hall, and even l'Institution des Catholique, whose principal, Armand Lanusse, commanded the Mescachebe company of the regiment.[14]

For the Union, capturing New Orleans in 1862 was a major military victory. Admiral David Farragut's flotilla took the Confederate's largest city, strategically placed at the mouth of the Mississippi, rather easily, as it turned out. However, occupation of this culturally complex, racially and sexually suspect city proved equally difficult for the troops and its inhabitants.

By 1860 interracial, multicultural New Orleans, a mix of whites of foreign origin, migrants from other states, slaves, freedmen, and free people of color, was the largest city in the South. Union General Benjamin Butler, a Massachusetts politician and lawyer before the war, restored order amid the chaos he found in the city. He established martial law and organized food and water distribution, sanitation, and yellow fever prevention. He demanded that locals take an oath of allegiance to the Union and either expelled or jailed men who showed disloyalty. The residents railed at his orders and found particularly galling his response to incidents of Confederate women insulting and even spitting on his troops in the streets: Butler issued an order that "when any female shall, by word, gesture, or movement, insult or show contempt for any officer or soldier of the United States, she shall be regarded and held liable to be treated as a woman of the town plying her avocation."[15]

Enforcement of the audacious "Woman Order" reduced the number of incidents, but the Confederates thereafter called him "Beast" Butler. With the Confederate retreat, in the ensuing chaos, slaves and refugees attached themselves to the Union forces. Some Native Guards officers met with Butler, who decided to reorganize and use the colored militia for the Union. Not knowing he regarded them as unequally as the Confederates had, assigning them to fatigue and garrison duty in sweltering locales deemed unfit for whites, the colored militia agreed to organize troops. Butler issued a general order on August 22, 1862, announcing the reactivation of the Louisiana militia into three new regiments and asking for volunteers. He promised them 160 acres of land or $100 with $38 in advance at the end of the war. They would receive equal pay with white soldiers of $13 per month for enlisted men and food rations for their families. An announcement in *L'Union de la Nouvelle Orleans*, the local French-language newspaper, asked particularly for sergeants and corporals who spoke English and French.[16]

Louis Charles Roudanez founded *L'Union* in September 1862 after he had grown wealthy from the municipal bond business and then studied medicine at the University of Paris; there he experienced the 1848 Revolution and developed a taste for radical politics. He largely financed the newspaper; the editor was Paul Trevigne, who was fluent in several languages and who taught for forty years at the l'Institution des Catholique. It published poems by local poets as well as news and commentary.

In 1864, the newspaper closed, but then Roudanez started the *New Orleans Tribune* and asked Jean-Charles Houzeau, a white astronomer and Belgian aristocrat in exile for his political views, to edit it. Houzeau started as *L'Union's* Northern correspondent and came from Philadelphia to New Orleans that same year. Roudanez's papers, which were published in French and English, with sometimes different stories, offered space for Colored Creoles to have a voice, perpetuating their identity and sense of community.[17]

By the end of September 1862, free people of color had organized the first Union regiment and organized two additional ones by mid-November 1862. Francois and Emerine decided that their oldest son, Louis Antoine, then nineteen, could join the First Regiment. He and his friends were excited about serving, although they had no military experience, like Union soldiers from elsewhere. Louis had only worked as a clerk in his father's store. He joined the First Regiment, Company B, as a newly minted young lieutenant.

In the regiment, Andre Cailloux raised a company of 100 men for Company E, in which he served as captain. Louis noted that some of the men who had joined the Confederate militia, twenty-six of the officers in all, did not join the Native Guards. Twenty-one of the former militiamen joined them in the Native Guards, but ten had been in the ranks and not in the officer corps. Only five of Louis Antoine's First Regiment officers—Cailloux, Edgard Davis, Octave Foy, Alcide Lewis, and Charles Sentmanat—had been in the Confederate militia. In all, more than 3,000—three out of four adult Colored Creole men—enlisted in Union Native Guards units. Much has been made of the Fifty-fourth Massachusetts Regiment featured in the film *Glory*, but Louis Antoine's and Andre Cailloux's First Native Guards was, apparently, the first official African American Union regiment.[18]

Louis Antoine served with a few Native Guards officers who, although they were free Negroes, were not of Colored Creole origin. Lieutenant James Ingraham, for example, was the son of a slave woman and a white man. English-speaking and a Methodist, he allied himself with the Colored Creoles. John Crowder was the son of Martha Spencer, a free black woman who grew up in Kentucky, and Jacob Crowder, also a free person of color. After Crowder's birth in Louisville, his father went off with the U.S. Army to Mexico and never returned. After two years, his mother obtained a divorce and moved to New Orleans. John worked as a cabin boy and a steward on steamboats on the Mississippi and as a porter in a jewelry store. Concealing his age, at sixteen, two years below the minimum age for a commissioned officer, he became a Second Lieutenant in the Native Guards.[19]

Rumor had it that the Colored Creole officers possessed enormous wealth. Not only was this untrue, but Snaer, for example, was still dependent on his father Francois. His father, however, was much more affluent than most of those with whom he served. Only Cailloux, who held $500, and Captain Louis Rey, who owned $200 worth in property, appeared in the 1859–1861 tax rolls. Noel Bacchus, the first sergeant of Company E, had $1,600 in real estate in 1860. Only Francis E. Dumas of Company B, a slave owner, fit the wealth description among the officers of the first Native Guards. He left the company on October 23, 1862, to become an officer in the Second Regiment, which left an opening for Louis Antoine to gain a promotion to Captain.[20]

The original recruits in the First Regiment, raised by Louis Antoine and the other colored officers, mostly free people of color, displayed a range of skin colors, reflecting their mixed race. Mostly freedmen were in the other two regiments. Large numbers of men in the

First Regiment were artisans: bricklayers, carpenters, cigar makers, and shoemakers. Thereafter, increasingly, runaway slaves entered all three regiments. The Colored Creole officers welcomed them. The traditional social distancing seemed to be eroded by the war, along with practical and then legal emancipation.[21]

Specifically why nineteen-year-old Louis Antoine and others joined the Union regiments is not clear. Along with the historical importance of military service to Colored Creole status, hard economic times may have meant that the pay and promises of aid to their families were attractive. The Union victory and the same necessity that made them previously publicly support the Confederate cause could have played a role. They may have believed, given the Union war aims, that success would bring equal rights and increased prestige to their community.

L'Union and then La Tribune followed the organization and actions of the colored regiments, mentioning Louis Antoine and the other officers in the French-language edition. L'Union supported the idea that the war would strike a blow for freedom and equality. The paper stood for full equality of rights for the free people of color and emancipation, with guidance and education, for the slaves. The colored community supported the troops as enthusiastically as they had their earlier Confederate regiment. At the time, of the total male population of free people of color in New Orleans, about 5,500, about 4,000 were between eighteen and forty-five. The 3,000 Native Guards in the Union Army included most of the age-eligible population.[22]

The Union Army experience proved uncomfortable from the first for Louis Antoine and his fellow Native Guards. Confederate-supporting local whites reacted angrily to their mobilization, yelling curses and insults at the men and then reporting that the soldiers engaged in impudent behavior toward white citizens. Complaints were made at Union headquarters and their white colonel, Spencer Stafford, responded that whites went out of the way to insult them, and police arrested them on the slightest pretense. Stafford, who served as Butler's Assistant Provost Marshal, had, upon his first assignment to the Native Guards, expressed reluctance because of his previous "prejudices." However, this changed. In December 1862, a few months after their organization, two petitions, one from the First and Second regiments and a separate one from the Third, asked for the placement of all colored troops together under his command. They wanted him because they trusted him; he had stood up for them.

The Native Guards tried to assert their equality in many ways, including attempts to ride on streetcars with whites instead of having to wait for "Negro cars" marked with a black star. Butler ordered the cars desegregated, but a local court set aside the order. Soldiers resented half- filled cars passing them while they waited for star cars. After a number of incidents, police officials decided that Native Guards officers could ride on white cars, but not enlisted men.[23]

Some overseers and slave owners ran the still-enslaved wives and children of freedmen soldiers off their plantations to fend for themselves. Others, believing that the presence of black soldiers would undermine productivity among their laborers, drove away such visitors at gunpoint. Also, the families of the soldiers suffered when paymasters denied the promised pay and when promised rations were sporadic or substandard. Butler tried to alleviate their plight by issuing orders and staying evictions, but the paymaster refused to pay the soldiers, claiming uncertainty about their legal status.[24]

White officers and troops freely insulted or abused the Native Guards. In addition, the troops were poorly equipped or not equipped at all. They could not obtain ammunition, mules, or wagons when other troops acquired them routinely. White officers of white troops refused to salute or defer to either the white or colored officers of the Native Guards no matter what the difference in rank. Their commander, Colonel Stafford, fed up with the distress of his soldiers and the behavior of the white Unionists, became furious when a white soldier serving as gate guard refused to let his men, who had been sent out to gather wood, return to the camp even though they had a pass. The guard shook one of the men roughly and called him insulting names. A soldier inside the base reported the altercation to the colonel, who rode up on horseback to insist that the men be admitted to the camp. When Stafford asked the captain in charge of the guard to explain the behavior of his soldier, the captain disrespectfully refused to give a satisfactory answer. The captain reported that Stafford rode his horse at him and knocked him to the ground.[25]

On October 25, 1862, the men left Camp Strong Station, assigned to open the railroad in the La Fourche district to forward supplies to General Godfrey Weitzel. The general had been ordered to occupy the rich sugar-producing areas and to keep supplies originating in Texas from reaching enemy forces in Louisiana. Weitzel did not want the Native Guards under his command and offered to resign, but to no avail. The Regiment found itself consigned to guard and backbreaking ditch- and trench-digging duty.

While guarding the railroads, Edgard Davis recalled how in late 1862 and early 1863, in cold wet weather, they suffered through wind-downed tents and water up to their knees. The press kept pointing out that persons of African descent were particularly fitted for swamp duty. Stafford urged Butler to let him bring his men, scattered along the railroad, together and to give them real military duty.[26]

By January 1863, they still had no pay and no relief from hard physical labor. In January Weitzel dispersed the companies of the Regiment among three forts for construction duty. Louis Antoine and his Company B, Cailloux and his company, and Companies F and G went to Fort Jackson on the right bank of the Mississippi River, below New Orleans in Plaquemines Parish, to make repairs and alterations. They were insulted and harassed by local whites daily. In February, seventy enlisted men in one day reported sick. Stafford reported faithfully on their decrepit condition with badly worn and tattered clothing, conditions that led to a deterioration of discipline.[27]

At Baton Rouge, after several months of service, they finally received pay on May 1, 1863, although less than they had been promised. The enlisted men received ten dollars per month, three dollars less than the white enlisted men. Negro officers received their promised equal pay of $60, but noncommissioned ones received no extra pay. However, finally, they could send money home.[28]

In the meantime, Louis Antoine and the other colored officers, who probably thought matters could not get worse, faced the arrival of General Nathaniel Banks in command, who shared the antipathy toward Negro officers expressed by other white officers. Banks, a New England politician who had thought military service would advance his career, had nothing but defeats to show for his efforts. He was sent to succeed "Beast" Butler, who had infuriated the white population, and was tasked to use conciliatory policies that would encourage Unionist sentiment among whites and to take control of the Mississippi River. Arriving to command the Department of the

Gulf in December 1862, he turned his attention to the colored officers in early 1863.

Louis Antoine and the other colored officers anxiously discussed Banks' announcement of February 1863 that having Negro officers undermined the service. He attacked the Second and Third Regiments first. After most refused his request to resign, he set up examining boards of some white officers of inferior rank to pass judgment on them. Most resigned faced with this indignity. By forcing them out, the white officers could receive promotions to their places.[29]

Louis Antoine and the other First Regiment officers were somewhat insulated at first, because Stafford and Lieutenant Colonel Chauncey Bassett had sympathized with them. Bassett, an old-school abolitionist, formerly served as a captain in the Sixth Michigan infantry. Stafford's complaints on behalf of his troops made him a pariah to the other white officers in the chain of command.[30]

Then the high command cashiered Colonel Stafford based on his loss of temper with white troops who harassed his men and disrespected their officers. His "intemperate behavior and language" led to his reassignment to detached hospital duty, and he was dismissed in May 1863 for conduct prejudicial to good order and military discipline. In January 1871, his dismissal was changed to an honorable discharge.[31]

Banks, aware that his defeats by Stonewall Jackson in Virginia had tarnished his reputation, and jealous of Ulysses Grant's growing reputation, needed a victory. He would help the Union take the Mississippi Valley from the rebels. Banks had not yet rid himself of most of the First and Third Regiment colored officers when he decided to advance from New Orleans to meet Grant at Vicksburg to split the Confederacy in half. Louis Antoine, Andre Cailloux, and their men were pleased that finally they would fight, for Banks had included them in his plans to take Port Hudson, a well-fortified Confederate stronghold on high bluffs on a bend in the river fourteen miles north of Baton Rouge. Banks ordered an attack beginning with an artillery barrage at six on the morning of May 27, followed by an infantry charge. At the same time Admiral David Farragut would begin a naval bombardment from the Mississippi River. But everything seemed to go wrong: Banks failed to ensure coordination between the forces or to understand that his own troops could not see each other or communicate as they were deployed.

When Louis Antoine, Cailloux, and their men arrived on May 26, 1863, to join the operation against Port Hudson, they found General William Dwight from Massachusetts in command. He had decided to test the "negro" question by exposing them in the middle of the battle. Dwight, a petty vindictive martinet, drank excessively and had nothing but contempt for his black troops. Cailloux's Company E would lead the charge; Louis Antoine's company would fight alongside them.

Dwight gave assignments to their regimental commanders and then, already drunk at seven in the morning, said he would observe from the rear. He also promised artillery, which never came, should the rebels pin down the troops. Colored Creole Anselmas Planciancios, given the standard and told to avoid surrender of the flags no matter what, had been baptized forty-one years earlier at St. Louis Cathedral. His wife was pregnant with their third child. He promised to carry the colors with honor "or report to God the reason why."

Cailloux urged his men on in French and English, but as they advanced they found not the smooth terrain Dwight had promised but a rugged bluff occupied by six companies of rebel troops. Also, they saw a second bluff with protected rifle pits occupied by sixty riflemen. To make matters worse, the Confederates had engineered a backwater from the Mississippi, forming a protective moat in front of the riflemen. An impassable swamp of cottonwoods and cypress and willows bordered the road along the right, and on the left stood an impregnable barrier of sharpened, wired-together felled trees, underbrush, and gullies. Confederate gunners had already routed the Union artillery battery. Louis Antoine and the other colored line officers led their troops forward despite direct Confederate gunfire. The Native Guards managed to discharge one volley and continued to charge as they were "dreadfully slaughtered."

Louis Antoine kept trying to move his troops forward and escaped injury himself but noticed Cailloux had one arm dangling, broken by a hit above the elbow. But Cailloux, too, continued to rally his troops, sword drawn, until felled by a shell to the head. A ball struck and killed Planciancios, the color guard, cutting the banner he carried in two and shaving away part of his skull. Two men nearby tried to retrieve the colors. One, Corporal Louis Leveiller, took a direct hit and fell dead. The other, Corporal Athanase Ulgere, retrieved the colors successfully. The embattled troops fell back on the Third Regiment and then retreated under heavy fire, running in disarray. Louis Antoine and the other colored officers stood their ground and tried to rally the troops, but some ran away.[32]

Louis Antoine and the surviving and uninjured Native Guards knew they were lucky. The Union Army suffered 708 killed, 3,336 wounded, and 329 captured or missing in the battle. On May 27, the First Regiment of the Native Guards suffered 35 killed, including Lieutenant John Crowder and Captain Andre Cailloux; 94 wounded; and 19 missing or captured, mostly from the 100 men in Cailloux's company. The Third Regiment suffered ten killed, thirty-eight wounded, and three missing or captured, mostly from Crowder's company. However, newspapers reported the May 27, 1863, assault widely as proving the courage of colored soldiers. The Confederates that night went out to search the colored dead who lay in front of them. Some soldiers from New Orleans recognized Cailloux: He had his officer's commission and eight dollars in greenbacks in his pocket.[33]

Louis Antoine and the other Native Guards had to observe Union details sent out to retrieve the bodies of the white troops as they left Cailloux, Crowder, and the other colored dead to lie in the vanguard where they had fallen. Banks refused a truce, which would have permitted the recovery of their bodies, so the corpses lay bloated and rotting in the sun until after the surrender of Port Hudson. On June 14 Banks tried another failed attack in which the decimated First Regiment did not participate.[34]

Banks moved to end the more independent, detached status of the Negro troops. Each unit would have 500 men to establish the discipline that Banks asserted Negroes needed. The First and Third Regiments became Corps d'Afrique effective June 3, 1863. This segregation of colored troops instead of serving alongside white regiments showed a decrease rather than an improvement in their status even in the midst of battle.[35]

Union recruiters took volunteers who came into their lines and also marched onto plantations and took slaves away at gunpoint to join the regiments. One of the contraband enlisted in St. James Parish was Adolph Tureaud, whose path would cross Louis Antoine's after the war. Tureaud's white grandfather had also sought refuge from Saint Domingue, but he ended up as a large plantation owner with a wife and eight children. His son, a contemporary of Louis Antoine's father Francois, had seven legitimate children and several children born of a relationship with Josephine, a young mulatto slave woman he bought from his mother-in-law. He manumitted her but not the child, a boy, Adolph, born in 1840. Adolph lived on the plantation with his mother and three siblings, all of whom his father baptized and gave the Tureaud name. Freed by the war, afterwards he returned to St. James Parish, where he became a farmer and had a son, Louis. He ran for office when the Republicans took over during Reconstruction. He, Louis Antoine, and other colored veterans served in the legislature together.[36]

In the months after the Battle of Port Hudson, Louis Antoine and his troops joined the other black soldiers building fortifications and digging rifle pits. Blistering heat, lack of clean water, the stench of death, and mosquitoes plagued them. On June 30, 1863, the Union command reassigned Louis Antoine to detached duty to the Freedman's Aid Society in New Orleans. Back home he found that his brother Pierre, his Pascal cousins, and other younger Colored Creoles had answered the Union call to organize regiments for the defense of New Orleans during the siege of Port Hudson. They served in the city from July 4 to August 13, 1863.[37]

Cailloux's valor made his fate a matter of great public interest. Louis Antoine and others had already carried word of the circumstances of his death through the Union news blackout into the city. L'Union helped to disseminate widely the story of his valiant service in the cause of liberty and the circumstances of his death. On July 4, the paper published a poem, "Captain Andre Cailloux and his Companions in arms."

Louis Antoine and the Colored Creole community mourned Cailloux, while Confederate New Orleans ridiculed him. They tried to drive a wedge between Colored Creoles and the Yankees, accurately arguing that "Negroes" had been urged to fight only to be massacred and then left on the field. Northern slave supporters, known as "Copperheads" and Confederates demeaned and besmirched Cailloux's memory and sacrifice endlessly. Claims that he and the others were cowards forced by Union bayonets at their back to confront death were abroad. A song written in Creole dialect called "Captaine Caillou" mocked Cailloux and white radicals. The blacks were naive, stupid, and timid, misled into thinking they could defeat the rebels. On the day of the funeral, journalist and Confederate apologist Henry Perry published a broadside equating Cailloux with an insect and describing his wife Felicie as a buxom scullery maid.[38]

The venom spread by Confederates and their sympathizers who opposed the war left undiminished the esteem afforded Cailloux by Louis Antoine and other Colored Creoles, who saw him as emblematic of their struggle for equal rights. Nothing about him or the circumstances of his death and funeral, of course, impressed Banks. Louis Antoine had to face the fact of Banks' continuing campaign against colored officers.

Three months after the Battle of Port Hudson, Banks wrote President Lincoln that when he arrived to command, the colored troops were "demoralized from various causes." Their officers were constantly in conflict with white troops, whose officers believed they should not remain in the service. Conflicts between white and black troops before the Battle of Port Hudson had arisen because of the character of the "Negro" officers, who were "unsuited for duty." Banks even omitted the First Regiment from the list of those entitled to inscribe Port Hudson on their regimental flags. Louis Antoine's soldiers continued to lack clothing, appropriate arms, and material support after the battle in which they had grievously suffered.[39]

Meanwhile, Banks continued to rid himself of colored officers in Louis Antoine's regiment just as he had earlier in the Second and Third Regiments. When colored officers were discharged or forced to resign, their troops often deserted, but this didn't stop Banks.[40]

Louis Antoine acted on a decision he made after Cailloux's funeral to remain silent about his racial identity when Banks renewed the project of removing colored officers from the Native Guards. When inquiries were addressed to Negro officers, Louis Antoine simply ignored them as if they did not apply to him. He left it to the command to identify and expel him. Finally, only a silent Louis Antoine remained in the First Regiment. His silence gave him the opportunity to serve as an officer, which probably accounts for his silence about the abuse his soldiers suffered.

Louis Antoine, a captain since March 1863, when Dumas left the regiment to join the Third Native Guards, returned from detached duty to the Freedman's Aid Society in New Orleans in September 1863. Dumas, a major serving as a staff officer, resigned in July 1863 when the other colored officers were ejected. Louis Antoine signed none of the protests submitted by the colored officers against their treatment and kept his own counsel about the inequities visited upon his troops. He saw the men under his command daily demoralized by the refusal to pay them what they had been promised, the manual labor they performed, and the lack of sufficient clothing to cover their backs as they dug and built fortifications. And yet, he avoided showing more than general sympathy for them, thereby concealing his own identity.

After the Battle of Port Hudson there were many desertions. Freedmen, former field slaves from throughout the South, who would not have known Louis Antoine as colored constituted the new recruits. Remaining an officer became easier because any remaining person of color from New Orleans probably left it up to him to hide his secret. Perhaps those who knew regarded it as justified deception of the white military command, who would have been alerted if they had read the French-language colored newspapers. The papers reported on the exploits of the men of color and especially their "Captaine Snaer."[41]

Louis Antoine watched Banks proceed with the humiliation of the remaining colored officers in the Native Guards, forcing them into resigning or drumming them out through a fraudulent process of "reviews." But he was committed to staying in the officer corps. To be sure, he believed in the ideology of human rights that demanded equality, and stepping forward would have asserted that view. But he decided instead to act on the strongly held view that only an individual could determine his own identity. By refusing to indicate he was colored, Louis Antoine soon found himself alone among a group of white Northern officers who took the colored officers' places.

Throughout the Union Army, about 100 "Negroes" served as commissioned officers, two thirds of whom were in the Native Guards regiments. These included New Orleans Creole Charles Sauvinet, who stayed with the Second Regiment as a staff officer at Ship Island, not leading troops in battle like Louis Antoine, until the end of the war. Another quarter of the officers were chaplains and surgeons.

Six Massachusetts officers received commissions in 1865, all but one after the war was over. Three other "Negro" officers served with an independent artillery battery at Fort Leavenworth.[42]

On February 22, 1864, assigned with his troops to garrison Port Hudson, Louis Antoine finally found a safe opportunity to complain about a matter involving race. He and other "officers of the United States Volunteer Army now holding positions in the colored military organization in Louisiana" petitioned the Congress to abolish slavery and enact "the advancement of the colored men to all civil and political rights enjoyed by white men." The signers of the petition included Negro officers shortly before they were expelled and white officers in the Regiment.[43]

Louis Antoine developed a cordial friendship with at least one of the white officers in his regiment, George Blight Halstead. He served with him for about two years before and after the Battle of Port Hudson. He kept a picture of Halstead inscribed to him in his personal papers. Halstead was from a well-off New Jersey family with ancestors who had fought in the Revolution and had been captured and imprisoned in Libby prison in 1862 in Virginia. After he was exchanged, he first worked for the adjutant general and then took an officer's appointment in the Native Guards. After his service there he was staff to commanders in a number of battles in Virginia and stayed in the service until 1866. Halstead, a lifelong bachelor, lived with his parents in New Jersey and was trained as a lawyer. When the Civil War began he was already forty-one years of age.[44]

Halstead summarized his experience in his pension application, which he filed for the first time in 1890. By August 9, 1894, the pension claims officer reviewing his claim for additional disability described him as having become "senile." He had known Halstead for several years and he was not "robust" and "is somewhat peculiar in his habits and retiring in disposition." After being discharged in the winter of 1866, he lived with his mother at least until the 1870s, when at some point he went to Minnesota and lived with his brother Frank on Lake Minnetonka in his home called the Hermitage. They were regarded by the locals, who called them hermits, as eccentrics. He apparently died in a fire at the Hermitage in 1901. Although Louis Antoine carried his photograph they never apparently kept in contact.[45]

Louis Antoine's new commander, Lieutenant Henry Merriam, formerly of the Maine Twentieth Volunteers, joined the regiment, renamed the Seventy-Third United States Colored Infantry, in the summer of 1864. Merriam was sympathetic to the suffering of his troops, but the arduous duty continued and so did desertions. In the late summer of 1864 white officers complained to higher authorities about the continued abuse of their Negro troops, but no amount of back-and-forth and protest relieved the men of the fatigue duty. They might as well have been engineers devoted to construction, but they served without the hearty diet engineers typically received to sustain physical labor. On May 27, Merriam reported an assault on his men by Union white troops. Amid the tensions it was difficult to keep white officers in a black regiment; they resigned the thankless duty because of the conditions and lengthy delays in promotion.[46]

Louis Antoine went on seven days' leave on October 10, 1864, to go to New Orleans because of severe illness in his family. Perhaps his always sickly sister Angela, who died in 1865, had fallen ill again. After his return, in November 1864, Secretary of War William Stanton finally responded favorably to pleas from the regiment's officers to allow Port Hudson to be emblazoned on the regimental banners.

On January 1, after white officers left and no others could be recruited, the regiment had only four captains and three lieutenants available for duty. During 1864, the lack of pay and poor working conditions and worry about their families had led 121 men to desert, although search parties had apprehended 43. Finally, Congress decided in June 1864 to pay Negro and white officers equally and retroactively to January 1, 1864, but not their enlisted men. The pay was slow in coming.[47]

When the Native Guards received orders to prepare for the field in February 1865, a number of men returned voluntarily from desertion. Merriam restored them with simple loss of pay and allowances for the time lost. He concluded that because morale had long been low due to unequal treatment, desertion was not unexpected. After President Lincoln offered amnesty in March 1865, sixty-seven more men returned to the regiment. In March also the Congress finally enacted a law granting equal pay to Negro soldiers from the time of their enlistment. Some, however, did not receive the bounty they were promised at enlistment until 1867.[48]

In March, the regiment received orders to join General John P. Hawkins' division of colored troops as part of a union operation against Fort Blakeley, Alabama. A week after arriving by steamer at Barrancas, Florida, on March 20, the regiment marched toward Fort Blakeley through northwest Florida and southern Alabama. A heavy rain made the roads and camp a swamp and wagons were mired in the mud. Going toward Pensacola they had to wade often up to their armpits, across a one- to three-mile Gulf inlet. Supply wagons lagged behind and rations ran out, reducing them to four days of eating corn roasted during the night. One lieutenant reported that he went two days without food and that his men were on half rations. The regiment arrived at Fort Blakeley on April 2, where a week-long siege ended successfully on April 9 as one of the last battles in the war.[49]

The regiment crashed through the Confederate fortifications and captured their rifle pits at Fort Blakeley. Merriam then volunteered to storm the fort before the general assault. The Native Guards went forward, capturing seven pieces of artillery and some prisoners. On April 9 the enemy's fire suddenly ceased, but when the troops advanced to take the fort, the firing began again. General Pile reported that the rebels threw down their weapons and ran toward the white troops as the African American regiment approached them. Within 30 minutes the 3,500 men and artillery at the fort had surrendered. The regiment lost two men who were killed, and two were wounded. Louis Antoine courageously led his men in the assault as they were the first to plant their regimental flag on the parapet, but he "took a ball in his left foot," leaving him disabled with shrapnel fragments.[50]

Louis Antoine was appointed Major by Brevet for "gallant conduct in the assault and capture of Fort Blakely, Ala. to date from April 9, 1865." Colonel Merriam received the Congressional Medal of Honor. Merriam wrote about Louis Antoine, "Captain Snaer fell with a severe wound at my feet as I reached the line. He refused to sheathe his sword or to be carried off the field . . . No braver officer has honored any flag." On April 16, 1865, *La Tribune's* French-language edition described the battle and praised "Captaine Louis Snaer" for his courageous leadership. Despite it all, Louis Antoine had managed to stay as an officer until the end.[51]

After the battle Louis Antoine's regiment marched to Montgomery, where they heard that on the very day they stormed Fort Blakeley, Robert E. Lee had surrendered at Appomattox. There they also learned of Abraham Lincoln's death. Under general orders, the regiment joined the rest of the Union military in wearing mourning badges. Bells in New Orleans tolled one hour starting at midnight and one hour before sundown. Salutes of twenty-one guns sounded in the city in tribute to the president and the men who took Fort Blakeley. *La Tribune* reported on the bravery of the regiment, Louis Antoine's leadership, and the loss of the president and like other papers draped its columns in black.[52]

Louis Antoine spent the next six days, after the April 9 battle, in a field hospital near Fort Blakeley and was then transferred to the U.S. General Hospital (Hotel St. Louis) in New Orleans. When he filed for a pension in August 1878, he described his wounds: "Received shell wound in left foot. Three metatarsal bones fractured. Left foot painful requiring constant surgical attention."[53]

From May 18, 1865, he was on a leave of absence in New Orleans, where his brother Pierre Anatole married Marie Cassagne on July 1 in St. Mary's Catholic Church. In July and August, Louis Antoine remained in the city, detached to work with the Freedmen's Bureau, until his honorable discharge on September 23, 1865. The military papers from beginning to end described him only as having a fair complexion, gray eyes, and light hair. The Army description books did not record race, and this helped to make Louis Antoine's passing possible.[54]

Demobilization of the Native Guards came just as the Colored Creole leadership in New Orleans had organized a shadow election to protest their exclusion from the ballot. On the evening of September 23rd, 250 former members of the regiment marched down Conti Street with fife and drum and stopped in front of *La Tribune* and cheered. The editor promised to battle "with pen and ink for the same noble cause" for which they had fought. A month later, at the conclusion of another march and rally by about 100 veterans, the men donated $500 to help defray expenses for the Friends of Universal Suffrage, an interracial political coalition of former soldiers and other loyalists organized in June 1865. Chapters of the Cailloux League, filled by returning veterans, donated money to the Friends.[55]

Also, spiritualist mediums linked to the Colored Creole leadership claimed they contacted Cailloux to give them inspiration in the struggle. For some individual French-speaking free people of color, American spiritualism offered an enlightened alternative to the increasing conservatism of the Catholic Church. Becoming increasingly popular in New Orleans in the 1850s, spiritualist leaders advocated a new Catholic faith based on universal brotherhood. Colored Creoles assumed leadership as spiritualist mediums. Nineteenth-century American spiritualism originated in New York in the mid-1840s and swept North America and Europe. A synthesis of European thinkers Charles Fourier, Franz Anton Mesmer, and Emanuel Swedenborg, they derived their inspiration from scientific advances of the seventeenth century. Newton's theory of universal gravitation was key.

Charles Testut, a white French émigré and literary colleague of Colored Creole writer Camille Thierry, brought the movement to the Colored Creole circles. In 1852 he had attended his first spiritualist gathering, and soon afterwards, receiving a spirit message, he formed his own circle. The Church, using the police, forced the spreading movement underground, where it flourished in private residences in the 1850s. In 1858, Henri Rey, age twenty-seven, a well-educated member of the Tremé's families and the brother of Native Guards Lieutenant Louis Rey, and other relatives converted to Spiritualism. The family had helped establish the Sisters of Holy Family, held a pew at St. Augustine's, and had financed one of the stained glass windows.[56]

Through Rey's circle came the spirit message from Cailloux, urging them on in the quest for equal rights. Guided by his spirit, free people of color hoped to gain the liberty and justice with the Union victory for which Andre Cailloux had given his life.[57]

Louis Antoine hoped that the freedom and opportunity he gained by refusing to identify his race could now be opened to the entire Snaer family, along with other Colored Creoles and the freed people. He would join with other former Native Guards officers in the political struggle ahead.

CHAPTER 5

....

Becoming "Negroes"

Former Native Guards officer Charles Sauvinet had accepted a position as head of the local branch of the Freedmen's Bank and had arrived by boat from New York in early 1866. He witnessed the start of a "massacre" in 1866. He reported looking out the window of his office on Carondelet Street at the marchers and seeing the police pass by; after "sufficient time" passed for them to get to the Mechanics' Institute, "the disturbances began." Sauvinet's porter called him "outdoors," saying "they are fighting."[1]

Although Sauvinet did not join in, striding along with three drummers, a fife, and a flag in front, other Native Guards veterans constituted the backbone of the marchers. First, a white man jostled a marcher, someone hit him, and then a shot was fired. Two-and-a-half hours of battle ensued as the marchers desperately tried to defend themselves by tossing bricks at the guns. The police and Confederate veterans joined white men and boys who even chased those marchers who attempted to escape.

Thirty-four Negroes and three white radicals were killed and more than 100 wounded in the riot. At least one of the dead and nine of the wounded were Native Guards veterans. General Philip Sheridan wanted to punish the perpetrators but found no support from President Johnson.[2]

The same fair skin that had permitted Louis Antoine to remain an officer saved his brother Seymour Snaer and some of the Colored Creoles from harm that day. Seymour, who described himself as keeping "a commission store in partnership with my brother," told the Congressional committee investigating the incident that he saw white men and police officers shoot several Negroes as they tried to escape from the attack in the hall and on his way home. When asked where he was born, he answered New Orleans. Asked about his descent, he answered, as best he knew, French and German, not mentioning his mixed race; as a result, he passed just as Louis Antoine had done in the Union officer corps. He said that as a Republican, he went to the Institute because he held sympathy with the goals. He affirmed his support for Negro voting rights and the disfranchisement of the former rebels. He told the committee that he escaped any injury that day except for a "little scratch" on his face. The police officers he passed by did not harm him. When asked if they could have if they had wanted to, Seymour answered, "Yes, they could have; they did not know me, I suppose." Essentially he avoided injury because the whites he encountered did not know he was a Colored Creole.[3]

The 1866 massacre was one of the bloodiest episodes on the road to black political participation during Reconstruction in Louisiana. The massacre, along with the passage of Black Codes and the Confederate resurgence in the other Southern states, enraged Northerners. They elected new Congressmen who passed the Reconstruction Acts of 1867, affirming Negro male suffrage. But the changes and conflicts that led to the massacre began earlier after the Union gained control of New Orleans in 1862 and then the state of Louisiana after 1863.

Much changed while Louis Antoine and other Native Guards were away in the Army. Although New Orleans was the region's commercial capital and largest city, during the Civil War the federal blockade of the port and the collapse of agriculture disrupted trade. Wartime occupation left the city dilapidated and tattered. The devastation in rural areas and the continuous influx of freed people into the city, after the Union victory in 1862, required a long period of adjustment. Union officials struggled to provide relief supplies and refugee camps. At the end of June 1863, Louis Antoine experienced these problems directly when he was on temporary assignment to detached duty with the Freedman's Aid Society in New Orleans. By early 1864, the ever-increasing number of freed people remained crowded into any housing they could find, often with little in the way of sanitary facilities.

Another significant change was that more Negroes had guns than before the war. Armed black soldiers entered and left the city, or had been organized for its defense, and when the war ended some kept their weapons. Moreover, Colored Creoles and former slaves had fought together on the battlefield. Now, with the Emancipation Proclamation and the Thirteenth Amendment, they were slaves no more, and the old three-tiered racial system had collapsed. Identity, citizenship, political rights, and economic opportunity were the issues of the hour.

Louis Antoine and other Colored Creole veterans, including those ejected from the officer corps, and their families represented a small number of people surrounded by freed people, and these issues mattered as they imagined their future. The Snaers, especially Louis Antoine and his brother Seymour, and other Colored Creoles found that they held influence out of all proportions to the size of their population and actively participated in the unfolding developments.

To deal with the immediate pressure of economic decline and the mounting refugee problem, Union officials adopted a program reminiscent of Louverture's decision to ask the freed people to keep working on the plantations during the Haitian Revolution in order to keep the economy from collapsing. Under this Union plan, General Banks signed agreements with loyal planters to have able-bodied Negroes found in New Orleans without visible means of support arrested and placed on plantations to work for $3 to $10 a month. Laborers had to have a pass to leave the plantation. The plan was designed to revive the commercial life of New Orleans and add funds to the Union treasury. The plantation owners could apply any needed discipline with the support of the Union soldiers. In exchange for their work and subjugation, the former slaves would receive food, clothing, and shelter in addition to wages. Banks also ordered basic education of plantation workers.[4]

Some African Americans supported the policy, but others saw it as no different from slavery. *La Tribune* pointed out that the freedman was at the total mercy of the planter, had to stay on the plantation, was bound by contract no matter what the conditions, and was forced to buy provisions from the master at whatever price, basically earning nothing for his work.[5]

Benjamin Flanders, who took over management of the plantations for the Treasury Department, said that when he met with planters, all they wanted to know was who would handle the whip under the new policy and how to keep the workers on the plantation and prevent them from visiting the city. He found that many of the workers, as under slavery, were ragged, lacked sufficient food, and in the end received no compensation. At this point economics coincided directly with political developments.[6]

Mobilization by former Native Guards officers, who had been removed by Banks, to gain suffrage for African Americans had started while Louis Antoine and Colored Creoles in the ranks were still in service. The organizers joined with the former slaves and white Republicans from the North, and local Unionists who had begun an equal rights movement, and they became leaders in the cause.

Shortly after the Union captured New Orleans in June 1862, white Unionists, consisting of no more than 10 percent of the population, organized meetings to stir Union sentiment and started Union clubs. Colored Creole leaders held meetings to plan political action as early as September 1862, when they formed the Native Guards regiments.

By the time Louis Antoine and his comrades stood before Port Hudson in the spring of 1863, delegates from the Union clubs had formed a Union Association with Thomas Durant, a prominent white lawyer and socialist, as president. Durant urged abolition of slavery with the encouragement of the Lincoln administration. Colored Creoles pressed the issue and *L'Union* published the minutes of the Association. Durant proceeded to register loyal white voters in order to have elections and a new constitution that would end military government in the state.[7]

While Louis Antoine remained in the Army, the former Native Guards officers focused on the political struggle. On November 5, 1863, during a meeting of free colored persons at Economy Hall, the headquarters of the Economy and Mutual Aid Association, P. B. S. Pinchback led the speakers and demanded political rights. The meeting sent a resolution to Governor George F. Shepley asking permission to register as voters, but received no response. In November 1863, *L'Union* asked that a proposed state constitutional convention include their enfranchisement and sponsored an interracial rally calling for the registration of free colored men.[8]

The equal rights movement based its suffrage claims on the Louisiana Purchase treaty guarantee of all rights, advantages, and immunities of citizenship to the territorial inhabitants. Jean Baptiste Roudanez, who later served as proprietor of *La Tribune*, made this argument before the Freedmen's Inquiry Commission in 1863. He also stressed the free colored men's intelligence, respectability, and loyalty and their history of military service. The advocates left out rights for freedmen, perhaps because their continued ambivalence about their own status and longstanding acceptance of a human rights ideology that condoned slavery, or for practical reasons.[9]

Radicals in the Colored Creole press routinely argued for the rights of slaves and free persons of color, but this did not always translate into action. For example, on September 1, 1863, the l'Institution des Catholique's board of directors denied the request of freedmen for the admission of their children to the school. There is no evidence that their position changed at any time during the war. (The Church, by the way, did not admit a former slave to the Colored Creole Sisters of the Holy Family until 1869, when a former cook at the archbishopric was admitted. She became Sister Mary Joachim in 1871, seven years after slavery was abolished.)[10]

In December 1863, President Lincoln grew impatient at the slow pace of Durant's efforts. He decided to begin Reconstruction in Louisiana by ordering General Banks to organize a new state government when 10 percent of those who had voted in 1860 took a loyalty oath to the Union. The order ignored the Colored Creoles' demand for suffrage. Under the 10 percent plan, delegates from the various Union organizations in the state met at Lyceum Hall on December 15 and formed the Louisiana State Convention of the Friends of Freedom. They allowed delegates from two clubs of free men of color to take seats.

In December 1863, the equal rights advocates began circulating a petition, which eventually contained 1,000 names of property-holding men, to demand suffrage for free men of color. Their contributions to national defense took center stage: twenty-seven of the signers had fought in the Battle of New Orleans.

On January 19, 1864, a meeting of the Union Association decided to lay the equal suffrage cause before President Lincoln. The 10 percent plan required election of state officers by February 22, 1864. Michael Hahn, the Union candidate, won the governorship. The Confederates also separately elected a governor, Henry Watkins, the last Confederate governor of Louisiana. In the gubernatorial election, Colored Creoles failed in the effort to make their suffrage claim an issue.

The petition that Snaer and his colleagues, white and colored, signed on February 22, 1864, at Port Hudson, petitioning Congress to abolish slavery and enact "the advancement of the colored men to all civil and political rights enjoyed by white men," reflected the leadership of the Native Guards officers in the effort.[11]

In Washington, radicals, including Senator Charles Sumner, persuaded the petitioners from New Orleans, Jean Baptiste Roudanez and Albert Bertonneau, a former officer in the Second Native Guards, to add a line asking for the vote for "especially those who have vindicated their right to vote by bearing arms." Roudanez and Bertonneau presented the petition to President Lincoln on March 12, 1864, and thereafter to the House and Senate. The next day Lincoln wrote a private note to Governor Hahn concerning the upcoming state convention: "I barely suggest for your private consideration whether some of the colored people might be let in . . . as for instance, the very intelligent, and especially those who have fought gallantly in our ranks."[12]

The 10 percent Unionist convention voted overwhelmingly to abolish slavery but deferred the suffrage question. Some members of the convention opposed granting African Americans any rights at all, insisting that slavery had been a benign institution beneficial to blacks. The convention finally adopted clauses allowing the legislature to enact equal suffrage, including formerly enslaved African Americans, and provisions for public education for all, which the legislature did not do.[13]

L'Union consistently pushed strongly for equal rights for all throughout the debate. When the paper shut down on July 19, 1864, some blamed hostility from local whites and threats on the life of the publisher and subscribers. However, Paul Trevigne, who had become the publisher, blamed the closure on "the apathy of potential subscribers, pro-Confederate Catholic priests; and the indifference of Union soldiers." The paper always had a small base of subscribers and was published primarily in French. Perhaps, also, the editorial style, based on the human rights rhetoric of the French Revolution, might have seemed anachronistic and impractical except to Colored Creole readers.[14]

After the convention completed its work on July 23, 1864, the new Louisiana constitution, without Negro suffrage, gained approval in a September election. The new legislature met in October, elected two senators, and adopted the Thirteenth Amendment. The president gave official recognition, but Congress refused to seat the senators. Throughout the summer and fall of 1864, some Colored Creoles continued to press for suffrage. They had available a revived journalistic voice when Roudanez and his brother founded *La Tribune* to succeed *L'Union* as a French- and English-language paper. Trevigne served briefly as editor until Roudanez persuaded Belgian scientist and social activist Jean Charles Houzeau to take over the paper in November 1864.

Until early 1868, *La Tribune* was a principal advocate for equality of rights for colored men in New Orleans. It also became a veritable official organ of the Republican Party and of the U.S. Government in Louisiana. The paper also covered the military activities of the Negro troops, including "our Louis Snaer," and the political efforts of Republicans, in both French and English.

A "quadroon" bill that Colored Creoles presented to the legislature, asking for recognition as white for persons having not more than one-fourth African blood, showed that some still thought in terms of the old three-tiered structure and had not accepted the new reality of race and emancipation. Traditionally, terms such as *mulattoes*, *mestizos*, and *octoroons* indicated degrees of non-white blood.[15] General Banks had proposed that if a federal court would decree that men with more white than colored blood could pass for white, they could be registered voters.

Then Charles Smith introduced the bill in the Senate as one way of enacting limited suffrage. New Orleans representative A. C. Hill noted that the bill would have excluded Andre Cailloux, the martyred hero of the community, a pure African. He thought the fight over the bill would simply divide the formerly free and the formerly enslaved, and that the two should stand together. Some Colored Creoles, however, kept believing that if they could separate from the freed people, they would have a political future and equal rights. Some had very close ties with Confederate whites and some had even served in the Confederacy.[16]

While the equal rights battle raged in New Orleans, on October 4, 1864, in Syracuse, New York, at the last of the protesting "Negro Conventions" that had been convened from time to time since 1830, the battle became more heated. Former Native Guards Captain James Ingraham, who was the son of a slave woman and a white man, spoke English, and was a Methodist, served as a delegate from Louisiana and fired up the convention. He displayed the blood-stained battle flag of the regiment he had taken from Port Hudson at Syracuse and in his other public appearances. Everyone identified it as Cailloux's, even though it had actually been borne by the slain color bearer Sergeant Planciancios. Ingraham spoke eloquently of the battle, helping to inspire the convention to create a National Equal Rights League. In New Orleans, Ingraham organized mass meetings to demand suffrage. Auxiliary Cailloux leagues were formed to support the league and to raise money.[17]

At a December 1864 mass meeting called by the National Equal Rights League, New Orleans Negroes organized a local branch, and Ingraham attacked a bill introduced in the state legislature to give suffrage to those persons having no more than one-fourth African blood. The "quadroon bill," he asserted, was "a firebrand thrown out to divide us," with preferences for the lightest colored. The audience, which included a large number of women, interrupted his speech with applause.[18]

Seymour Rene Snaer was an active participant in the meetings, including the January 1865 Convention of Colored Men of Louisiana organized to discuss giving support to the National Equal Rights League. Some of the wealthiest and most prominent Colored Creoles attended, according to a published attendance list of eighty-three names. They included Dr. Roudanez; landowners Aristide Mary and Thomy Lafon, Arnold Bertonneau, and Victor McCarty; the future Lieutenant Governor Oscar Dunn; and Jordan Noble, the War of 1812 drummer boy at Chalmette. The convention elected Ingraham president.[19]

La Tribune trumpeted the solidarity between free and freed persons at the convention. However, Colored Creoles again presented to the legislature the "quadroon" bill. Over the objections *of La Tribune* on February 17, 1865, they introduced this petition for partial suffrage into the legislature. It died in committee.[20]

Most of the Colored Creoles came to understand that any political future they might have was based on the prospects and freedom and security of the freedmen. Politically, they had all become "Negroes" with emancipation. Morality, racial sensibility, and practicality engendered Colored Creole empathy for the plight of the freed people. The Louisiana Equal Rights League promoted not just their political participation, but also their moral, educational, and industrial development. Well-to-do Colored Creoles mobilized to aid the less fortunate freed people. Some played important roles in the Freedmen's Aid Association and cooperated with the poor to organize schools, old people's homes, and orphanages.[21]

The League sent agents to parishes to check on the condition of the freed people and appealed to military officials for the redress of their grievances. They also established a Bureau of Industry to aid needy Negroes in New Orleans. In the first monthly report in March 1865, Ingraham, as Superintendent, declared that during February the Bureau had received and spent $251.15 in obtaining rations for 190 of the 192 persons who applied for them. He also wrote letters for thirty-six persons, obtained employment for thirty-two of the thirty-seven persons who applied for it, obtained passes for twenty-two, and was instrumental in obtaining the release of several persons from jail. Additionally, he obtained wood and coal for several people and gave general assistance to 586 others to alleviate the suffering.

For the rural areas, members of the Equal Rights League, the *Tribune*, and other white Unionists developed a proposal unlike the Union Army's contract labor plan, which they considered abusive. In 1864, the *Tribune* called upon well-off free Negroes to form a Farmer's Association to buy up abandoned plantations and lease them to the freedmen, who would work for shares. Not only would this be a good investment, but it would bind their interests to those of the freedmen and give them an opportunity to break the power of the old planters. It would also help the freedmen learn to become self-reliant.

Under the *Tribune* plan, the laborers would feed and clothe themselves, be free to move about, and receive monthly or weekly wages in addition to a share of the crop. The several groups interested in this plan formed the New Orleans Freedmen's Aid Association on February 27, 1865. The plan used some of the ideas of Charles Fourier's socialist community.[22]

To give loans and furnish supplies, education, and advice to the freedmen, the Association established a bank, into which each of the sixty members paid $20 annual dues. Some of the wealthiest New Orleans Colored Creoles were members of the Association, including broker Aristide Mary and Roudanez. Benjamin Flanders and Thomas J. Durant were the best-known white men among the sixty members. They solicited money from Northerners and other freedmen's associations. By August 1865 they had rented several plantations and given freedmen provisions and seed and awarded prizes for industry and zeal. The plan gave an opportunity for Colored Creoles to bond with the freed people in the changed picture after emancipation, but the Association established only four small plantations before the federal decision to return plantations to their owners after the war ended their efforts. However, the funders continually sounded the call for industry, family, and morality and no dependency among the freed people.[23]

New Orleans' economy recovered from the War slowly. The deterioration of the levees, the collapse of sugar production, and a series of epidemics and floods stalled growth. The collapse of sugar production and the weakness of tobacco sales offered a stark contrast to the resurgent strength of cotton production and trade. But from 1868 to the nationwide panic of 1873, New Orleans had only a modest period of recovery and prosperity.

The rise of the railroads diverted much of the agricultural traffic from the Midwest and up and down the river from New Orleans, but the waterfront remained the center of the city's commercial life. Agricultural goods, whether arriving by rail or steamboat, were transported to Northern or European markets by ship. Dockworkers were an essential part of the process. Blacks, mostly freed now as opposed to the slaves who worked before the war, did the heavy work as roustabouts on the steamboats on the Mississippi. The screwmen, who knew the intricacies of packing the most cotton safely with jackscrews and then seeing to its careful unloading, were still at the top. Longshoremen, the largest group, received cotton from the screwmen and unloaded sugar and other goods themselves. Black scale hands assisted white weighers and assistant weighers.[24]

In New Orleans freed people found their economic opportunities limited in the postwar environment by white unions, corrupt city officials, and racist employers. Labor unions excluded anyone of African descent and attacked anyone who it appeared might take jobs from whites, including attacks on Negro stevedores on the docks in 1867.[25]

Negro workers organized several unions of longshoremen and teamsters between 1865 and 1877. Following the pattern of free colored people before the war, they also established several new mutual aid associations to bury the dead, aid the sick, and provide social outlets for families. They also participated in several strikes, some with white workers and others in competition for higher wages.[26]

In May 1867, Negro longshoremen struck against white and Negro contractors who hired them to unload ships when they tried to pay them less than they had agreed to. They chased the contractors off the docks and marched to the Freedman's Bureau office to complain. But General Joseph Mower ordered them to stop the disruption and stationed soldiers along the docks. When the contractors hired replacement workers ("scabs"), the black workers ran them off. The general quieted matters by ordering that the striking workers be paid fairly.

The black workers struck again in 1872, boarding a ship loaded with scabs. Then a series of strikes among both black and white workers occurred in 1880. There were attempts to form a union with black and white workers, but these efforts were undermined by scabs.[27]

Most of the Snaers fared well economically throughout Reconstruction. Louis Antoine lived much of the time at the longtime Tremé residence on St. Claude. His brother Peter, who apparently like most in the period apprenticed with another dentist, ran a dental practice nearby, supporting his wife, Mary Cassagne, and their children. Seymour tried various occupations, including working as a cigar merchant, before becoming a lawyer.[28]

Until she died in 1865, Louis Antoine's sister Angela had lived with the family of Samuel, Louis' disabled half-brother who throughout his career as a musician and composer had financial difficulties. Samuel's wife, Marie Noel, who possessed valuable real estate she inherited from her mother, died in 1867. Unable to pay the latest mortgage, he lost the property in a sale for the debt. His household included two children, Joseph Samuel and Leopold, who may have been named for Leopold Guichard.[29]

Francois, described as a capitalist in the 1870 Census, remained financially well off. He was worth $10,000 in real property and $4,000 in personal property. His store still sold groceries, tinware, dry goods, and alcoholic beverages. In their household, the family engaged two Negro servants: a cook, Esther Thomas, age forty-five, and a housekeeper, Emily Samuel. He also employed a store clerk: a mulatto, Fernand Calico. His son Victor, who also clerked, and Victoria Rose still resided with their parents. Victoria taught at the Clio Street Public school, in midcity up from the Tremé. The Reconstruction government had established mandatory desegregated schools in the city for the first time.[30]

Some Colored Creoles were among the New Orleans residents who suffered severe economic distress during the war. Felicie Cailloux, the widow of the hero Andre Cailloux, symbolized the suffering some families experienced. She spent more than a year trying to obtain his back pay and years seeking a pension for his service. Letters of introduction to General Banks availed her nothing. In 1867 the government denied her a pension because of a clerical error on her application caused by her inability to read English. Finally, in 1871, she began receiving a pension of $20 per month. She died three years later on October 19, 1874.[31]

Seymour Rene, like other Negroes who followed advice to save eagerly, kept an account in the branch of the Freedmen's Bank. During its seven-year existence, freedmen and former free people of color made more than 10,000 deposits from bounties, lottery tickets, associations, and churches. By 1867, more than $1,994,340 had been deposited. When the bank collapsed in 1874, Seymour and the other depositors lost everything.[32]

The bank, chartered by Congress in 1865 and supported by community leaders, held out the hope that saving would pave the way for economic sufficiency, but when the bank collapsed, Negro businesses and businessmen saw everything disappear in a snap. The collapse of the bank hit hardest those who trusted the government and began saving to buy homes or start businesses. Uneducated laborers sold their deposit books to speculators for ten cents on the dollar.[33]

The crash also psychologically damaged the Negro community, as many would never trust a bank again. The *Louisianan*, a defender of the bank, wrote that its failure had "caused on the part of our people, not only a feeling of distrust for other moneyed corporations, but has created a feeling of apathy in regard to saving and intensified the desire to spend in a round of pleasure, the earnings of a week, after the expenses of the household have been met."[34]

Distrust of the bank and depreciation of property values added to the devastation among Negroes throughout the 1860s and 1870s. Total property held by Negroes declined from $655,820 in 1860 to $560,243 in 1870. Only forty-four held more than $3,000 in property in 1860 and only nine in 1870. However, some Colored Creoles actually prospered during the Republican era. Those who already had property and could keep it made gains. They accumulated property and held on to and expanded their real estate. Colored Creole wealth was directly tied to the support, education, and financial aid provided by their white or mixed-race relatives before the war. Many became skilled laborers before the war, and after the war they continued their dominance in many fields. Six in 1870 had land worth more than $40,000, while in 1860 there had been none.[35]

The 1870 city directory listed 169 colored businesses; all but three were one-owner concerns, and seventy-five were located in the home of the owner. They included coffeehouses, restaurants, rooming houses, and cigar stores. The grocers, including the Snaers, were one of the most successful groups. In the 1870 Census, while twenty-two of the thirty-five colored grocers owned $3,000 or less of property, six, including the Snaers, owned more than $5,000.

Seven of the eight enterprises listed in the 1870 city directory, including the Snaers, had residences located with their business. A few Colored Creoles, like Aristide Mary, owned stock and operated as brokers and commission merchants, making loans at interest to businesses and traders across racial lines, and possessed the greatest wealth.[36]

Colored Creoles and other free Negroes had long been skilled artisans, and they maintained strength in various occupations. In 1870, they still exceeded 25.5 percent of the labor force as steam boatmen, draymen, masons, bakers, carpenters and joiners, cigar makers, plasterers, barbers, hairdressers, and gardeners.[37]

The political struggle for Colored Creoles became as difficult as dealing with the economic dislocations. In June 1865, Durant and others had formed a Friends of Universal Suffrage to work for giving Negro men the right to vote. By September they held a statewide election for delegates to a Republican convention. It was convened on September 25 with white and colored delegates, two days after the shadow election organized to protest the exclusion of Negroes from the ballot. Colored Creoles remained part of an interracial coalition to gain the right to vote through the end of 1865 and into 1866. The 1866 massacre led to Congressional Reconstruction and Negro male suffrage and political participation for the first time in the 1868 elections.[38]

Great political ferment inspired African Americans in the run-up to the elections afterwards. The Union League and political clubs, mass meetings and speakers, and the selection of Negro registrars designated by the Freedmen's Bureau all added to the excitement. At the local level in towns and cities they learned how to organize local councils or branches. They would listen to a speaker, adjourn to form a council, and learn the rituals. There were announcements and newspaper readings for the illiterate. In addition to the experience gained in politics and the local councils that discussed everything, including wages, churches developed as political institutions.[39]

Women had been active participants in the equal rights meetings throughout the struggle to gain suffrage, although they could not vote. Women understood what was at stake, including educational opportunities for their children. E. Franklin Frazier described how freedwomen asserted themselves during the election of 1868: "if a husband refused to wear a picture of Republican presidential candidate, former Union General Ulysses S. Grant, around the old plantation, in the presence of the old slave Master, and/or the overseer, his wife would wear it. If he would not give it to her she would walk all the way to town to buy, beg, or borrow one to wear."[40]

Negroes saw the political activities as defining events. Men, women, and children crowded the audiences in the state houses. They expected a new day of opportunity and empowerment. Each of the constitutional conventions called in the Southern states had Negro members, but Louisiana, along with South Carolina, had a non-white majority. In most states, Negroes constituted a small minority. In six states, native whites were in the majority. Some Negro members were slaves and others free, some were emigrants from the North, and many were veterans of the Union Army. Colored Creoles played a leading role. The conventions took a moderate conciliatory position toward white Confederates, even supporting their enfranchisement.

The state constitutions approved by the Reconstruction conventions, including the one in Louisiana, were much more progressive than the constitutions of antebellum days. They abolished property qualifications for voting and holding office; some abolished imprisonment for debt. Public school systems and modernized local government were also included. These constitutions were apparently so highly regarded that even when Reconstruction was overthrown by white supremacists, their basic provisions were maintained.

In Louisiana, the constitutional convention established under the 1867 Reconstruction Act consisted of ninety-eight delegates, half white and half of African descent, several of whom were Union military veterans. Louis Sosthene Jonathan Snaer, likely the son of Francois and Marie Rochefort, represented St. Martin Parish in the convention. Leopold Guichard, whose son Robert later married Francois' daughter Victoria Rose Snaer, represented St. Bernard Parish. The convention enshrined universal suffrage for men in the new constitution. In the constitution Republican idealism, an integral part of the Colored Creole tradition, featured prominently. It provided that "all persons shall enjoy equal rights and privileges upon any conveyance of a public character." It also required all members of the general assembly and other officers to take an oath upon entering office to respect the political and civil equality of "all men." The Bill of Rights provided that all citizens shall enjoy the same civil, political, and public rights.[41]

Temporarily, in the face of mutual adversity and opportunity, the break between Colored Creoles and freedmen seemed healed. But for the upcoming elections under the new constitution, against the advice of Houzeau, who still thought solidarity with the greater mass of former slaves was a better route, Roudanez and *La Tribune* decided to support an independent ticket in 1868. The slate ran against Henry Warmoth and Oscar Dunn, a well-off free Negro plasterer and contractor who had become active in politics in the race for governor and lieutenant governor. Warmoth, an adventurer and a carpetbagger from Illinois, studied law before entering the Union Army as a lieutenant colonel at age twenty-three. He left the army, settled in Louisiana, and soon became a leader of the Republican Party. He catered to the freed people, whom he knew numerically were the future power base, and they supported him.[42]

Warmoth allied himself with rising leaders of the English-speaking and Protestant freedmen, such as Dunn and Pinchback. Roudanez and *La Tribune* ran the Colored Creole Francis Ernest Dumas, who served in the Native Guards but had been a wealthy slave owner, and spoke only French, at the top of the ticket. When he lost by two votes he decided against supporting the Republican ticket. Warmoth won the nomination by two votes. Along with Dunn and Warmoth, the Party nominated Antoine Dubuclet, a wealthy Colored Creole plantation owner, for treasurer. Dumas decided to run for lieutenant governor with white Unionist James Govan Taliaferro for governor. Taliaferro had lived in Louisiana for sixty years. He had publicly argued against secession in 1861 and had presided at the 1868 convention.

Houzeau correctly surmised that Dumas' ownership of slaves and Taliaferro's opposition to the Thirteenth Amendment abolishing slavery (although he opposed secession) meant they would get nowhere and divide the Party. Warmoth's ticket won by a landslide and then the Republican Party and Unionists withdrew their support from *La Tribune*, which ceased publication.[43]

After the state constitutional convention, the legislature met in New Orleans on June 29, 1868, ratified the Fourteenth Amendment, and elected two senators, William Pitt Kellogg and John S. Harris, who took their seats in July. New Orleans became the capital of the state until Redemption returned it to Baton Rouge in1880. Despite the presence of the Union troops still stationed throughout the state, the Democrats succeeded in choosing electors for Horatio Seymour and Francis Preston Blair Jr. for the fall 1868 presidential election, which Ulysses Grant won.

The Snaers' prospects depended, as did that of other Colored Creoles, on the outcome of the rancorous politics for control of Louisiana. On the one side stood Warmoth and his large freedmen base; on the other stood Roudanez, *L'Union*, and the other Colored Creoles, including the Snaers, using French Enlightenment ideas to seek a complete revolution toward equality. Warmoth essentially routed them, helped by Pinchback and Oscar Dunn.

After turning against them in his inaugural address, Governor Henry Warmoth admonished Negroes not to intrude socially on whites. Then he vetoed the legislature's equal public accommodations bill, which made it a crime to refuse service to Negroes. He said he wanted to repel the spirit of Saint Domingue; black government. The bill, modified to provide for damages instead, passed in February 1869.

From the passage of the 1867 Reconstruction Act legalizing black male suffrage, Union veterans and supporters competed to acquire a range of government jobs. The Colored Creoles benefitted from the two-tiered structure and their own superior education compared to the formerly enslaved. In the jostling, Louis Antoine and Seymour at first succeeded in obtaining only minor posts, Seymour as a post office clerk and Louis as a commissary agent. In April 1868, Louis Antoine ran for the post of clerk of the Fifth District Court against Louis Powers. Powers won the election, but Louis Antoine challenged his right to hold the office based on the fact that Powers was a former Confederate. The suit ended without a decision when the sheriff claimed he could not find Snaer to serve the papers. Right before the election in June 1868, Louis Antoine went on vacation to St. Louis by steamboat, which had long been common among well-off Colored Creoles. He and his brothers began deciding whether to stay in New Orleans to compete in the crowded political field or to look elsewhere in the state.[44]

By 1870, three Snaers, Louis Antoine, Seymour, and a younger brother Alex, had moved away from New Orleans. Their involvement in the political and economic conflict between and among Colored Creoles and freed people, Seymour's close shave in the 1866 massacre, Louis Antoine's survival of the war, and their family history all perhaps encouraged their risk taking. They left the city around this time for Iberia Parish, which had just been organized from parts of two other parishes, and sought new opportunities there.[45]

In 1870, the census taker noted that Louis Antoine Snaer, age twenty-seven, was living in Iberia Parish and serving as a tax collector. The 1870 Census recorded the value of his personal estate as $1,000. He lived with the family of Samuel Wakefield, another person of mixed race who later served in the Reconstruction legislature and then held several political appointments in the parish. The Snaer brothers would find opportunity but also tragedy on this new frontier away from home.

CHAPTER 6

....

Opportunity and Tragedy in Iberia Parish

I n June 1873, in Iberia Parish, Louisiana, Seymour Rene Snaer, then a 28-year-old lawyer, had a worse experience than his narrow escape from the 1866 massacre: He faced down a mob of about a thousand people demanding a lynching. The mob wanted to avenge the murder of his own brother, despite his pleas for peace. The day before, robbers had murdered 24-year-old Jean Jacques Beluche Alexamore "Alex" Snaer and his white business partner, Daniel Francois Lanet, at a grocery store they operated near the Teche River, five miles south of New Iberia.

Marauding robbers like those who killed Snaer and Lanet became common in rural areas in the South, where poverty and root-lessness prevailed after the war. The Democrat-controlled anti-Republican *Louisiana Sugar Bowl* newspaper reported that four "negroes" beat Snaer and Lanet to death, robbed their store and safe, and set the store on fire.

"Colored" Constables Paul Soule and Eli Boutte suspected the murderers had tried robbing the store previously and had been "frus-trated" by an encounter with Snaer. The constables arrested Polycarp, identified as one of the earlier intruders, and took him before Justice Albert Bolivar. He confessed after being told he would probably be hanged by the "infuriated crowd," which had gathered outside, unless he told the whole story.

Polycarp identified his accomplices as "Ozome," Martin Patterson, and Adrien Frilot. Upon their arrest for robbery and murder, the three denied their guilt. The constables, brandishing pistols, herded their captives toward the New Iberia jail. Seymour Snaer told the crowd outside the jail that after Polycarp had identified the other assailants, he promised to "intercede for his life."[1]

The Reverends Jessup and Le Croisque arrived on the scene to reinforce Seymour Snaer's message. They pleaded for calm, and Jessup asked that only lawful means be used. The crowd spared Polycarp but seized and lynched Patterson, Ozome, and Frilot, hanging them from a tree, while the crowd yelled "we cannot expect justice from the law."

The funeral of Lanet and Snaer drew a large crowd, including the lynchers, who then buried them in the Catholic cemetery. Two weeks later, the press reported that Constables Soule and Boutte said the four men who committed the crime belonged to a gang that operated in the area. The constables thought that since they had captured half the band, the others would be less likely to continue their marauding. Polycarp, who had escaped a lynching, was tried and found guilty and imprisoned for life.[2]

Polycarp, from jail, said the robbers had already selected their next victim. The *Sugar Bowl* newspaper, fomenting hysteria, suggested that "This knowledge should cause all planters and others living in the country, to make it a rule to never keep money at their houses, and let it generally be known [that there is no money there] as a matter of precaution."

One of the robbers had induced Alex Snaer to come outside from behind the counter, telling him that he had a message from a girl in the neighborhood. Snaer expressed disinterest and started to turn away when the robber who had called him "struck him a blow which staggered him to the floor. As he was rising, another attacker caught him and cut his throat. After the first blow, the men inside struck down Lanet, a small man, so that the double murder took a matter of minutes." Then they robbed the store, covered the floor and bodies with coal oil, ignited the place, and fled.[3]

The *Sugar Bowl* reported that some of the "colored people" decided one of these men who murdered Snaer and Lanet completely lacked any "redeeming quality." Probably Frilot, he had apparently "very often visited New Orleans, and was always furnished lodgings and meals at the Snaer family house by their father Francois, who always regarded him as a friend, as the unfortunate merchants always believed their murderers to be." The robbery and murder fit into the pattern of a series of criminal violations. Under impoverished post-war economic conditions and with slavery at an end and limited opportunity, thefts and robberies increased, most often accompanied by violence. In fact, gang violence from white outlaws and black and interracial bands increased all over the South in the uncertain conditions of the period.[4]

As discussed earlier, the Snaer brothers had migrated to Iberia Parish in search of opportunities on a new frontier. Louis Antoine used his veteran military hero status and Republican Party credentials to gain a number of posts. He served as a director of the Iberia Parish Public Schools, as secretary to the parish school directors, and a tax collector. In 1870, the value of his personal estate was $1,000. He lived with the family of Samuel Wakefield, a mulatto cooper (a maker of casks and barrels), and his wife and three children. By January 1872, he had been elected representative from the parish to the state legislature, serving through the extra session of 1878.[5] Along with five other former Native Guards officers, he served in the Republican state legislature along with four other Union veterans, including Adolphe Tureaud, the grandfather of leading twentieth-century civil rights litigator A. P. Tureaud, who represented Saint James Parish.[6] President Grant rewarded Wakefield, a politically active Republican, with an appointment in 1871 as Iberia deputy postmaster. He later became postmaster, a job that paid $1,200 a year.[7] Alex Snaer successfully ran for justice of the peace before joining Lanet in running the grocery store. Lanet, a Frenchman,, lived in New Iberia with the French family of Mary and Jules Poirson. He was about 50 years of age and owned about $1,000 in personal property at the time of his murder.[8]

Iberia Parish, organized from parts of two other parishes, offered better chances for political and economic advancement than the crowded field in New Orleans. New Iberia, first settled on the banks of Bayou Teche in 1779 by Spaniards from Malaga, Spain, became, after the Louisiana Purchase, simply New Town. In 1814, the federal government opened the first post office and officially named it New Iberia. It became a commerce center due to its central location between St. Martinville and New Orleans. It was located at the start of a twenty-five-mile bend in the river that flowed easterly, then northerly and finally westward, passing less than two miles from where the bend began. For merchants, it was cheaper to dock in New Iberia and unload

Southern Louisiana showing new Orleans and Iberia Parish.

goods onto wagons and carts, then take their goods up and around. In 1820, the steamboat *Teche* arrived in New Iberia and became the principal means of transport for the next sixty years.[9]

Throughout the Civil War, New Iberia and surrounding areas suffered pillaging in turn by the Confederate and Union armies. Union forces stripped the area of anything of value, loading it onto wagons and transporting it to New Orleans.[10]

Agriculture took time to recover, as it did elsewhere. The Mississippi River flooded in 1865 and 1866, destroying the cotton, corn, and sugarcane crops; those that survived froze during the harsher than normal winter in 1865–66. Insects took care of the little left.

In 1867, yellow fever swept through the Teche country, killing thousands within months. In 1868 the state established Iberia Parish with New Iberia as the seat of parish government. In 1870, a fire erupted on Main Street, destroying half of New Iberia's downtown businesses. At the time the Snaers arrived in the parish, however, the town had started to rebound.[11]

For Seymour and Louis, the murder of their brother cast a pall over their migration from home. However, they avoided the continuous political conflict in New Orleans between warring Republican Party forces, which began after the 1868 election of Warmoth to the governorship. On November 22, 1871, Oscar Dunn, the Negro lieutenant governor, then forty-six, who had broken with Warmoth, died mysteriously. Partisans believed he had been poisoned. Warmoth and P. B. S. Pinchback, who was president pro tempore of the state Senate and became acting lieutenant governor, continued to jockey for political control. In the run-up to the 1872 election, Governor Warmoth, seeing the reaction against Reconstruction approaching, switched to the Democrats and matter-of-factly declared his gubernatorial choice as Conservative Democrat John McNery. Pinchback led the Senate in bringing impeachment charges for illegal activities during the 1872 election against Warmouth. Pinchback then became governor for 35 days from December 9, 1872, until January 13, 1873, when he handed over the office to Walter P. Kellogg, whom the Republicans declared the winner of the gubernatorial election of 1872.[12]

After Kellogg prevailed in the 1872 election, when Republican officeholders attempted to assume their posts around the state, ex-Confederate whites responded with violence, intimidating, assaulting, and even killing blacks and white Republicans. The violence included the Colfax Riot, the deadliest event following the 1872 election, which claimed the lives of more than 105 men. In the wake of the election, a white militia overpowered the state militia that was in control of the Colfax parish courthouse in April 1873. They murdered large numbers of Negro militia men even after they surrendered. A Congressional military report identified eighty-one Negro men who had been murdered and estimated that another fifteen to twenty bodies had been discarded in the nearby Red River.[13]

In *Cruikshank v. U.S.* (1875), a case growing out of the massacre, three white ringleaders were brought to trial and convicted under the federal Enforcement Act of 1870, which made it a crime to interfere with any citizen's constitutional rights. The defendants appealed what they felt to be faulty indictments. Their convictions were reversed on the basis that there had been no state action and thus no violation of the Fourteenth Amendment.[14]

In instances when Republicans were able to peacefully take office, many were intimidated by the "night riders" into refusing to act as public servants in fear that their lives and the lives of their families would be taken. Kellogg followed Warmoth's perfidy by mostly ignoring Negroes after his election. Pinchback and others accused him of trying to run a white supremacist organization in the Republican Party. White vigilantes kept up their attacks on Republicans, and violence and riots increased.

The Democratic Party also used the courts to attack Republican policies. The Slaughterhouse Cases, decided in 1873, resulted in the first Supreme Court decision interpreting the Fourteenth Amendment. But the case was also an attack on a bill passed by the Republican legislature in March 1869 to grant a monopoly to the slaughtering business in New Orleans. The white New Orleans butchers who opposed the law were predominantly recent immigrants from Gascony, France, referred to locally as foreign French; they represented the third wave of ethnic French immigration to New Orleans after the original colonial settlers and the Saint Domingue refugees. While butchers had long been loathed in the city for using their powerful lobby to avoid such a cleanup in the past, the social and political circumstances of Reconstruction garnered them support from conservative Anglo-Protestant whites. They claimed the slaughterhouse ordinance was another example of the federally backed Reconstruction government imposing its will on whites. Additionally, since private slaughterhouses in town would be shut down, the white owners of these facilities would be placed on an equal footing with aspiring black butchers who had equal access to the municipally sanctioned facility downriver. The case represented the consolidation of ethnic-white immigrants under the Anglo-Protestant–dominated Democratic Party. With a new common foe to be found in New Orleans after emancipation, ethnic rivalries of the past were transformed into a simpler racial rhetoric.[15]

Between the politics of white supremacists and radical Republicans, the transition period of the 1870s was a time when some New Orleans residents sought compromise. The contested 1872 gubernatorial election was so rife with fraud on the part of both parties, historian T. Harry Williams opined, that "deciding a victor . . . would have puzzled even a Solomon." As trade languished, a biracial group of civic leaders came forward with the proposition that if Negroes were to be free citizens, as the law prescribed, it would be best for the economy and society of New Orleans to quickly reach compromises that would result in a peaceful, working government for the city.

Members of the unification, or fusionist, movement, which began in earnest in 1873, sought to unite the races of Louisiana behind the Democratic Party in order to cast off the rule of Republican carpet-baggers, as federal rule was seen by many, especially whites, as the main source of the economic downturn. This "unification" would be accomplished by way of white acceptance of civil rights for Negroes, including the desegregated schools established for the first time during Reconstruction, and thereby, with black votes, outvoting the extreme, white supremacist wing of the Democratic Party. Negro membership in the committee was mostly composed of wealthy Colored Creoles. The movement soured with increased white supremacist organizing to overthrow Reconstruction.[16]

Violence quickly displaced the idea of unification. Soon, infight-ing among various factions of the Republican Party; mounting public debts, which had begun to grow even before the war; and elections marred by fraud in both parties created a crisis in Louisiana that mir-rored the fall of Republican governments across the South. African Americans in rural Louisiana were increasingly the targets of ritual-ized violence. Radicals across the state lost political power as the ex-Confederates organized in the Democratic Party became better able to manipulate elections. Reactionaries were in a position to undo the social and political advances of federal Reconstruction.

As part of their strategy white supremacists, disgruntled with Republican control, organized the White League, which opened a chapter in New Orleans on July 1, 1874. Immediately after the Civil War, reactionaries in rural parishes had formed the Knights of the White Camellia, an organization similar to the Ku Klux Klan, in Georgia and Tennessee. Later, larger groups with public membership such as the Crescent City Democratic Club paved the way for the White League (which the Crescent City Democratic Club would eventually join as the Crescent City White League). The White League was a paramilitary organization that adopted the name of the Louisiana state militia, parallel to the integrated and legitimate militia that they would eventually fight on Canal Street in New Orleans.

The martial air of the White League was matched by a rhetoric that often boiled down the complexities of Reconstruction Louisiana to black-and-white terms (literally), but the members were careful to emphasize that they sought only to end what they labeled ineffective federal rule. Although their aims were appealing to many conservative whites and ethnic immigrants, the White League was decidedly an upper-class affair. Based in part on the circle of conservative elites who had served in the Civil War and during the 1866 New Orleans riot that killed Negro protestors trying to gain the right to vote, the organization was extremely successful in attracting new members. The memberships largely comprised men age 16 to 25 who had not served in the war but romanticized the Confederates' "lost cause." The League members attempted to demonize whites who opposed them in Democratic newspapers as "Carpetbaggers and Scalawags."[17]

As tensions heightened and conciliatory efforts failed, Democrats fueled the frenzy by spreading rumors of a black league organized to attack whites. In New Orleans, the resulting Battle of Liberty Place, which occurred on September 14, 1874, at the foot of Canal Street, was reminiscent of the Civil War, with organized columns of the White League advancing on the integrated Metropolitan Police and the black state militia, led by former Confederate General and now Republican James Longstreet. A suspiciously well-timed freight train along the river gave the White League cover to gain a tactical advantage in the battle, and soon afterward the Metropolitan Police fell back from their position, followed by the black militia. Governor Kellogg and General Longstreet were forced to seek shelter in the federal Custom House.[18]

In the end, three days later, federal troops ejected the White League and reinstated Kellogg as governor, but the White League made moves to claim the moral and political victory. While the White League's call to rally at the Clay statue on Canal Street had been heeded by 6,000 white New Orleans residents of numerous ethnicities, whether Creoles, German, Jewish, Irish, Italian, or foreign-French, power was concentrated in the hands of relatively small groups of Protestant Anglo-Americans organized not only in the White League but also in the secretive Boston and Pickwick social clubs.[19]

All the while, the Snaer brothers tried to stay above the fray. First elected in 1872 to represent Iberia Parish in the state House of Representatives, Louis Antoine ignored attacks on him by the Democratic-controlled parish newspaper, the *Sugar Bowl*. When Alex was murdered, the newspaper suggested that the episode should serve as a lesson to him about the dangerous propensities of freed people. He served through the turmoil until the extra session of 1878. He chaired the Parochial Affairs committee in the 1873 session, which handled legislative involvement with local issues from across the state, and a committee to examine whether banking games or lotteries were tolerated in Orleans Parish in the 1874 session. He also championed a bill to ask Congress to help in suppressing slavery in Cuba, the last Spanish colony to end slavery. He added a provision asking that the other former slave states join in the resolution, which won unanimous approval. He unsuccessfully tried to gain tax relief for delinquent taxpayers. He also joined with Robert Guichard, who later married his sister, Victoria Rose, to ask for a clear definition of the boundaries of St. Bernard Parish.[20]

While Louis Antoine served in the legislature, Seymour continued his private practice of law with two experienced white attorneys, E. K. Washington and Simeon Belden. Belden, born in Massachusetts in 1833, moved to Louisiana before the war. Admitted to the Bar in 1856, he became a staunch Republican. Called by opponents a scalawag, he ran on the ticket in the first election after the 1868 constitution went into effect when Henry Warmoth won the governorship. Elected attorney general, he served with Lt. Governor Oscar Dunn, Secretary of State George Bovee, Auditor G. M. Wickliffe, Treasurer Antoine Dubuclet, and Superintendent of Education the Rev. T. W. Conway. Belden as attorney general defended the state law regulating slaughterhouses for public health reasons, referred to earlier.[21]

Washington was born in Pennsylvania in 1823 but moved to New Orleans and identified the city as his residence when applying for a passport in 1857. He was listed officially as "ordered into the service of the State of Louisiana" in the Confederate Louisiana Third Infantry Regiment as a third lieutenant. However, there is no record of the regiment's service in the usual regimental histories.[22]

Colored Creole racial identity became an issue in the important case of *Hall v. DeCuir*, which was handled by Seymour Snaer and

Washington. It was finally resolved by the U.S. Supreme Court. The case, which began in the lower court in 1872, arose from a complaint about a violation of the Civil Rights Act of 1869, which prohibited race discrimination in public facilities. Seymour Snaer and Washington's client was Mrs. Josephine DeCuir, the sister of the state treasurer. She asked for damages of $75,000 for a violation of her civil rights during a trip on the steamboat *La Fourche*. She traveled by boat from New Orleans to the Hermitage landing in Point Coupee on July 20, 1872. Her attorney, Washington, was traveling with her to look at some papers connected with the succession of her late husband, Antoine DeCuir Jr.

Mrs. DeCuir's circumstances showed how much things had changed for Colored Creoles as a result of the war. She and her late husband, who died in 1865, had long been among the wealthiest free people of color. Before the war, nearly one in three Colored Creoles was a slave owner. Some, like the Snaers, had one or two household slaves, and others had hundreds of slaves working on large planta- tions. Some were benevolent masters; others treated their slaves as harshly as the most brutal white masters. They also married among themselves. For example, Antoine DeCuir and Antoine Dubuclet, the richest Colored Creoles in Pointe Coupee Parish, signed formal four-page contracts in French for the marriage of Josephine and Antoine DeCuir Jr. They had owned more than a thousand acres of fertile land along a river in Pointe Coupee Parish, raised sugarcane, corn, and rice, and produced wool and molasses.[23]

Their total estate, including real property, machinery, livestock, and 112 slaves, had been worth in excess of $150,000, at a time when owning $2,000 worth of property was wealthy. After DeCuir died during the last year of the war, his widow had taken over as mistress of the once-great plantation. But in the spring of 1871, she listened to the final bids recorded for her plantation house, stables, cabins, ma- chinery, and sugarhouse and the remaining 840 acres of her planta- tion. In a single day the accumulations of a lifetime had disappeared before the auctioneer's gavel. In the final tally she received only $25,752 for her land and other holdings, an amount that failed to cover the estate's outstanding debts, which had accumulated since the emancipation of their slaves and the collapse of the Southern economy.[24]

Washington represented Mrs. DeCuir in an appeal regarding her husband's estate. She had first hired other attorneys and claimed they did not take her wishes into account, but the state Supreme Court found that she had waited too long to complain: Over a year had elapsed, and the estate had been closed and could not be reopened.

When the discrimination case went to trial, Washington testified that when she first came to his office on the estate matter, he assumed she was white based on her physical appearance and her manner: "[S]he was well dressed and her manner appeared to be lady-like. I had not the remotest intimation she was a person of color." He added: "It would not have made me any difference if I had."[25]

Due to his assumption about her race, Washington, when he booked the passage, did not check to see whether the boat captain assigned persons of color to inferior sleeping quarters. After boarding the boat and seeing she had not arrived, he walked ashore to talk with Seymour Snaer and "noticed some hesitation" on his part. Seymour told him that if Mrs. DeCuir went on the boat "she would be mortified." Washington then "apprehended that she was a woman of color."

Washington told the clerk she was a woman of color and asked if she could have accommodations in the ladies' cabin; he was told she could not. He rushed back to tell Seymour to warn her not to come on the boat, but she was already on board. Seymour took a different boat to Point Coupee. Mrs. DeCuir was denied passage in the ladies; cabin and spent the overnight trip on a deck chair in a common area of the boat. She paid first-class fare upon arriving at her destination.[26]

Mrs. DeCuir, according to the record, was a "Lady of color, genteel in her manners, modest in her deportment, neat in her appearance, and quite fair for one of mixed blood. Her features are rather delicate, with a nose which indicates a decided preponderance of the Caucasian and Indian blood. The blackness and length of the hair, which is straight, confirm this idea." Interestingly, some of the Snaers who claim descent from Samuel believe that their great-great-grandfather Joseph married an Indian woman. Claims of Indian ancestry, some of which are entirely valid, are not uncommon among blacks. Claiming Caucasian and Indian ancestry would add to Mrs. DeCuir's distinction from Negroes to make her treatment even more abhorrent.[27]

Joseph Snaer, son of Samuel, father of David ("Papa D").

Emma Mitchell (Bend), wife of Joseph, wearing dress she made.

The steamboat captain, Baranco, testified that Mrs. DeCuir had been on the *La Fourche* and had stayed outside. He had reminded her of the rule and she had replied "she had been in France a good while, and there she was treated like a white lady." The captain testified that in his view she was "a yellow woman. Anyone could see she was a colored woman by looking at her."

He also testified that he knew her deceased husband as a colored man. She was a medium bright mulatto, and he had never seen white persons as dark as her. Seymour Snaer asked, "Have you not seen some people darker than Madame DeCuir claiming to be white?" When he answered in the negative, Seymour Snaer asked, "Do you know Mr. Sauvinet [Charles] of this city?" Former Native Guards officer Sauvinet, who was apparently about Mrs. DeCuir's color, was well known. He had won his civil rights suit under the Reconstruction law for denial of access in a bar on the basis of race.[28]

In his deposition for Mrs. DeCuir, Aristide DuConge, another Colored Creole, reported that he traveled to St. Louis on the Mississippi just before the 1868 election on the same line "with Major [Louis Antoine] Snaer." DuConge, age twenty-nine, was Louis Antoine's neighbor on Royal Street. His testimony, given in French, was translated by Seymour Snaer. He testified that he and Louis took passage and paid the fare, obtained a cabin-room, ate at the first-class table, and received the same treatment as the other passengers. Seymour Snaer asked him if he was "a reputed colored man." DuConge pointed out that "my complexion is white, but I claim to be a colored man." He had about the same skin tone as Seymour Snaer, whom he knew as a "colored man."

Asked about his hair he said, "I know thousands of white men who have more curly hair than I have, and then some, of course, straighter . . . I know thousands of colored men darker than I am who have the same kind of hair which I have." When asked the color of his hair, he responded, "about Brown." When asked if he had any features of a Negro, he responded, "I don't know, I am reputed to be a colored man, and have always been known as a colored man, and I cannot enjoy the same privileges as those reputed to be white. I don't know that I can pass better for a white man or a colored man." Asked about his features, DuConge said, "I have the same features" as other colored people in New Orleans.[29]

Louis Antoine, said DuConge, was "known in all the city of New Orleans as a colored man." DuConge's statements affirmed that no one questioned their right to first-class treatment on the boat, nor did he and Louis Antoine hide their colored identity. Louis no longer dissembled about being a Colored Creole after he left the army. With the end of the war and emancipation, Colored Creoles were, like the freedmen and women, all "Negro" citizens and the voting base of the Republican Party in the South.

Counsel for the defendant pressed DuConge to say he appeared white, which led to the treatment on the boat he had described. But, he answered, "there must be a difference, because they call me a colored person and another man a white man." In the cabins on the boat, DuConge said class was the distinction, not race: "these colored people were rich." They would have staterooms in the gentlemen's cabin but would not eat at the cabin table or associate with the other cabin passengers.[30]

Forty-seven-year-old P. G. Deslonde testified that "It is worse than it was before the war. Before the war, being a rich planter and patronizing boats, we had some kind of comfort; since the war generally the planters made very little crops and they do not patronize these boats to a great extent. In fact I can travel just as well as any man on one certain boat on this river; that is all; but not with the proper fare that should be extended to me," even when his "pockets were full of gold." He went on: "For giving my freight to the captain, he will invite me to take a private stateroom." He was then asked what his standing was, to which he replied, "I am secretary of state now." And you count yourself a rich man, counsel asked. "No, I count myself a poor man to-day," Deslonde said. He knew Mrs. DeCuir and regarded her as of "copper color."[31]

Essentially, Mrs. DeCuir and DuConge went beyond what Louis Antoine did when he refused to identify himself as of African descent at the behest of the U.S. Army. They relied on the principle of equality of human rights, but also the principle that no one has the right to determine an individual's identity and then make decisions based on the identification. As far as they were concerned, mixed race was an identity. They also had a statute to back up their beliefs. The court found that the steamboat line had violated the equal rights and privileges in any public conveyance clause of Article 13 of the Louisiana

Constitution. They also found a violation of the 1869 equal accommodations act as interpreted in an earlier decision.[32] Mrs. DeCuir was awarded $1,000 and costs. The steamboat line appealed the decision to the state Supreme Court but lost in June 1873. The company then appealed to the U.S. Supreme Court, which in 1877 ruled against Mrs. DeCuir. The Court found that the Louisiana statute prohibiting race discrimination on a steamboat plying from New Orleans to Vicksburg, which had various landings, including one at Hermitage landing, was unconstitutional because it interfered with commerce among the states. Mrs. DeCuir did not testify in her case; instead, witnesses attested to her status as a lady. Gender entered the case in testimony concerning her respectability. Having the "physical form of the woman before them" in the trial court was not a reason for her success: The Louisiana courts were interpreting a Reconstruction statute and were Reconstruction judges. In the U.S. Supreme Court, she, like other women who lost discrimination cases on appeal, was black and gender did not matter. The evidence in this case and the eventual outcome typified the decline in status the Colored Creoles had suffered. Now lumped with formerly enslaved persons, all were denied equal rights.[33]

By the time of the U.S. Supreme Court decision, seven years after the auction of the estate, Mrs. DeCuir was living in reduced circumstances. She lived in the Marigny in New Orleans with her daughter and her son, whom the Census reported as a portrait painter, and boarders. The Supreme Court clerk noted trouble collecting court costs of a few hundred dollars from her. Her lawyers said she had no money, but rumor had it that "she had more money than God."[34]

Seymour Snaer continued to spend time in New Orleans, Terrebonne, and La Fourche, practicing law in each locale and remaining politically active. He unsuccessfully ran for the statehouse Fifth Ward representative from New Orleans in the 1874 election. He was very much involved when P. B. S. Pinchback, after his acting governorship, was elected in 1874 to the U.S. House of Representatives and then the U.S. Senate, where Democrats in control refused to seat him. When Pinchback returned to New Orleans to a wildly enthusiastic reception from African Americans in March 1875, Seymour was among the important greeters. After a crowd met him at the train, including the lieutenant governor and other officials, they went to lawyer George Paris's house for an elegant repast and toasts. The colored members of the legislature and other political officials gathered there. Seymour toasted Pinchback, acknowledging that their manhood, liberties, and citizenship were at stake in the fight for his seat, and drank to the wish that he be admitted to the seat. Despite the political infighting, the press reported that Seymour served as district attorney of Terrebonne and La Fourche, the Nineteenth Judicial District, starting in 1877.[35]

After the ex-Confederates completed their takeover in the 1876 elections, in October 1877 Seymour testified in Congressional hearings established to deal with ballot challenges in federal elections in the violence-torn state. Seymour told the committee that he lived in Terre Bonne in April 1877, but during the 1876 election he lived in La Fourche and ran for district attorney on the Republican ticket; he lost as the Democrats took over the state. He answered Democrats' charges that black women were either casting their husband's ballots or inappropriately urging them to vote. Actually, white Democrats intimidated black voters to reduce their ability to vote. He said he had heard "speakers throughout the campaign say that the colored people would have more protection under the Republican government than under the Democratic government."[36]

Seymour told the Congressional committee that "black women say or they would express themselves in such a way, that they had children, and they knew by the prejudice the Democrats had against the colored people that if the Democratic Party came into power they would not have probably the occasion to give the proper education to their children and would not live so happily as under the Republican administration."[37]

Louis Antoine testified in the same hearings, denouncing as false Democratic claims that in Iberia in the Third Congressional District, Republicans had intimidated blacks who wanted to vote Democratic. In answer to questions, he told the committee that, instead, he saw intimidation "on the part of the democratic party, or rather democrats" toward "colored men."[38]

He also responded that he knew of no reports that colored women threatened to leave their husbands if they voted for the Democratic ticket. Throughout the period of struggle to gain the vote and during the election strife thereafter, Negro women, former slaves, and former free people of color who could not vote, in fact, urged on the colored men. He said the real problem was that "Some of them were afraid to ask for [Republican tickets] openly." But he would not divulge their names or the names of their employers "for fear of losing their employment."[39]

Samuel Wakefield, the postmaster with whose family Louis had lived, testified that the 1876 election was fair. He had heard "a colored man say he was promised twenty-five cents to vote the Democratic ticket" and that after he voted "when he came out for his money they wouldn't give it to him." He also said the local Republicans made a deal with a district judge in 1874 that he would protect them from molestation as they voted.[40]

In December 1873 Victoria Rose married Leopold Guichard's son, Robert Guichard, who served in the Reconstruction legislature along with Louis Antoine from 1870 through 1878. George Pierre,

Victoria Rose sister of Louis Antoine, Pierre and Seymour and half sister of Samuel.

the second youngest of Francois and Anne Emerine's children, began appearing in city directories as a cigar maker. Another son, Victor, married Louisa Joneau in December 1876. Louis Joneau and Louis Antoine stood as principal and surety to attest to their ages as over 21 when Victor received the marriage license. Louisa died within the next three weeks at age twenty-two. On June 31, 1878, Victor married Adele Litaud. In 1877, at age 21, Omer, their third youngest son, had, like Victoria, begun to teach in one of the still desegregated public schools established during Reconstruction.[41]

The Snaer family, along with other Colored Creoles and freed people, now had to readjust to new social and economic realities. The Compromise of 1877 gave the presidency to Rutherford B. Hayes. He kept his promise to withdraw the remaining Union troops from the South. The white ex-Confederates who had used violence and intimidation to suppress the Negro vote and to drive Republicans from office were able to fully accomplish their goal. They "redeemed" the government, wresting it away from Republicans and taking power for themselves. Political ambitions ended for the Snaers. New choices about how to pursue opportunity and equal rights challenged the Colored Creole community.

CHAPTER 7

....

Mulattoes and Colored Creoles

For the Snaers and other Colored Creoles and African Americans in New Orleans, the Nadir that began in the 1870s became ever more depressing. The U.S. Supreme Court had struck down the desegregation law passed by the Reconstruction legislature in the *DeCuir* case. Economic dislocations began to worsen after some initial prosperity. With the Democratic takeover in 1877, Seymour and Louis Antoine Snaer lost the political positions they had gained in migrating to Iberia Parish. As an endpoint to the turmoil since the Republican political victory with the 1868 constitution, ex-Confederates completely overthrew the Republican government with the Compromise of 1877. Rutherford B. Hayes, keeping the promises he made as part of the bargain that gave him the presidency, withdrew the last federal troops from Louisiana. The constitutional convention in 1879 drafted a new "Redeemer" constitution that eliminated the protections of equal civil and political rights guaranteed by Republicans in the 1867 constitution.

Colored Creoles, typically devout Catholics, had seen the Catholic diocese support slavery and the Confederacy. Now the church, led by Archbishop Napoleon Joseph Perché, rejoiced at the end of Reconstruction and a return to white supremacy. Adding insult to injury, the Archbishop, in a pastoral letter dated May 1, 1877, prescribed the singing of a thanksgiving prayer in all the churches for the "pacification of the state."[1]

In 1878 a convention of 200 Negro delegates met at New Orleans to discuss the idea of a mass exodus of blacks westward. Speakers at the convention discussed the violence in rural parishes and how the threat of emigration might threaten white planters enough to make life more tolerable in those parishes where life was the least secure. However, while some black Louisianans joined the 1879 migration to Kansas, most were either unwilling or unable to relocate.[2]

Many Colored Creoles, who had maintained a vibrant community despite the population decreases due to the restrictions on emancipation and migration from elsewhere in the late antebellum period and the travails of war, lost their way. They had adjusted to the change from the old three-tiered system to political solidarity with slave-descended African Americans during Reconstruction. They had benefitted by obtaining leadership positions and political patronage and had hoped for a permanent change to equal rights for all. They had difficulty enduring the backlash that submerged their hopes with the triumph of the Democratic Party and white supremacists.

To be sure, their small group had all become for political purposes black or Negro during Republican rule, but Colored Creoles and the African-descended majority did not form easy relationships or a cohesive community. Color, class, language, culture, philosophy, and the history of slavery created barriers. Colored Creoles were better educated, and educated new leaders only gradually emerged from the ex-slaves to carry on the struggle for full citizenship. Nostalgia and blame casting, such as that which divided Pinchback, Dumas, and the supporters and opponents of the quadroon bill during Reconstruction, left festering wounds.

The course of Reconstruction was problematic from the beginning. Legalities in the Thirteenth, Fourteenth, and Fifteenth Amendments were important, but the failure to give the slaves compensation left them still dependent on former masters for work and a living. White supremacists proved more resilient than the federal government, and the Northern public tired of the divisions of war. After nine short years of Reconstruction, when federal troops withdrew, blacks and mulattoes suffered.

The Snaers, like other Colored Creoles, who were still called mulattoes in the Census, shared the pain of adjustment and economic hard times. Seymour and Louis Snaer had benefitted, along with other former Union soldiers, from his Republican Party and veteran status. By becoming politically "Negro" like slave-descended African

Americans, Colored Creoles had been elected to office, exercised leadership, and enjoyed the equal rights they had long sought. But that period was over. Now they, like all people of African descent, faced a complete denial of their rights and could not even return to the border space between whites and slaves.

Some Colored Creoles who had prospered during Reconstruction extended the advantages they had before the war. Many had become skilled laborers in the antebellum period, and after the war they continued their dominance in many fields. They were accustomed to owning land and businesses, including coffeehouses, restaurants, rooming houses, and cigar stores. The grocers, including the Snaers, remained one of the most successful groups, operating businesses at or next to their residences. Those who had profited as brokers and commission merchants during Reconstruction were still the wealthiest.[3]

Negro artisans, many of whom were Colored Creoles, maintained strength in some jobs despite the end of Reconstruction. By 1880 they still held one fourth of the skilled trade jobs. But workers of African descent, formerly free and freed, found it harder to compete against native-born whites. Competition from whites also hit the foreign-born hardest. The percentage of all foreign-born workers in 1880 dropped by between 12 to 50 percentage points from where it had been in 1870 for occupations such as butchers, shoemakers, tinsmiths, blacksmiths, coopers, and painters, among others.Negro butchers and wheelwrights suffered great losses, but shoemakers, cabinetmakers, coopers, and machinists did have gains. Even with the competition, Negro workers, many of them Colored Creoles, continued to dominate many of these jobs because they could learn trades from relatives or by becoming apprentices to Negro artisans. Wages, however, remained low and costs high, and by 1880 even these workers faced long stretches of unemployment. They were unable to patronize the stores and other businesses owned by Colored Creoles as frequently, which caused a decline in their profitably.[4]

Negro workers, particularly longshoremen and teamsters, continued to organize labor unions after Reconstruction. Free people of color also founded several new mutual aid associations to bury the dead, aid the sick, and provide social outlets for families. They also participated in several strikes in 1877 and 1880 for higher wages.

In October 1880, Negro waiters struck at the St. Charles Hotel for an increase in their wages, plus food and lodging. They lost their jobs with the hiring of white women who undercut their salaries.[5]

Despite political inequality, violence, discrimination, and economic coercion in their daily lives, between 1877 and the 1890s, Negroes in New Orleans and some other Southern communities occasionally exercised some rights. There are examples of how some voted; held numerous minor offices; rode side by side with whites on trains, streetcars, and common carriers; served on juries with whites; and even occasionally used public dining rooms, restaurants, saloons, and waiting rooms. Not until the 1890s did segregation become almost absolute.[6]

Louisiana and New Orleans largely followed the pattern elsewhere. Non-whites maintained some political influence by receiving federal patronage appointments and participating in Republican national presidential nominating conventions as delegates. The number of Negro officeholders declined with the end of Reconstruction, but between 1868 and 1896 Negroes remained at about 45 percent of registered voters. Although registered, however, they increasingly could not actually vote because of the violence, intimidation, and illegal suppression that existed. Then in 1898 the Democrats added a grandfather clause to the state constitution, with complicated requirements for anyone whose ancestors had not voted before January 1867. After the U.S. Supreme Court declared that grandfather clauses violated the Fourteenth Amendment, Louisiana and other Southern states routinely used tests and devices to keep non-whites from voting. For example, in Louisiana in 1896, there were 130,344 Negro registered voters and 164,884 whites; in New Orleans there were 14,153 registered Negroes. In 1900 there were only 5,320 Negro registered voters statewide, with 1,482 of those in New Orleans. By 1904 there were only 660 Negroes registered in New Orleans. Disenfranchisement meant that political power was no longer possible for people of African descent, whether they were Colored Creoles, mixed-race people, or Negroes.[7]

As Reconstruction ended, Seymour and Louis Antoine Snaer decided that despite the difficult environment, it was time to start their own families. On January 18, 1877, twenty-eight-year-old Seymour married twenty-year-old Marie Lalande, a Colored Creole and the daughter of Euphraisie and Louis Lalande, at St. Augustine

Seymour Rene Snaer, son of Francois, brother of Louis Antoine, half brother of Samuel.

Marie Lalande, wife of Seymour Rene, mother of Seymour Louis and great grandmother of Denise.

Church. After the birth of their son, Seymour Louis, at the end of that year she became ill. She died of myelitis, a now-manageable inflammation of the spinal cord, after only two years of marriage, on June 18, 1879.[8]

On November 30, 1878, Louis married Marie Antoinette Emma Gandolfi, daughter of Joseph Peter Gandolfi and Elizabeth Lorenza Presas, at St. Augustine Church. The marriage certificate did not include race; however, in previous censuses, Louis and Marie had been listed in their respective mixed-race families as free persons of color. After the end of Reconstruction, race mattered more. In 1880 the census taker listed Louis Antoine, his wife, and their one-year-old son Louis in their separate household as white, which could be what he observed without asking questions. Although we can't know that the Snaers knew what was recorded, it appears that Louis Antoine chose again to pass as white, as he had during his Army career. His time as "Colored" during the Reconstruction period was over.

Louis Antoine's wife Marie Antoinette Emma Gandolfi.

One of Louis and Marie's eight children, Emma, as an adult, recalled her Gandolfi grandmother's story about her origins as French and Spanish and her Gandolfi grandfather as Italian. Actually she was of mixed race, which she hid, just like the Snaers. Her father, Juan Presas of Catalonia, arrived in New Orleans in 1823 as a ship captain. He had married a free woman of color, Zoe Maria Rose Dazema, from Saint Domingue in about 1797. In New Orleans Juan Presas continued in the shipping business. In 1848 he registered as the owner of the schooner *Fairy*. He died in 1864 at age seventy-four, and the family buried him in St. Louis cemetery No. 2. His wife Zoe died in 1878.[9]

The Gandolfi brothers, druggists Joseph and Felix, immigrated from Sardinia, and Joseph married Emma's grandmother, Elizabeth, but the Presases were of mixed race like the Snaers. The 1870 census confirms the mulatto ancestry of Louis Antoine's wife, Emma. In the house situated next to the Society of the Family of Saints, the Gondolfi and Preses families lived together, including Elizabeth Gandolfi and her children and the widow Zoe Presas and her daughter. The census taker described each individual as mulatto. Louis Antoine's wife, like her husband, although fair enough to pass, had mulatto ancestry through her grandmother, Zoe. At Joseph Presas's birth, Louisiana records recorded him as colored, but by 1910 he was passing for white in New Orleans and died white in Chicago in 1923.[10]

The death of Seymour Snaer's wife left him to care for their two-year-old son, Seymour Louis, while practicing law. In addition to their work on the DeCuir case, some of the matters he handled with his partner E. K. Washington were decided ultimately in the Louisiana Supreme Court. For example, they represented the heirs of Charles P. Boutté (his children and grandchildren) on appeal from a decision of the Orleans Parish court, in which they sought possession of his estate. The executor refused to transfer the property even though the will had been probated in 1871. The debts were deemed small and the property "inconsiderable." He refused to wind up the estate even though those who had been given legacies consented and there were no objections made by creditors. The executor, who received fees for managing the estate, said he wanted to keep the funds until he was certain that no claims would arise, but years had passed. The state Supreme Court reversed, finding for Snaer and Washington's clients.

The Court decided that everyone who stood to benefit, including the surviving widow, wanted closure. They could post security for any possible late-arriving claims and take possession of the estate.[11]

Seymour's last recorded appearance for the state, from his work as Terrebonne and La Fourche district attorney, occurred in April 1880. He asked the court to deny the appeal of Scott Ross from a murder conviction. Ross had received a sentence of life imprisonment for shooting and killing William Anderson. Ross' counsel alleged a number of procedural errors, but the court refused to overturn the verdict.

Louis Antoine and his family moved to what his daughter Emma later described as a "Well Furnished house" on Royal Street in the Marigny, opening a hardware store on the lower floor of the building. Emma and the older of their eight children went to Catholic school, Holy Trinity, where they were taught by Benedictine nuns; the younger ones went to St. Ann's kindergarten.

In 1878, after filing for the first time as a former officer in the military, Louis Antoine began receiving a pension of $5 per month for the injury to his foot. Thereafter he "kept a grocery store" for his brother-in-law Robert Guichard, his sister Victoria Rose's husband, in Plaquemines and in Cincinnati; "he would come home to visit." Then, like other Union veterans, in a period when veterans, even those of African descent, could still obtain Republican patronage posts, he used his status and connections to acquire a federal job. He became a storekeeper, guarding warehouses and weighing taxable goods for the U.S. Internal Revenue Department.[12]

Louis Antoine maintained his membership in the veterans' fraternal and political organization, the Grand Army of the Republic (GAR), wearing its pin in his formal photographs. The GAR became an important force in the fight for increases in veterans' pensions. Usually black and white veterans, like Louis Antoine, who had federal jobs joined and remained members. The GAR. named one of the posts in New Orleans in honor of Andre Cailloux and another for Anselmas Planciancois, the flag bearer at Port Hudson.[13]

Some Native Guards veterans found a refuge in other parts of the federal civilian workforce. Algernon Sidney Badger, who first led the Metropolitan Police established under Republican rule, had hired Native Guards veterans, including officers Octave Rey and Eugene Rapp. After the Democratic takeover of the state in 1877, President

Louis Antoine wearing his GAR medal.

Hayes' administration gave Badger the patronage post of postmaster and then collector of customs. With Republican control of jobs at the Custom House, except during Democrat Grover Cleveland's first presidency from March 1885 to March 1889, Colored Creoles, especially veterans and Reconstruction political officials, could find employment. In 1879, former Lieutenant Governor C. C. Antoine held an appointment as warehouse clerk at $2,000 a year. Arnold Bertonneau, who had just lost his 1878 suit seeking admission of his two sons to desegregate a school, also received a post.[14]

In 1879, eminent Creole writer Rodolphe Lucien Desdunes obtained a job with the Customs Service as a messenger, with a salary of $600 a year. The service dropped him from the rolls in August 1885 after Cleveland took office, but he returned to the service as a clerk after the election of Republican Benjamin Harrison.[15]

Cleveland's presidency did not seem to affect Louis Antoine's employment. Perhaps since he had been a military hero and served to the end of the war, his bosses misidentified him as a white man. In 1882 he had become an inspector of customs, and by 1885 he had become an assistant weigher at the Custom House, jobs previously held by white men.

An atmosphere of interracial collaboration and solidarity among the more than 10,000 workingmen at the docks had taken over for the first time, resulting in a cotton workers' strike for higher wages in September 1881. On the tenth day of the strike, police Sergeant Thomas Reynolds shot and killed Negro union teamster James Hawkins. At Hawkins' funeral in a Negro church an interracial crowd gathered. In the procession thereafter to the cemetery, hundreds of white screwmen and yardmen took part. This supportive atmosphere, which was prevalent during Louis Antoine's work as an inspector and weigher at the port, began to break down after 1884 due to overwork, craft and unskilled labor issues, and racial conflict. A general strike in November 1892 lasted for eleven days. The economic depression of 1893 only added to the difficulty.[16]

The era of interracial cooperation and labor solidarity continued, but with difficulty. The craft unions survived the collapse of the general strike better than the unions of unskilled Negro workers. The labor movement continued despite the depressions of the 1890s and the effect of white supremacy and overt racism in political and civil society until the collapse of union power in the 1920s. However, the labor and management disputes and the turmoil on the docks seemed incessant. For Louis Antoine and some of the other Snaers, living in New Orleans became increasingly problematic.[17]

Seymour Rene's personal problems mounted after the 1879 death of his wife, Marie Lalande. The 1880 Census recorded that he lived in Bayou Blue, Terrebonne, Louisiana, along with his son Seymour Louis, who was then three; Celestene Avet, a sister-in-law, who kept house; Elodie, her daughter, then sixteen; and Seymour Rene's younger brother, twenty-three-year-old Omer Joseph, a teacher. They were all, reflecting post-Reconstruction's binary categorization, recorded as black, whereas earlier, Celeste, Elodie, and the other Lalandes had all been listed as mulattoes.[18] Celeste had probably moved into the household to care for his son. Shortly thereafter, on November 3, 1880, the

Terrebonne Parish clerk issued a marriage bond for Seymour Rene and Celeste's daughter, Elodie. By the following month, however, Seymour began to show signs of epilepsy. The press in Houma, the Terrebonne Parish seat, reported that he had signed an order requesting goods from Max Beer and Fellman as "district attorney Nineteenth Judicial District" even though he "is an idiot," currently holds no office, and "though insane is not dangerous."[19] The same paper reported on December 5, 1880, that Seymour, "who is suffering from mania and who so mysteriously disappeared after having ordered the goods from Beer and Fellman," had "turned up in Donaldsonville with a little boy, apparently three years of age" (his son was three at the time). They thought he was on his way to Houma on the steamer *Yazoo*.[20]

Seymour Rene was probably picked up on the streets by police officials. Police codes like that of New Orleans, dating from 1808, provided that "furious madmen" found roaming the streets should be brought in to the mayor or justice of the peace. if found insane they were given to their nearest relative to be kept in good and secure custody. If no relative could be found, they were kept by officials—meaning in jail. Paupers or persons who had no estates, of course, had no judicial proceedings.

The *New Orleans Item* reported on March 25, 1881, that a trial for Seymour's removal from office on the charge of insanity was held and that the question of his insanity had been discussed for some months: "He acted in a peculiar way for a sane man, purchasing merchandise for which he had no use."[21]

Seymour ended up in the asylum as a result of commitment by his wife Elodie, who also received assignment as his guardian or curator. Under the Louisiana civil code of 1808, modeled after the Napoleonic code, persons above puberty who were subject to "an habitual state of madness or insanity" could have someone assigned to "taking charge of their own persons" and administering their estates. Relatives of a person thought insane were permitted to apply for a prohibition called an "interdiction" for this purpose.

The parish judge had sole power to determine the person's condition, after questioning the individual. According to the 1808 code, if he wished he could "appoint skilled physicians or other personnel" to provide a diagnosis. If the judge found the person insane, a "curator" would be appointed to gather and oversee the use of any resources the patient possessed for "mitigating his suffering and accelerating his cure." Depending on the patient's state and his resources, the judge could order home care or hospitalization or, if the individual was determined dangerous, confinement in jail. The 1808 code remained in force after Louisiana became a state.

According to a decision and order of the Nineteenth Judicial District Court of Louisiana of Terrebonne Parish, Seymour Rene was interdicted March 28, 1881, on his wife's petition. Since she met all of the requirements, the court appointed her his curator, without bond, with an order for inventory of the property on December 16, 1882. There is no recorded explanation for her action in sending him to the state mental hospital instead of obtaining private treatment or for the lack of intervention by his relatives in New Orleans.

Previously considered demonic possession, epilepsy became regarded as a form of insanity in the nineteenth century. Patients could be categorized as "insane, suffering from Stupidity, bordering on Idiocy, caused by epilepsy" or "insane, suffering from Epileptic Insanity," as they were in the records of patients transferred to East Louisiana State Hospital in the 1880s from commitment in New Orleans. In these records, a thirty-eight-year-old epileptic insanity patient was described as having spasms for nearly seven months, "resulting in an impairment of his mind. He is a cart driver by occupation but unable to attend to his work. He has been in the habit of drinking."[22]

For the mentally ill and those considered so, including epileptics, issues about lack of treatment and abuse came to public attention when Dorothea Dix took up the cause in Massachusetts in 1843. She became the most influential psychiatric reformer of the nineteenth century. She was responsible for the funding or enlargement of thirty-two mental hospitals in the United States and Europe, including the establishment in Louisiana of the state mental hospital.

Louisiana established the Lunatic Asylum for the Criminally Insane in Jackson in East Feliciana Parish in 1847. Supporters argued that it had a salubrious climate, not swampy and subject to yellow fever like New Orleans. East and West Felicianas are the closest piney woods hill parishes to New Orleans. They are accessible by water from most of the state, but also are not threatened by high water. Centenary College was located there, and the first session of the constitutional convention of 1844–45 had met in Jackson. Commitment was indeterminate—ostensibly until cured. Patients were charged $10 a month unless adjudged unable to pay. The wealthy sent their mentally ill relatives to hospitals in the North for treatment and hospitalization. Funding was limited. Seymour, like the other patients, suffered from a lack of staffing and thus care until he died in 1885.[23]

During Reconstruction and the end of slavery, the number of African American patients in asylums increased, but there is no record of requests or funding provided from the Freedmen's Bureau. Biased asylum directors, ignoring the fact that blacks who were mentally ill went untreated during slavery, attributed the increase to the deleterious effects of emancipation. The legislature under Reconstruction tried to have more state oversight to improve conditions, but local people opposed any interference with their control of the board. Segregated race quarters that weren't needed during slavery were established in the 1880s. Seymour Rene, apparently regarded as white, essentially passed in the mental hospital. He was an exception, also, in that few professionals were ever recorded in the patient population.[24]

Seymour Rene also arrived at the hospital at a time when the legislature decided to solve a public relations problem by ordering the relocation of the patients in New Orleans to the state asylum. They appropriated $60,000 a year for 1883 and 1884 for the purpose, which was not enough to improve conditions for the patients already there. The patient census was 244 in April 1884 but rose to 600 two years later.

The legislature responded to an investigation of mental health treatment made public by George Washington Cable, a well-known fiction writer; his books included *Old Creole Days*. He turned his attention to social reform, becoming involved in mental hospital reform, and became an advocate for the social causes he felt needed attention. Conditions at the New Orleans jail for mental patients were long known to be deplorable. In April 1881 Cable was selected for special grand jury duty and became secretary of the jury. A special grand jury independently investigates the possibility of criminal action or political corruption. These juries made inquiries and had before reported on abuses in public institutions. He had the mayor ask him to inspect prisons and asylums. When he was selected for grand jury duty he got the group to investigate prisons and asylums in the North and make recommendations. He wrote and publicized a report describing scant funds, corruption, and ineptness, and comparing conditions in New Orleans with those in the North. The legislative response was to send the New Orleans patients to East Feliciana State.[25]

Most wards at the asylum lacked furniture; patients slept on mattresses on the floor. The patients had inadequate clothing and many had no shoes. The wards were heated by fireplaces, but only until bedtime, for fear of smoke and fire. The hospital had nothing but bucket brigades for the delivery of water. Candles provided the only light at night. Incandescent lights were installed, along with a water force pump and delivery system, sometime after April 1885, when Seymour died.[26]

On April 13, 1885, Rene Seymour, the name on his birth certificate (although he was named for the pirate Rene Beluche, he preferred to use Seymour as his first name), "colored," died in the state insane asylum, with epilepsy recorded as the cause. He was forty-one years of age, although his death certificate reported him as age thirty-eight.[27]

His wife Elodie opened his succession. The appraisers valued his estate at $450. His land sat on the right bank of Bayou Terrebonne, about a half-mile below the town of Houma, the seat of Terrebonne Parish. Three white widows' properties bounded Snaer's meandering eight acres, valued at $400. Snaer's household and kitchen goods were appraised at $40 and his books at $10. It was a modest but valuable estate.[28]

The 1890 Census was burned in an archival fire, but in 1900, Elodie, a schoolteacher age thirty-seven, still lived in Terrebonne, with her brother Ernest Avet, age forty-one, a day laborer, and her grandmother, Euphraisie Lalande. The two white neighbors still lived there, but two black families had also taken up residence nearby. Elodie died in Terrebonne in 1946.

Seymour represented the longstanding ideal of justice and equal rights that were part of Colored Creole heritage. Whether during the 1866 massacre and his testimony thereafter, his insistence on due process after the murder of his brother, and his principled behavior as a lawyer, Seymour was a remarkable man.

CHAPTER 8

Just Americans

In 1896, the people of New Orleans anxiously awaited the U. S. Supreme Court decision in *Plessy v. Ferguson*. When the court decided that segregation was legal, it struck at the heart of the Colored Creoles' hope that discrimination on the basis of race would be forbidden. Justice Henry Billings Brown for the Court stated that the Fourteenth Amendment "could not have been intended to abolish distinctions based upon color, or to enforce social, as distinguished from political, equality, or a commingling of the two races upon terms unsatisfactory to either." Therefore, "Laws permitting, and even requiring, their separation in places where they are liable to be brought into contact do not necessarily imply the inferiority of either race to the other, and have been generally, if not universally, recognized as within the competency of the state legislatures in the exercise of their police power." Instead of individual freedom to identify oneself and to be treated equally without regard to race, *Plessy* allowed the state to declare who is "a white and who a colored person," and to segregate accordingly.

Some of the Snaers had left Louisiana after Reconstruction. This time, with deep disappointment, and seeing no way to avoid Jim Crow segregation, Louis Antoine Snaer left for good, taking his family to California.[1]

The Snaer family began to disperse and break apart at a time when being a Colored Creole seemed to count for nothing and the community was under great stress. Seymour and Louis Antoine's half-brother, Samuel the musician, had died in 1881. After his wife's death, he had married Felecia, who was born in Louisiana and had an Italian father and mother. They had four children: Maurice, born in 1874; Felix, born in 1876; and Raymond, age one in 1880; and Marie, five months in 1880.[2]

In the early 1880s, at a time when a number of Colored Creoles fled the Democratic takeover of the state, Pierre Snaer, the dentist, took his family to Gonzalez, Texas, where they became white. They apparently did not attempt to intervene in Seymour's illness and his interdiction. But after Seymour's death, his son, Seymour Louis, who did not like his stepmother, Elodie, went to live with his aunt, Victoria Guichard, and her family. The Snaers also did not pay taxes on the St. Claude Street property in 1879 and thereafter, or, after Francois' death in 1880, on additional property toward Bayou St. John in the Tremé that he had bought in 1837.

Pierre Anatole.

The Snaer children, Francois' heirs, sold both properties and any tax liabilities at some point, probably after 1891, when his widow, Anne Emerine, was still living at 232 St. Claude Street, probably with Emilio, the youngest son. She died in 1895. The children had scattered, moving away or living about the city with their own families.[3]

In addition to their own problems in Iberia Parish, word came to the Snaers of trouble in Samuel Wakefield's family. He had taken in and helped the brothers when they went to Iberia. Given white supremacists' control, his son, Adolph, who had a position as a customs inspector under the Republicans, switched to the Democrats, who named him clerk of the court in 1884. They touted his switch and then ejected him, claiming that a police jury found irregularities in his office. Then in 1889 vigilantes shot and killed Samuel Wakefield, who remained an unrepentant Republican. Whites accused him of shooting his white supervisor at a door and blinds manufacturing plant.[4]

Despite hard times, New Orleans' African Americans did not stop agitating against segregation in the 1890s, although they repeatedly lost. Colored Creoles remained disturbed that they could not even fall back on the privileges they had enjoyed before the war. The U.S. Census still counted mixed-race people separate from blacks or Negroes as it had done since 1850. In fact, it was not until after the 1920 Census that the "one-drop rule" was used and the mulatto category disappeared. But their former status counted for nothing as the screws of discrimination were turned tighter and tighter.[5]

In this same period, when a few, mostly poor African Americans left Louisiana to join the 1879 exodus to Kansas, Colored Creoles who left were attracted largely to California or Chicago, where the most direct train routes from New Orleans led, or elsewhere.[6]

As conditions became more and more difficult, Colored Creoles who appeared white identified themselves as white, moved to white neighborhoods, and never looked back. Hundreds of mulattoes recorded themselves for the first time as white in the 1875 state census. Aristide Mary, disgusted with unscrupulous black and white politicians, grew increasingly disconsolate as times changed. He tried earnestly but failed to keep a segregated state university, Southern, for

Negroes from being established in 1879. P. B. S. Pinchback supported the university, making peace with the new racial order.[7] By the end of the century, colored New Orleans residents began making lists of families of African descent who were passing as white and whose children did not know of their background. Others took different routes in dealing with their despair, beginning with the Democratic takeover after the election of 1876. While Seymour's epilepsy led to his institutionalization, other Colored Creoles were driven to actual mental illness by their new circumstances and related issues as Reconstruction came to an end. Francois Lacroix simply stopped taking care of his affairs and lost his property; he died in 1876. Charles Sauvinet served in various appointive offices under the Republicans and always remained ambiguous about race as a free man of color, although he identified himself, indirectly, as colored by filing the discrimination lawsuit against the Bank bar and coffeehouse, which he won. He never recovered when white supremacy took over. In the spring of 1878, Sauvinet's son was diagnosed with tuberculosis. Sauvinet did not believe the doctor's view that his son might recover, and when they returned home from the doctor's, he went into his bedroom, lay down, and shot himself with a pistol. The coroner marked a "C" for his race on the death certificate. He did the same for Sauvinet's son, who died three weeks later, although his mother had registered him at birth as white.[8]

Louis Antoine also tried to accommodate to the new racial reality. He accepted when Democratic Governor Alfred Wiltz, elected under the constitution overthrowing Reconstruction, appointed him, as black, to Southern University's board in May 1880. Wiltz's term is notable mainly for his support of the corrupt lottery that controlled the legislature, the neglect of public education, the continuation of black disenfranchisement, and the embezzlement of state funds by his ally, state Treasurer Edward A. Burke.[9]

In 1889 Aristide Mary, Louis Martinet, Rodolphe Desdunes, and others organized the Comité des Citoyens (Committee of Citizens) to test the constitutionality of the separate-car law enacted by the Redeemer legislature. Martinet, from St. Martinville, was the son of Marie Louise, a woman of color, and Hipolite Martinet, a Belgian immigrant. His father, a carpenter, owned real estate worth

$1,000 in 1860. Louis had several siblings; all were mulatto except Hipolite, who was white. His father owned slaves.[10]

After the war, Martinet attended Straight University Law School and obtained admission to the Bar by 1880. He also trained to become a physician. In 1888, after Reconstruction, he opened his office as a notary public on Exchange Alley. The notary's office used the law without involving courts. Free people of color used notary records in Saint Domingue and in Louisiana as relatively inexpensive means of documenting legal transactions. The notaries' records provided a basis for affirming legality. He formalized legal decisions, including property transfers, inheritances, and chartering of the mutual aid associations that abounded in the city. His notarized record of the establishment of Callie House's New Orleans Ex-Slave Pension Association left the only clear record of that chapter. Martinet's clients included the colored community in Tremé and the Marigny, where the Snaers, shoemaker Homer Plessy, and schoolteacher and cigar seller Rodolphe Desdunes lived.[11]

Railroads opposed the separate-car law because providing racially segregated train cars was expensive and inefficient. The Pullman Car Company paid for the successful defense of one of their conductors who did not send a colored passenger to a separate car: The Louisiana Supreme Court decided that the law was unconstitutional as interfering with interstate travel.[12]

The Comité, which wanted the law voided altogether so as to desegregate intrastate transportation, picked Homer Plessy to violate the law because he was not of discernible African descent. Therefore, the railroad would be required to identify him as a colored man. Their basic objection as Colored Creoles was, of course, the denial of "public rights," including the right to go and come freely that they had embraced historically. But they also insisted on refusing to let the government determine identity for nefarious reasons. Colored Creoles had long experience in the "defining away" of their privileges and identity in Saint Domingue, in antebellum Louisiana, and in the post-Reconstruction turn to white supremacy.

Essentially, what the Comité wanted was what Louis Antoine insisted upon when he refused to identify himself so the military could exclude him from the officer corps. It was also what his fellow Creole officers did when they identified themselves but insisted they should not be removed. It was what Seymour Rene and E. K. Washington invoked on behalf of Josephine DeCuir in insisting that the steamboat captain could not identify her as colored in order to exclude her from the ladies' cabin. Labeling a person in order to exclude him or her was inadmissible they insisted.

The U.S. Supreme Court's affirmation of segregation had dire personal consequences. In late December 1892 the Louisiana Supreme Court decided against *Plessy*. Five months later, Aristide Mary committed suicide. The Catholic Church refused him burial and his funeral took place at his brother's house on Ann Street.

Louis Antoine began to feel increasingly ill. He filed an additional claim for an increase in his pension. He had developed asthma, catarrh of the stomach, and rheumatism, all of which his physician attributed to his service in addition to the effects of the gunshot in his foot. He asked two enlisted men from the Union Army Company he commanded, Leon Populus and Albert Victor, to file affidavits attesting to the severe conditions and related illnesses they all suffered during the war.[13]

Albert Bertonneau and Aristide Duconge, fellow Colored Creoles and longtime friends of Louis Antoine's, supported his claim. They attested to knowing him for years, having been his neighbors since the Civil War. They said he often suffered from coughing and wheezing and could do no "more than half of what an able-bodied man could." Their endorsement and other evidence got Snaer an added one-twelfth disability benefit from the U.S. Pension Bureau, making his total five-twelfths of a full pension.[14]

By 1893, Louis Antoine felt no better. Increasingly frustrated with the social and economic constraints they faced, Louis Antoine took his family to the Pacific Northwest. They moved to Oregon, where the black population was less than 2,000, and they lived as white. Oregon, with its huge cannery industry, had ports where he could work as a customs official just as he had in New Orleans. His children attended public school. Pierre Louis, later known as Louis Peter, was fourteen, Emma eleven, Felix eight, Lily five, and Victoria two. Emma recalled that their grandmother found Oregon too rainy and cold. Depressed by the weather and homesick, they decided to move back to Louisiana.

Louis' friend, Arnold Bertonneau, who had carried the equal rights petition to President Lincoln after serving in the Native Guards, had been distraught since he unsuccessfully sued the New Orleans school board for refusing to admit his children on account of race in 1877. He abandoned New Orleans and his race and moved to Pasadena, California. When he died in 1912, his death certificate identified him as white. Others also left the city, including Paul Broyard, the son of Henry Broyard; Henry had served as an enlisted man in Louis Antoine's regiment at Fort Blakeley. Henry, a white man, passed for colored so that he could legally marry his colored wife, but his appearance was no more remarkable than Louis' and that of the other colored men in the regiment. Henry died in 1873. By the 1890s Paul had become a very successful construction contractor, employing the male members of his extended family and caring for his widowed mother. He left with his wife and six children for California and lived as white.[15]

In 1894 the state made interracial marriage illegal again, as it had been before Republican Reconstruction. In 1895 the Catholic Church announced the segregation of all services. By the time of the *Plessy v. Ferguson* decision in 1896, things had gotten even worse. The Court decided to reject the discrimination theories the Colored Creoles advanced and to endorse state-imposed racial segregation.[16]

In deciding to uphold segregation in *Plessy*, the Court gave short shrift to the Comité's lawyer's arguments. Justice Henry Brown's majority opinion stated: "The power to assign [a passenger] to a particular coach obviously implies the power to determine to which race the passenger belongs." Also implicated was "the power to determine who, under the laws of the particular state, is to be deemed a white, and who a colored, person . . . This question, though indicated in the brief of the plaintiff in error, does not properly arise upon the record in this case."

Plessy, his appeal lost, paid a fine of $25 in 1897. The next year at a state constitutional convention, delegates laid down the legal blueprint for the future. As the chair of the judiciary committee declared, "our mission was to establish the supremacy of the white race." In 1906 segregated streetcars reappeared in New Orleans.[17]

After *Plessy*, Louis Antoine and his family moved to northern California. Their transition was made easier because Robert Guichard and Louis Antoine's sister, Victoria Rose, had already taken Seymour's son, Seymour Louis, and their own seven children to California.

The Snaers became white permanently, both privately and publicly. They lived quietly, first in San Francisco, and raised their family with no discussion of their African heritage. Louis Antoine clerked in the "large fruit and vegetable concern" his brother-in-law Robert Guichard established.[18]

Louis Antoine and his family moved to 1232 Fifteenth Avenue in Oakland, where they lived until he retired. Oakland was the terminus of the transcontinental railroad and had a thriving commercial sector. The children went to Catholic school.[19] Emma graduated from Our Lady of Lourdes High School at 1500 East Fifteenth Street, not far from their home. Her younger sisters, Lillian Josephine and Victoria Margaret, were also educated there, which was operated by the Sisters of Mercy of the Union starting in 1877. (The school closed in 1931, but after fundraising and rebuilding it reopened as St. Anthony's Catholic School.) Lillian Josephine became a Sister of Mercy teaching nun with the name Sister Mary Catherine. In the early years, the school served a mixed Irish and Portuguese population of students; by the time the "white" Snaer children attended, it had become increasingly Portuguese, and in recent years it has served an Asian and Latino population.[20]

Emma did clerical work for the California Hospital Company at Seventh and Market Streets until the Great San Francisco Fire in 1906. She took a job with the fire insurance companies that had moved to Oakland and worked for nine years before moving to Seattle with her brother, Louis Peter, and his family. The Oakland neighborhood, including Fifteenth Street, where the Snaers lived, is now mostly Vietnamese, and the address where they lived is shared by the Kenworth Storage and Transportation Company and an aquarium supplier.[21]

The younger Snaers, the children of Francois and Emerine, had great difficulty trying to walk the color line. Their different experiences arose from their search to identify themselves as they pleased despite oppressive laws and societal claims. Omer Joseph, born in 1856, sought to balance his desire to live in New Orleans against his refusal to deal with Jim Crow discrimination, a common problem of Colored Creoles at the time. His descendants ended up passing for white, and his own death certificate identified him as white. Omer Joseph married Caroline Reggio in 1883 when she was twenty-two

Emma Ann Marguerite, younger daughter of Louis Antoine.

and he was twenty-seven. In the 1880 Census, her mother, also named Caroline Reggio, is listed as from England and white and supported by her son, Henry, age twenty-one, a schoolteacher. She had two daughters, age seventeen and twenty-one. Once Caroline married Omer, they lived near St. Claude Avenue and Music Street in the Seventh Ward.[22]

Chester Snaer, born in 1895, and Violet Antoinette Snaer, born in April 1897, lived in the household of Henry Reggio's family as niece and nephew. They were identified as Omer's children, but their mother was not listed. The entire family was recorded by the census taker as white, although Violet is recorded as colored on her birth certificate, and probably so was Chester, whose record has not been found.[23]

In 1891, Omer Joseph had been working as a marble cutter on North Galvez Street, between Onzaga and D'Abadie Streets. Caroline (wife of Omer Joseph Snaer) died in 1899. Omer Joseph appears in the 1900 Census in San Francisco as a white gardener living and working in the household of George Mannier, who was of French origin. However, in the 1902 New Orleans city directory, Omer Joseph and Chester lived as renters at 3203 Iberville Street.[24]

Omer's descendants in Mississippi changed their surname and became white, and ignored calls from family members. They just wanted to be left alone lest their "redneck relatives" find out about their origins. Chester became "Chester Schneider" and was listed in the 1920 Census as white and a carpenter with a white wife, Eleanor, and a child, Violet, born that year. Chester died in Jackson, Mississippi, in 1985.[25]

In the 1930 Census Omer was listed as "Omer Schneider," white and living in Biloxi with other Schneiders, including Chester and Violet. He died in Mississippi in October 1940.[26]

In New Orleans, Francois' son, Victor Joseph, born in 1850, was listed as a cigar maker in the 1886 city directory. His only other employment before that had been as a clerk in his father's store and, in 1870, as a streetcar conductor living in Mandeville. His brother, George, was also a conductor. Since Negroes could not work in these occupations, they were certainly identified, at work at least, as white. Emile, Francois' youngest son, born in 1862 (his middle name was probably Auguste), stayed at 232 St. Claude Avenue while his mother was alive and worked as a cigar maker. He moved to New York and was a white cigar maker at his death in November 1916.

While according to some family lore Victor Joseph Snaer died in 1891, a press report in 1887 from Bluefields, Nicaragua (at the time a Miskito reserve created by British and American agreement), noted his death there. The reserve was an area of thriving commercial activity based on banana and wood production. There was plenty of work for artisans and laborers and great rewards for investors.[27]

Victor Snaer (who may have been Victor Joseph's son, born in 1878), in 1902 worked as a motorman on the electric trains that had started operating in 1893. He too must have been identified as white. William, the son of the dentist, Peter, moved to the Philippines. Another son, Hamilton, moved back to New Orleans from Texas, working first as a mason. By 1910 he and his wife Lititia had both become white. He worked first as a mason and then as a shoemaker; her brother, George, an insurance agent, lived with them. Hamilton died in New Orleans in 1924.[28]

Seymour R. Snaer's son, Seymour Louis, had been taken to the Bay Area by his aunt, Victoria, to become white. But he, like his uncle, Omer Joseph, felt conflicted over being identified without regard to his mixed race. In 1900, when he was twenty-three, he returned to New Orleans, became black again, and boarded in a black household with Alfred, a tinsmith, and Antoinette Bezou, a seamstress, in the 1500 block of Hospital Street. He took up the occupation of druggist. According to his granddaughter, "he seemed to have many different jobs throughout his career." There are several "mysteries" about him; she noted that at one point he went by the name "Martin Snaer."[29]

Later, Seymour Louis returned to California and whiteness. He became a salesman in the oil industry, worked at the Guichard grocery store, married a white woman, and had a son, Seymour W., born in 1909. Seymour W., educated at the University of California, Berkeley, became a prize-winning photographer at the *San Francisco Examiner*. Louis Antoine's great-grandchildren knew Seymour and they visited each other when they were children, all self-identifying as white. By 1930, Seymour Louis had suffered several strokes and was cared for in Our Lady's Home for Aged Men and Women in Oakland. He died there in 1940. Denise, the daughter of photographer Seymour W., is a successful landscape architect who also teaches sandcasting at a West Oakland industrial arts school to disadvantaged children in public housing. They learn welding, blacksmithing, and building their own bikes in the hope of expanding their ideas of what is possible.[30]

Louis Antoine, calling himself Louis Anthony Snaer, was living in Oakland in 1912 and receiving a pension of $20 per month, which was increased to $24 per month starting June 19, 1912. In 1915, he and his wife moved to southern California to live with his son, Pierre, known as Louis Peter. Victoria Margaret, their youngest daughter, lived with them. Their direct descendants, all white, including Louis Peter's grandson Larry Niekamp, live in California and Texas today.[31]

After Louis Anthony died of bronchial pneumonia on June 18, 1917, in Los Angeles, Marie Antoinette Emma, age sixty, wrote to the Commissioner of Pensions on December 8, 1917, that she was "very

Seymour Louis, son of Seymour Rene and Marie Lalande, at work in one of the Guichard groceries.

Seymour William, son of Seymour Louis grandson of Seymour Rene, and father of Denise.

Denise Snaer Gauder, great-granddaughter of Seymour Rene and Marie Lalande.

Louis Peter, oldest son of Louis Antoine.

Larry Niekamp, Louis Antoine's great-grandson.

anxious to receive the pension, as my husband has left me no other means." She supplied a sworn statement of Louis' sister, Victoria, and her husband, Guichard, that they had known her since childhood and knew that she and Louis had been husband and wife. She received the pension.[32]

Edgard Davis, from Louis Antoine's Native Guards regiment, died a few months before him, in February 1917. Davis, who also appeared white, acknowledged his African ancestry along with the other colored officers who were ejected from the service. However, by the turn of the century, after *Plessy*, he and his family had also crossed the line. Like some other Colored Creoles, they became white just by moving to a different neighborhood in New Orleans.

The Snaers, children of Francois' second marriage to Anne Emerine, like other Colored Creoles, searched for equal rights under a series of legal and practical circumstances. They had lived under French law and the changes brought by the French Revolution and the Haitian Revolution; then under Cuban law and Spanish law; in the United States under antebellum law and during the Civil War; and finally under Reconstruction and Jim Crow. Their question was always the same: Could they be who *they* said they were and have equal rights and opportunities?

Perhaps those Snaers and other Colored Creoles who left New Orleans for good and took advantage of their fair skin were just being practical. They did not have to suffer the consequences of their race in the age of Jim Crow, like their relatives who continued to live in New Orleans. But they too paid a price: Abandoning their history meant losing traditions, ideals, and sources of inspiration. For instance, Louis Antoine's family knew something of his military record and possessed his sword but did not know how he negotiated the system to remain the only colored officer known to lead troops in battle throughout the war. Seymour Rene's courage, ideals, accomplishments, and suffering went unacknowledged and unexplored. The family didn't know that Samuel, the child of Francois and Marie Catherine Rochefort, coped with his disability and his uniqueness as a composer and musician. When his children and grandchildren asked Louis Antoine about their heritage, he gave no answer beyond "we're just Americans."

Those Snaers from Francois' first family who stayed in New Orleans, and other Creoles, had to find ways to sustain themselves economically. They also had to maintain a social and cultural life despite the fact that they were disconnected from active participation in the political process and lived in a society that segregated them legally as inferiors. At every turn they had to negotiate the difficult racial terrain. Creoles had a history of cultural cohesion and social networks to rely on that slave-descended African Americans were just developing. Both groups needed to join together as one community if they ever hoped to achieve political involvement or to gain equal rights. It would not be easy.

CHAPTER 9

At Home or Away:
We Are Who We Say We Are

"You couldn't work in the department stores, the men couldn't drive a bus, you couldn't work for the telephone company, you couldn't work for the Public Service, so if you didn't do menial labor, or housework, or learn to be a cigar maker, or you weren't lucky enough to get an education to teach, well, you were in very bad luck because then these people had nothing to do. You see, they didn't give the poor colored people jobs." This is how Eugenia Lacarra, a third-generation cigar maker, described the exploitation and struggles of black workers in early-twentieth-century New Orleans. Color-based discrimination tempted some Colored Creoles, including some Snaers, to pass.[1]

Despite the difficulty of securing work, New Orleans was a prosperous city. Until the Great Depression, it remained the wealthiest in the South due to its internationally competitive Cotton Exchange, the active port, and large banks. The city's diversity was also one of its strengths. Artists, writers, and other bohemians migrated to the Italian-dominated French Quarter, where housing was quaint and inexpensive. The smells of baking bread and bananas permeated the area; United Fruit was the largest user of the port. There were fine restaurants and working-class cafés. Prostitutes plied their trade in the hedges surrounding Jackson Square. Downriver were the working-class whites who earned their living from the port, sugar and timber mills, and the slaughterhouses. Uptown, along St. Charles Avenue and into the Garden District, white elites, descended from the owners of American upriver plantations, predominated.[2]

On Broad Street, Negro doctors, lawyers, dentists, and pharmacists held a monopoly by serving the segregated market. They hired their own relatives first. A few Negroes, primarily Creoles, held federal patronage jobs in the Custom House or post office or became teachers. Some had jobs in the city and parochial schools. Even those jobs, however, were few in number. Creoles still controlled the building trades well into the twentieth century. Emilio Snaer, Francois' youngest son from his second marriage, Louis Antoine and Seymour Rene's brother, worked as a cigar maker. In slack times, he and others followed the jobs to New York or Tampa for several months at a time, returning to New Orleans when work dried up or their health failed. Pulmonary disease was common among cigar makers: Emilio died from it in 1916 while in New York.[3]

The precariousness of employment for blacks and the lack of good-paying jobs meant that both men and women had to work, and those who could pass as white sometimes did. For women, entry into the public workplace exposed them to sexual harassment and exploitation and had no legal protection on account of their race. Public work also threatened a possible loss of respectability. Creole mothers and aunts taught tailoring to girls in the family, who would perform sewing or piecework at home. Gradually, as more women became employed, paid jobs became acceptable for Colored Creole women. As men left cigar factories for other work, black and Colored Creole women took their places. In the 1910s and 1920s most poor women of color worked in laundries, cigar factories, or food processing facilities, or in domestic service. In segregated workplaces where both white and black women were employed, doing roughly similar work, white women earned more.[4]

Passing was stressful, whether it was done full time or part time. James Montoya (1891–1919), a cigar maker whose father was also a cigar maker, explained that passing "was not easy, it was hard. You'd be around there and the whites would be talking about Negroes and you'd have to take it. Once I had been seen at night . . . and I was later asked what was I doing with all those niggers. I told them that it was none of their damn business who I was with. They never asked me that anymore but I didn't like it."[5]

Passing or attempting to do so while staying in the city has a long local history. From 1926, Howard University Professor Camille

Lucie Nickerson (1888–1982), who used the stage name the "Louisiana Lady," regularly performed a ditty about passing she heard in New Orleans, where she grew up. The song is about Toucoutou, a beautiful "octoroon" who refused to marry a suitor who was very dark. In disguise, he went to a ball and sang this song to embarrass her publicly: "There is no soap strong enough to whiten your dark skin." In the antebellum period Creoles interpreted the song to assure whites that they rejected passing. By the time Nickerson heard it, however, the song was just a witty acknowledgment of the reality and risks of passing.

Omer Joseph, a younger brother of Louis Antoine and Seymour Rene, was light enough that he took the risks required to pass for white. Like other working-class Colored Creoles, at first he did so part time or discontinuously instead of adopting a new identity, as some other relatives did. Passing for white continuously allowed access to more lucrative and less physically arduous employment. It also meant that children could, unchallenged, attend white schools and families could attend white churches.[6] Eventually Omer Joseph decided to pass full time and moved uptown. He married Caroline Reggio and never appeared to have contact with the colored Snaers again. Some New Orleans residents insist they can still identify whose families took that path: They were as distinct and separated from their communities as those who became white in their migrations north and west.

The Colored Creoles who left New Orleans from the end of Reconstruction through the Great Migration but stayed colored became artisans, physicians, lawyers, teachers, and dentists, joining the new growing class of professional Negroes in the North, relieved from the burden of Southern repression. Those who moved and passed for white included some, however, like Louis Antoine, who had no work credentials beyond clerical and administrative experience in the Customs Service or the post office and in marketing in his brother-in-law Robert Guichard's very successful fruit and vegetable business. Louis Antoine's brother, Peter, had become an experienced dentist before he migrated and passed. Some who migrated and passed, like Louis Antoine, were collecting military pensions. His daughters, all of whom passed, became housewives or worked in other occupations reserved for women of the day. Emma became a clerk or secretary and

Lily took vows as a nun, which was not unusual for Catholics. Lawyer Seymour Rene's son, Seymour Louis, became a salesman. In addition to economic concerns, there were other reasons why blacks chose to leave or to pass. Episodic murder and assault reminiscent of the white supremacists' violence earlier but now done openly by police, had a chilling effect on blacks in the city. The Robert Charles Riot of 1900 sent a direct message to blacks. Charles, originally a Mississippian, advocated self-defense and emigration to Liberia in response to racial discrimination. On the evening of July 23, 1900, three white police officers harassed Charles and a friend, Leonard Pierce, for sitting on a porch in a white neighborhood. During the encounter a police officer and Charles exchanged gunfire, but neither was killed. Charles fled. When police found Charles at his home, he was armed with a rifle. He killed two officers, including the police chief, and escaped. The police began a manhunt. The next day whites, arriving at the location where the policemen were killed, demanded the lynching of Charles. Mobs of whites roamed the city attacking blacks for three days. By July 25, the mob had killed three African Americans, eleven others were hospitalized, and more than fifty had suffered injuries. Local newspapers blamed blacks for the violence. Some blacks provided assistance to Charles and expressed sympathy in the wake of growing restrictions on voting and civil rights. On July 27, the police and the mob surrounded a house where they had located Charles. After exchanges of fire, and with Charles refusing to surrender, the police burned the building. When Charles fled to escape the fire, a Tulane University medical student in the mob shot and killed him. Then the rest of the frenzied mob beat and fired their weapons repeatedly at his body.

Blacks were fearful and on edge. They had experienced a long history of racial violence. They also saw that a whole group could be attacked when someone white and in authority was brutalized. In 1890 Irish Police Chief David G. Hennessy was ambushed as he walked home, and in a dying declaration he identified his assailants as "Dagoes." Police rounded up dozens of Sicilians, nineteen of whom were jailed and indicted for murder. Six of the nine brought to trial in February 1891 were acquitted, and the court ordered a mistrial in the cases of three others. Based on some outstanding indictments, however, they all were returned to jail. Amid public charges of jury tampering, intimidation, and bribery, a mob of 6,000 to 8,000 stormed the jail the next morning. They shot and killed nine of the Sicilians, including five who had not been brought to trial. They dragged two others outside and hanged them. The Italian government protested and there was even talk of war, but the U.S. government disavowed any responsibility. Eventually, the federal government paid an indemnity to the survivors of one victim who had Italian citizenship. These lynchings, although they targeted Sicilians, served as warning enough of what could happen to blacks if any complicity with Charles was even rumored.[7]

Black anti-lynching activist Ida Wells-Barnett investigated the death of Charles. In a pamphlet published just a month after the riot, she insisted that Charles acted on his belief in self-defense, based on his advocacy work and literature. He did not believe in violence or retribution against whites. He was not a criminal or someone bent on irrational acts of violence. Local blacks, however, did not use Wells-Barnett's report to come to Charles's defense. A minister preached a widely publicized sermon titled "Afterthoughts, or Lessons from the Riot," which used Charles's life as a warning: "There was certainly no excuse for Charles's resistance," the preacher insisted. Disputing Wells-Barnett, he stated clearly that he did not think Charles was a "hero." Mindful of the need not to upset whites, the minister decried Charles's defiance and pleaded for the abandonment of "constant harping over past wrongs," which he believed would lead to the "destruction" of blacks.

The summer of 1900 brought not only the Charles incident but also anxieties over the prospect of even more Jim Crow regulations. Whites began a campaign to segregate New Orleans' streetcars. Streetcars had been the site for segregation struggles for decades. The cars had been briefly segregated after the war, when Colored Creoles who had been in the Native Guards protested their exclusion. The Republican Reconstruction legislature outlawed segregation, but with the *Plessy v. Ferguson* decision in 1896, segregation in public transportation was again permitted. Georgia passed the first streetcar law in 1891 and by 1900 seven Southern states had such laws. Cities also had their own ordinances. Early in July 1900, when the state legislature began discussing a new separate-car bill, local white residents worried that some "Conductors will make serious blunders by assigning dark-complexioned white people (of whom there are many in this city) to negro cars."[8] Some white men would simply not wait for a white car to approach, leading to integration. Ignoring these issues, in 1902 a new state law imposed segregation on streetcars throughout the state. Other Southern states followed Louisiana's example and passed similar laws. The streetcar boycotts organized in New Orleans and other cities by Creoles and African Americans were unsuccessful in ending segregation.[9]

The color divide in the Snaer family reappeared in draft registrations for World War I: There were white Snaers registered in California and Texas and colored Snaers in New Orleans. A colored Snaer in the military recalled that an officer told him "if you keep identifying yourself as a Negro no one will find you if something happens because you don't look like a Negro and they'll be looking for a Negro."[10]

The younger sons of Francois from his second marriage, and most of the descendants of Samuel Snaer, the musician, his son from his first marriage, decided to remain colored and in New Orleans after their white relatives left. These New Orleans Snaers were listed in the Census every ten years as mulattoes and after that as Negro or black when the mulatto category was abolished in 1920. They stayed because since their ancestors had migrated from Saint Domingue and Cuba in 1809, they enjoyed the built environment, some of which they had helped to construct, the culture and language, and their organizations and schools. Relationships with friends and relatives, some of whom were too dark to pass, were too important to abandon easily. Even when these Snaers appeared white, and were frequently misidentified, they stayed colored and maintained networks with each other, including dark-skinned relatives.[11]

After Samuel's wife, Marie, died, he married Felecia, a mulatto whose father was Italian. She continued to live in New Orleans until her death in 1919. One of their children, Morris, born in 1874, a printer, and his brother Felix, who died in 1901, never lived elsewhere.[12] Samuel's son, Leopold, a tour wagon driver and carpenter, stayed in the city, moving around in the Quarter and the Marigny until his death in 1933. In 1920, he was using his carpentry skills as a cabinet maker in a furniture store; his wife Wilhemina was a homemaker. By 1930, with harder economic times, he and his wife moved in with her relatives. She became a washerwoman and he found work as a repairman in a furniture store.[13]

Colored Creoles continued to pass on their skills to sons or other relatives who followed in their footsteps. Samuel's grandson, David, born in 1887, was a carpenter like his uncle, Leopold, and many other Colored Creoles, including Louis Tureaud, the father of Alexander Pierre (A. P.) Tureaud, who became New Orleans' leading civil rights lawyer. His wife, Sophie, was a seamstress, like numerous other Colored Creole women, including the mother of New Orleans' first African American mayor, Ernest "Dutch" Morial. Samuel Snaer's grandson, David, and his wife Lillian Perossier, living in New Orleans, had ten children, all of whom appeared white except for Curtis, born in 1927, the darkest. Their son David Jr., born in 1915, moved back and forth across the color line, unlike his siblings who identified as black. He was like his uncle Omer Joseph and his cousin

David, son of Joseph Samuel.

David and his wife, Lillian Perossier.

David and Lillian's five daughters: Hilda, America (Mae), Lillian, Bernice "Bunny" and Ruth.

America (Mae) and her mother Lillian.

David and Lillian's ten children: Bunny, Ruth, Lillian, Hilda, Mae, Kenneth, Bobby, Curtis, Roy and David.

David and Lillian's five sons: Robert, Curtis, David, Roy and Kenneth.

Seymour Louis, Seymour Rene's son, who in his youth went back to New Orleans briefly as colored before becoming permanently white in California. David Jr. had both a black family and a white family.[14]

David and Lillian's children as adults had a variety of occupations, some traditional among Colored Creoles. Mae and Hilda were seamstresses like their mother. Bernice and Ruth were housewives, although Ruth worked as a professional dancer briefly before she married and Bernice as a seamstress "extraordinaire" according to her family. Roy was a high school carpentry teacher. Curtis became a facility manager and Kenneth a postal worker.[15]

Some of these Snaers, although they decided to remain colored, exhibited the color consciousness characteristic of many Creoles. For example, Ruth's son Arol ("Glennie") married Aroline Miller's mother Valerye, over objections that she was too dark. They eventually divorced.[16]

After the migrants left New Orleans, blacks, descendants of former slaves, and Colored Creoles continued to live in largely separate worlds within the city's seventeen wards. Creoles were concentrated in

David Jr.'s first wife, June.

David Jr.'s second wife, Bridgette.

Roy's daughter, Yvonne Snaer, the grand-daughter of David and Lillian.

Roy with his niece, Arolon Miller.

Ruth Snaer, David and Lillian's daughter.

Ruth's son, Arol "Glennie" Miller as a child.

Valerye Faye Jackson, Arol Miller's first wife and mother of Arolon.

Arolon Miller.

the Seventh Ward. French and English were still spoken below Canal Street in their neighborhoods.

As blacks contended with discrimination and stifled economic opportunity, they had no influence in the local political arena. Excluded by legal and illegal means, the 127,923 black registered voters in New Orleans in 1888 (compared to 126,884 whites) by 1904 had been reduced to only 1,342. By 1940, when blacks constituted about one third of the city's total population of 495,000, only 400 were registered to vote. The numbers show their complete powerlessness. They paid taxes but experienced brazen inequality in the allocation of governmental resources. Descendants of slaves and Colored Creoles held different perspectives on the best way to pursue change. They had joined together for political advantage during Reconstruction, but under Jim Crow their paths diverged again. Louis Antoine Snaer, Aristide Mary, Arnold Bertonneau, Louis Martinet, and their contemporaries had insisted on the Creole tradition of equality of human rights. Louis Antoine had compromised his values by accepting an appointment to the board of segregated Southern University, but that was as far as he would go. But descendants of slaves, as freed people, accepted practicality: They wanted a university, even if it was segregated, to increase the numbers of educated blacks.[17]

The Snaer descendants who stayed colored did not resent their relatives who left or those who passed. As Thomas Sears, whose daughter married into the Snaer family, put it, "whites wouldn't let them be free and equal so it was the fault of the whites and they shouldn't be blamed." They did not deserve condemnation whatever compromises they made.[18]

With the Democrats in control and segregation imposed, it took time and experience before Creoles and blacks could be allies again. Until they did, there was no hope of overcoming Jim Crow restrictions. They did not start to come together until the 1940s. But in the meanwhile, in the absence of a political voice, the Snaers and other blacks expressed themselves using the available venues. The church was one of these places: Catholic for the Creoles and Protestant for the others, who were the majority. There were also cultural and social activities, and these institutions provided civic engagement. The relationships that were developed maintained and enhanced morale and formed a basis for solidarity and the social movements of the future.

The Mardi Gras Indian tradition, as a significant cultural expression with political consciousness, grew in importance in New Orleans among African Americans in the early 1900s. The Mardi Gras Indians developed into secret tribal societies, identified by particular handmade costumes, with chiefs and other officials who established and maintained traditional routines.[19] Mardi Gras Indians depict slaves' and American Indians' resistance to their suppression. Their music, rituals and secret language exhibit African, Caribbean, and Creole Louisiana influence and respect toward Indians. At first the rituals included violence, either mock or real, between the tribes of downtown Creoles and uptown blacks. Then, either because of policing or because caste differences eroded, the Indians competed only with chants, marches, and costumes as assertions of dignity, protest, and rebellion.

New Orleans jazz, as an authentic style, can be dated at least from the opening of the Storyville red-light district in 1897. Samuel Snaer's grandson Joseph played the trumpet in one of the bands. The players brought with them a wealth of different music experiences, both secular and religious. The marching band was directly responsible for the manner of performing the New Orleans ensemble style. Historians cite a background of West African culture and a heritage of two centuries of learning and making music at dances, weddings, baptisms, picnics, parties and funerals. From plantation religion came spirituals; from experience came the blues. Ragtime, the syncopated piano music that originated in the Midwest, flourished throughout the South about the same time that the Storyville district did (1897–1917). The New Orleans ensembles and their immediate successors played a conglomeration of religious and secular, notated and improvised music. In its heyday, Storyville had two newspapers and its own Carnival ball, and houses of prostitution advertised both themselves and the bands that played in them. The development of jazz, culturally and materially, enhanced the lives of all blacks in these difficult times.[20]

Benevolent societies dated from antebellum times among free people of color and played both a service and entertainment role. They provided burial and health assistance for members and also organized street parades and balls or concerts at the organization's hall. The celebrations included music and offered a venue for the development of jazz.[21]

Samuel's descendant Albert Snaer, born in 1902, played in New Orleans jazz bands until he moved to New York. His experiences were like those of many other New Orleans musicians. So many of them moved to Chicago that they strongly influenced the rise of jazz there, and the New Orleans ensemble style developed to its fullest expression. With the Great Migration in 1917, when Southern blacks went north for jobs in defense industries, jazzmen followed them and then wrote back to musician friends in New Orleans urging them to come north. With tales of how good it was to be in Chicago, major New Orleans jazzmen such as Sidney Bechet and Kid Ory (with whom Louis Armstrong played) arrived in Chicago. Daniel Desdunes (who had joined his father Rodolphe Desdunes' Citizens' Committee effort to test interstate railroad segregation in 1892) migrated too but did not stay in Chicago. He had worked as a professional musician in New Orleans and played in jazz bands before moving to Omaha, Nebraska ,where he became a teacher and bandleader.

The New Orleans style of collective improvisation was eclipsed in the mid-1920s by solo improvisation and the development of Big Band jazz. The 1930s eventually gave rise to the swing era, but in the late 1940s there was a revival of interest in early jazz, Dixieland, or the New Orleans style. Albert Snaer adjusted to these trends. By the 1940s he was in New York playing in theater bands and living in a rooming house with other musicians, while his wife and children remained in New Orleans. While many musicians and other black New Orleans residents did leave the city, a majority stayed in their culturally diverse and architecturally appealing home despite the racial suppression.[22]

Colored Creoles in New Orleans cherished respectability, refinement, and education. They shared such ideals with blacks generally. Descendants of former slaves wanted the respect accorded to people with cultivated manners and tastes who were enlightened and well read. Many Creoles were proud of their cultured and well-schooled forebears demanding equal rights. Changing times, World War I, and then the Great Migration created a spirit of militancy that slowly affected New Orleans. After 1925, both uplifting ideology and militancy were important.[23]

In the decades after World War I, the black population of New Orleans almost tripled. Migrants from the rural South saw it as the

Promised Land. The Mississippi River flood of 1927 and then the Great Depression accelerated the trend. Most blacks were paid less than the average white worker and even less than Creoles in some occupations and suffered dramatically higher mortality rates. They could afford to live only in the city's worst housing, with a lack of sanitation facilities. Their children attended public schools and they belonged to Protestant churches. They were generally poorer than Creoles of color. However, by the 1920s, because of their larger population, they tended to dominate the business and professional class. They spoke English and socialized in national clubs and organizations, including the Prince Hall Masons, the Grand United Order of Odd Fellows, and the Colored Knights of Pythias. These organizations allowed persons of any religion to join. Walter Cohen, a Catholic Creole, belonged to the Knights of Pythias, the Odd Fellows, the Elks, and the NAACP and was an honorary member of the Autocrat and San Jacinto clubs.

As the neighborhood around it changed, the congregation of St. Augustine Church, the Snaers' home church, became mostly Italian. The colored Snaers, like other Creole families, went, some very reluctantly, to Corpus Christi, about a mile away, the segregated church the Catholic archdiocese established in 1916. The Church maintained segregation in all public parades and ceremonies. Some Catholics simply stopped attending church. However, Colored Creoles remained Catholic even when they stopped speaking French. They stayed faithful to the church in part because it ran schools and Xavier University, although segregated, for their children.

A Negro League baseball team played in the city occasionally. Lucian Snaer, a descendant of Samuel, along with Leon Augustine of New Orleans became two of six colored umpires hired by the National Negro League in 1923. Their hiring resulted from a successful campaign by the *Chicago Defender* to replace the all-white umpires the league used. Creole social life included clubs that engaged in social and benevolent activities. Some Snaers belonged to the Young Men's Vidalia Benevolent Association, formed in 1886. Many Creole men belonged to one of the oldest secret societies in the world, the Masons.[24]

Creole society remained exclusive and close-knit. The Creoles retained a strong sense of cultural preservation, which included speaking some French, attending Catholic churches, and socializing among themselves. These goals meant that the organizations continued to exist through good and bad times economically.

Many Colored Creoles sought solace in a world of their own hoping to avoid race discrimination. As Howard University sociologist E. Franklin Frazier wrote of the black middle class, they substituted pretensions for reality. These Creoles did not want their children to attend school with "Negroes," those who happened to have dark skin. The colored Snaers said they did not draw distinctions and accepted all of their family members. But the Creoles Frazier discussed hoped somehow to remain separate from "Negroes," even if they had dark-skinned relatives whom they tried to ignore. Colored Creole author Rodolphe Desdunes, writing in 1911 in *Our People and Our History*, described these Creoles as clinging to the old three-race system and being obsessed with keeping up appearances. Such a Creole, he argued, turned into an "amalgamated Negro" who was "a fool in his own house" and "who esteemed nothing so much as the fairness of his skin and the supple strains of his hair." Brown skin was acceptable only if the family was well known and had wealth and "refinement." Gradually most colored Creoles became friends with blacks because they had the same occupation or met at school. Even though some scholars dismiss views about color as mythical, the subject remains openly discussed to this day in bars and barber and beauty shops, especially after Hurricane Katrina hit New Orleans and the comparative darkness of those most harmed became evident.[25]

Only slowly did Colored Creoles and slave-descended African Americans begin to work together on social problems The separate economy, the development of black insurance companies as important economic institutions, and the role of black professionals, doctors, and pharmacists eased the way. The insurance companies thrived because white insurance companies avoided blacks, fearing that their life expectancies were too low. The African American companies had Colored Creoles and slave-descended blacks on their boards. The members began to socialize and in some cases their children married. By 1925, these two groups had begun to reach consensus about the need to confront the city government on such issues as the lack of recreational facilities and decent schools for African Americans. Achieving integration would require sophisticated strategies and innovative tactics.

Becoming Black

David Snaer, Samuel Snaer's grandson, had had enough. His eldest child, America, called Mae, had already moved away and wondered why her parents didn't follow. But by the 1940s his wife had died and he was ready. He moved to Chicago, first taking part of his family, leaving the youngest, Kenneth, behind with the Colored Creole Sears family next door. Then on to California they went, and Kenneth later joined them. But still, except for his son David, who had two families, one black and one white, they stayed colored, despite their appearances. It was not just jobs and the economy that led them to leave New Orleans, but persistent problems like the dilapidated, overcrowded schools, the absence of recreational facilities for their children, inadequate health services, erratic trash pickup, unpaved or worn-out streets, and the police violence.

Year after year, the government ignored the complaints of African Americans, whether Creole or descendants of slaves. An exception came after the February 1930 murder of a fourteen-year-old black girl, Hattie McCray, by a white police officer, Charles Guerand, after she resisted his repeated sexual advances. He shot her in the kitchen of the diner where she worked as a dishwasher as she ran from him. The incident was denounced across racial lines and was covered in the local white press and in black newspapers nationwide. White church leaders and African Americans across class and color lines, including Colored Creoles, demanded justice. Protestors contributed to the Civic Federation and the local NAACP chapter to hire a special prosecutor. They hired a white lawyer who was a close friend of the

America (Mae).

presiding judge and who had been an assistant district attorney, keeping black lawyers out of the case. The strategy worked: The all-white male jury convicted Guerand and the judge imposed a death sentence. However, Guerand's lawyers appealed, claiming diminished capacity through mental illness or drunkenness, and created sympathy for the convicted cop. He spent five years under treatment in the state hospital for the insane. Thereafter, the white and black public lost interest in the case; Guerand served a short prison sentence and returned to New Orleans, where he lived quietly as a cabinetmaker and an active member of the millmen's union.[1]

At first, Walter Cohen and George Lucas were the African American leaders. Cohen was a successful Creole, a Republican Party patronage distributor, a "work within the system" man. Lucas was a non-Creole, a well-off physician, and president of the local NAACP.

Their cautious approach to requesting improvements reigned until about ten years after Cohen's death in 1930 and Lucas's death in 1931. In addition to the NAACP branch of which Lucas was president, they organized a Federation of Civic Leagues to advance the issues. The Federation made repeated but unsuccessful appeals using the equal rights arguments traditionally pressed by Colored Creoles and the argument that African Americans paid taxes but received totally inadequate unequal public services.

Even when the New Deal programs of the 1930s gave funds to local communities to build schools, officials ignored African Americans' segregated schools. This was true even though the *Plessy v. Ferguson* ruling required that any federal money given to Louisiana and New Orleans be distributed equally to both races.[2]

The Federation of Civic Leagues' efforts to provide recreational facilities for blacks were also unsuccessful. In 1929, all of the parks in the city except one, in the uptown section, were reserved for whites. The city had only one public swimming pool for a population of 130,000 blacks, and there were no black beaches. The Snaers and other black children played in the streets and swam in the bayous. Despite complaints, protests, and the drowning deaths of sixteen blacks, it was not until 1934 that the city opened a black beach. Unlike white beaches, it had no lifeguard stations or lights along the water's edge. It was immediately crowded, however, as blacks had no other public beach.[3]

On the flagrant episodes of racial violence, African American leaders took little action. Between 1925 and 1929, Lucas occasionally reported incidents of violence, along with such matters as the ineffective government flood-relief efforts in 1927, to the NAACP's national office, but he failed to organize concerted action.[4]

The violence was a continuing problem. From February to August 1932, four black men were killed, three of them shot by police. One, who had been arrested for "unknown reasons," was shot on the street and died in Charity Hospital. A twenty-nine-year-old black man was shot to death by a white gas station owner whose complaint was that the Negro "didn't listen to him," according to the police report. A white pharmacist told the police to arrest a black man who could not pay his pharmacy bill. The man objected to the arrest, and the pharmacist told the police that the man and his brother were both "bad niggers." He told the police to shoot the arrested man, and so they killed him. In August, a popular young black athlete died at Charity Hospital from wounds inflicted by an "accidental" discharge of a motorcycle officer's gun. The NAACP failed to act in any of the cases.

The Louisiana *Weekly* newspaper, which reported these incidents, became the community's most consistent voice, highlighting the issues and advocating for better leadership and more vigorous action. The paper was founded by businessman Constant Charles Dejoie Sr. and school principal Orlando Capitola Ward Taylor on September 19, 1925. It promised to document and report on the daily lives and struggles of blacks in New Orleans. Local black-owned businesses took out ample advertisements, including Dejoie's Cut Rate Pharmacy.[5]

At first the paper supported Cohen and Lucas and encouraged them in their demands. But after they died and the Great Depression brought greater unemployment and poverty, new approaches seemed necessary. Few beleaguered African Americans in the Crescent City noted the return of Alexander Pierre Tureaud to New Orleans in 1926. But the coming of this freshly qualified 27-year-old attorney marked the beginning of significant changes in the community activism.

Tureaud was a contemporary of lawyer Seymour Rene Snaer's white grandson, Seymour William, whose father, Seymour Louis, had been taken to California as a child to pass. Like them he appeared white. But, proud of his black and white ancestry and of Creole culture, instead of staying in the North and passing, A. P. came home determined to regenerate civil rights activism. Tureaud joined by marriage the circle of the Dejoies. In 1931 he married Lucille Dejoie, a pharmacist whose father was CC, the newspaper owner's cousin.[6]

Tureaud had a family history very different from that of the Snaers, although he proudly asserted his Creoleness. His grandfather Adolph, like Louis Antoine and Pierre Snaer, had served in the Union Army. But, unlike the Snaers, Adolph had been a plantation slave owned by his father, A. P.'s great-grandfather, who fled Saint Domingue during the Haitian Revolution, and a mulatto woman slave. A. P., born in 1899, was the fifth son of the twelve children in his family. He was an able student. He migrated north after high school and worked on the railroad and then at other odd jobs in New York, finally becoming a junior clerk at the Justice Department in Washington. There he decided to become a lawyer. He graduated from Howard University School of Law and became involved in civil rights organizations and met leaders in the field before returning to New Orleans.[7]

His mother and home drew him back to New Orleans at a time when African Americans sorely needed leadership. His family was torn apart racially like the Snaers and other Colored Creoles. While A. P. was away, four of his sisters crossed the color line and lived as white. One stayed white in New Orleans and married and had a sizeable family; the others left. As the passing sisters requested, the family destroyed all photos and documents that would identify them as colored. His sister Victoria, after years in New York, moved back to New Orleans and became a secretary to A. P. in his law practice. A. P. and his sister were the only ones in his family who went beyond the eighth grade; his father, brothers, and other male relatives were all tradesmen and skilled laborers, not professionals. Supported by a job at the Custom House arranged by Walter Cohen, the colored Republican leader and dispenser of patronage, he was ready to start a law practice and find ways to attack discrimination.[8]

The *Weekly* gradually abandoned its support of the local NAACP branch and other black leaders in the period. The local NAACP's failure to act on the issues that plagued African Americans ultimately had a positive effect: The ineffective leaders were replaced, the NAACP branch was reinvigorated, and a new local civil rights movement was launched to address the injustices blacks faced with the rise of legalized segregation and blacks' expulsion from the political process.

In 1930 only 27 percent of the roughly 1.3 million whites in Louisiana were registered voters, but whites still firmly controlled politics. Only 0.2 percent of the roughly 800,000 blacks were registered to vote. The 1931 figures, compiled by the registrar of voters in New Orleans, showed the same sort of disparity. The black vote represented less than one seventieth of the total registered voters in New Orleans. Almost 97 percent of the roughly 34,000 registered voters were Democrats. The black voters were Republicans, who made up only about 3.5 percent of the registrants. The constraints enacted into law to suppress the black vote worked. Without needing the votes of blacks, local officials saw no reason to concern themselves with the problems that they raised.

Not until 1939 did positive change begin, when A. P. Tureaud and a few newer young members of the NAACP branch organized into what they called "The Group." They included truck drivers, insurance agents, postal carriers, doormen, artisans, and tradesmen, who had always been among elite Colored Creoles, and a few teachers and other professionals. They believed that all blacks had to join together without regard to wealth, status, education, group distinctions, or color as they had done during Reconstruction to achieve equal rights. Although they lost the 1939 NAACP branch presidential election, they demonstrated enough clout that the winner, moderate J. Edwin "Chummy" Wilkins, a pharmacist, appointed Tureaud as the branch legal adviser.

By 1942 Tureaud, at the urging of Thurgood Marshall, the legal director of the national NAACP, began to devote full time to his law practice. It was important for African Americans to gain voting rights, which would give them leverage for hiring black police officers and reforming police practices and other issues, but in the meantime the NAACP could respond to teachers who were NAACP members in attacking salary discrimination. Tureaud became the lead attorney representing black teachers seeking equal pay. He was on his way in using the law to make social change in New Orleans and the rest of Louisiana.

The 1941 suit *McKelpin v. Orleans Parish School Board* challenged the discrepancy in pay between black and white schoolteachers: For the same work, whites received on average $1,1120.65 more. On June 14, 1941, Tureaud filed suit against the Orleans Parish School Board on behalf of teacher Joseph McKelpin. He argued that discrimination in teachers' salaries based on race was a violation of the equal protection clause. In the end he negotiated a two-year plan that would close the gap in teachers' pay by 50 percent each year.[9]

The NAACP branch became a well-organized and aggressive organization. The members accepted Tureaud's belief that the way to gain equal rights was by demanding and confronting whites through legal challenges to race discrimination. Soon the branch became a large and influential chapter and maintained strong ties with the national office.

Tureaud used diplomatic biracial appeals and political activity, but his main focus was on the legal battles that he and other NAACP attorneys fought. He also filed police brutality complaints in record numbers against the New Orleans police.[10]

Legal challenges, and the influx of black migrants from the rural South to New Orleans after World War II, helped in the revival of the black vote. New Orleans' black population increased, even while blacks were migrating to the North, from about 162,000 (one third of the population) in 1940 to about 183,000 (32 percent of the population) in 1950. By 1960 blacks represented 37 percent of the population, increasing to 67 percent by 2000. The percentages increased as "white flight" took hold in the 1950s and 1960s. As the population and the number of voters increased, change began to occur. Four-term reform mayor DeLesseps "Chep" Morrison's victory margin in 1946 was only 4,000 votes. In 1948 there 13,000 registered black voters in New Orleans and by 1950 twice that number. Morrison adopted a posture of seeming responsiveness to African American problems. He made some helpful decisions but did not want to create disorder that would disrupt business, so he opposed the desegregation of schools, transportation, and lunch counters. Early in his administration, Morrison supported the construction of a suburban-style black neighborhood, Pontchartrain Park; built public housing for low-income blacks; and spent money on street and infrastructure improvements in black neighborhoods. The city also built playgrounds, swimming pools, and recreational centers for African Americans. These actions earned him the enmity of hardline segregationists, although the facilities remained segregated and received less funding than civic projects in white neighborhoods.[11]

Tureaud filed suit for a black applicant to the police department who had been rejected even though he achieved one of the highest test scores on record. Mayor Morrison, in response, appointed the applicant and one other colored policeman. But unlike the Reconstruction colored officers who policed both whites and blacks, one observer noted that the mayor assigned them "to the juvenile bureau . . . dressed them in plain clothes, and tucked them away in a predominantly black district where very few white voters dared to venture. This cautious manipulation worked superbly. They were hardly noticed." Gradually more black police officers were added, and by 1955 there were twenty-five, who worked under strict supervision and heavy scrutiny. But they worked for a department that had poorly paid officers overall and that seemed consistently mired in scandal.[12]

The integration of the New Orleans public schools involved a heated ten-year battle with public protests. Turead sued on behalf of black parents in Bush v. Orleans parish School Board in 1952. He suspended his efforts until after *Brown v. Board of Education* was decided in 1954. Not until November 1960, did school segregation come to an end under federal court order in New Orleans. Four black first graders, including Ruby Bridges, entered all white schools under the protection of federal marshals as they were heckled and jeered by white crowds.[13]

Because of segregation in the private sector, African Americans in New Orleans owned a wide variety of businesses: Grocery and general merchandise stores, insurance companies, dry cleaners, radio repair shops, restaurants, taxicab companies, funeral homes, dentists, and physicians served the black community and provided jobs. Caterers, tailors, roofers, and plasterers provided services to whites and blacks.[14]

But African Americans remained excluded from many jobs in New Orleans, as in the rest of the South. Firefighters and bank tellers and clerks were solely white jobs, as were bus drivers until 1961. Many unions still excluded blacks from jobs and apprenticeships. Blacks could still find work in the post office as clerks, and black teachers fared better after Tureaud's victory in equalizing salaries.

By the time the "sit-ins" and then Black Power came along in the 1960s, Tureaud, once considered a radical, seemed old-fashioned, too proud of being a Creole and too committed to orderly progress and politeness. The student movement built on what had been won through the courts, and NAACP lawyers defended them successfully when they were arrested.

On September 30, 1963, during the March for Freedom to City Hall, Oretha Castle was carried out of the building in a chair when she and her sister refused to leave. Ernest "Dutch" Morial marched alongside her. Morial was a Colored Creole whom Tureaud had taken into his law practice when he became the first non-white graduate of LSU Law School in 1954. He was president of the NAACP branch from 1962 to 1965 and had served as Chairman of the Committee to

Prevent Police Brutality to Negro Citizens during Morrison's administration, thus responding to one of the key issues for black residents. The white business elite cooperated by securing a parade permit and warning the white citizens' council away. However, not one city official greeted the marchers at City Hall. Morial had been mentored by Tureaud and respected him but he understood and supported the strategies of the direct action movement. Telling his fellow Creoles that "we are all black" now, he understood that healing the breach between the Colored Creoles and other African Americans was necessary for progress.[15]

Morial had established a reputation as an able and respected lawyer. He had been elected to the Louisiana Court of Appeals, among other offices. In 1977, with 20 percent of the white vote added to the black vote, he won a runoff and was elected the first African American mayor of New Orleans.[16]

Morial was part of New Orleans' powerful Colored Creole community, from which Tureaud and other political leaders had also come. His father, a cigarmaker, was the son of a white man and a Colored Creole house servant. Morial's father married a seamstress. Ernest, born in 1929, was their eldest child. They had all been described as mulattoes in censuses before 1930, when everyone with African descent became a Negro.

The Morials, like A. P. Tureaud, some of the Snaers, and many other Colored Creoles and slave-descended African Americans, did not even think of leaving New Orleans permanently during the Great Migration. This was true even though one fifth of his graduating class from Xavier University in 1951 went to California, and so did three of his five siblings. Marc Morial, his son, says he never knew his two aunts, who became white. A brother went to sea and never came back, a typical Colored Creole family story.

Dutch Morial adhered to the traditional Colored Creole belief in human rights for all. As a lawyer, like Tureaud he saw civil rights as a means of achieving that goal. With their role in ending segregation by using the courts and in the direct action protest movement, the influence of Colored Creoles far surpassed anything those who left could ever imagine. The white and colored Snaers in California and elsewhere looked on from afar. Omer Joseph's relatives, now white and renamed, lived in Mississippi and could view the developments

Larry Niekamp (left) and Kenneth Snaer (right) meet for the first time at the 2003 family reunion.

closer at hand. Those African Americans who stayed in New Orleans and all over the South while others moved away became the heart and soul of the civil rights movement. With help from Northerners, black and white, and some local whites who were longtime supporters of liberal causes, they changed the South to a hospitable place that descendants of migrants could return to in the late twentieth century and after. In New Orleans that required healing the divide between slave-descended African Americans and colored Creoles. There would be lingering episodes and negative attitudes from time to time, but a major change had been made—and it would mostly stick.[17]

In California, the Snaers, who had remained African American despite skin color that would permit them to pass, occasionally struck their own blow against discrimination. Samuel Snaer's great-great-grandson, David Snaer's son, Kenneth, a mail carrier, in 1970 joined a protest against the refusal to promote blacks to the supervisory ranks. One of managers asked why he joined the other blacks when he could pass. He answered that he had no desire to be anything except black, and everyone should be treated equally. Eventually he was promoted to postmaster.[18]

NOTES

....

Preface

1. Werner Sollors, in *Beyond Ethnicity: Consent and Descent in American Culture* (New York: Oxford University Press, 1986), 241, describes the "tragic mulatto" stereotype as simultaneously racist in its embodiment of white values and revolutionary in asserting the humanity of mixed-race people: overdetermined as white in sentiment, "coloured" in appearance, yet ultimately ambiguous in terms of what they convey.

2. Ibid., Kenji Yoshino, *Covering: The Hidden Assault on Our Civil Rights* (New York: Random House, 2007).

3. Virginia Dominguez, *White by Definition: Social Classification in Creole Louisiana* (New Brunswick, NJ: Rutgers University Press, 1986), 163–166; see the discussion in Carroll Smith-Rosenberg, *This Violent Empire: The Birth of an American National Identity* (Chapel Hill: University of North Carolina Press, 2012).

4. Dominguez, *White by Definition*, p. 149.

5. See, for example, Isabel Wilkerson, *The Warmth of Other Suns; The Epic Story of America's Great Migration* (New York: Random House, 2010); Joe William Trotter Jr. ed., *The Great Migration in Historical Perspective: New Dimensions of Race, Class, and Gender* (Bloomington: Indiana University Press, 1991).

6. See discussion in Pierre Force, "The House on Bayou Road: Atlantic Creole Networks in the Eighteenth and Nineteenth Centuries." *Journal of American History* (2013), vol. 100, 21–45.

Chapter 1: Becoming Colored Creole

1. John E. Dawson and G. Shea, eds., *The Operations of the French Fleet Under the Count de Grasse in 1781–82 as described in two Contemporaneous Journals* (New York, 1864), 56–58, quoted in Rayford Logan, *Diplomatic Relations of the United States with Haiti, 1776–1891* (Chapel Hill: University of North Carolina Press, 1941), 4. The spelling of the Snaer name was Anglicized in American documents, dropping cedillas and accent marks. However, the family continued to pronounce Francois, Rene and other birth names in French.

2. Nathalie Dessens, *From Saint Domingue to New Orleans: Migration and Influences* (Gainesville: University of Florida Press, 2007), 10, and notes there cited.

3. Médéric-Louis-Elie Moreau de Saint-Méry, *Description topographique, physique, civile, politique et historique de la partie française de l'isle Saint-Domingue.* B. Maurel and E. Taillemite, eds. 3 vols. Paris: Société de l'histoire des Colonies Françaises, 1958.

4. John Garrigus, *Before Haiti: Race and Citizenship in French Saint-Domingue* (New York: Palgrave Macmillan, 2006), 51–66, 141–162. Snaer is an Old Dutch word for daughter-in-law. Its current Dutch meaning is string. A Francois Snaer traveled on April 15, 1778, by boat from Rotterdam (Aix en Provence, Centre des Archives d'Outre Mer, Archives departmentales de la Gironde). Snaer descendants claimed variously French or Dutch origin for the name Snaer. Many Dutch buccaneers, merchants, artisans, and farmers came to Saint Domingue from the Dutch island of Curaçao. The family's oral tradition insists her last name was Flique, but that seems to be a corruption of another name, perhaps Phillipe. In the 1880 Census, the census taker lists Francois V's parents, who would be Francois and Marie Eugenie, as French. Catherine Niekamp in Familysearch.org lists Francois' birth date as either 1777 or 1780. The succession of Marie Rothschild in Chapter III discusses their marriage. Jennifer Heuer, "The One-Drop Rule in Reverse: Interracial Marriages in Napoleonic and Restoration France," *Law and History Review* (2009), vol. 27, note 15; Sue Peabody, "*Négresse, Mulâtrese, Citoyenne*: Gender and Emancipation in the French Caribbean, 1650–1848," in Diana Paton and Pamela Scully, eds., *Gender and Slave Emancipation in the Atlantic World* (Durham, NC, and London: Duke University Press, 2005), 56–78. The 1685 Code Noir didn't prohibit interracial marriages. The revision in 1724 did outlaw them in Louisiana, but the Snaers were apparently married in Saint Domingue. Werner Sollors, *Neither Black*

Nor White Yet Both: Thematic Explorations of Interracial Literature (Cambridge, MA: Harvard University Press, 1999), 396.

5. Moreau, *Description*, p. 107; Heuer, "The One-Drop Rule," note 15 and notes there cited; Peabody, *"Négresse, Mulâtrese, Citoyenne,"* 56–78. The 1685 Code Noir did not prohibit interracial marriages. Molly M. Hermann, "The French Colonial Question and the Disintegration of White Supremacy in the Colony of Saint Domingue 1789–1792," M.A. thesis, University of North Carolina–Wilmington History Department (2005), 36.

6. James E. McClellan III, *Colonialism and Science: Saint Domingue in the Old Regime* (Chicago, IL: University of Chicago Press, 2010), 48–50, and notes there cited; Hermann, "The French Colonial Question," 23, and notes there cited. 465,429 slaves and 27,548 free people of color, both black and of mixed race, vastly outnumbered the 30,826 white population.

7. David Geggus, "Slave and Free Women in Saint Domingue," in Darlene Clark Hine and Barry Gaspar, eds., *More Than Chattel: Black Women and Slavery in the Americas* (Bloomington: Indiana University Press, 1996), 270, note 84 citing Moreau.

8. Susan M. Soochow, "Economic roles of the free women of Cap Français," in Hine and Gaspar, *More Than Chattel,* 279–297.

9. Ibid., 280.

10. Garrigus, *Before Haiti*, Chapter 6.

11. Ibid.

12. Ibid., Chapter 2.

13. Ibid., 143–160; Hermann, "The French Colonial Question," p. 35–36.

14. Ibid.

15. Ibid., 166.

16. Hermann, "The French Colonial Question," 36–37, and notes there cited.

17. Ibid. Peabody, *"Négresse, Mulâtrese, Citoyenne,"* 56–78; See Chapter III's discussion of the succession of Marie Rothschild.

18. Ibid., 228–236.

19. On the Haitian Revolution see Laurent DuBois, *Avengers of the New World: The Story of the Haitian Revolution* (Cambridge, MA: Harvard University Press, 2005), and C. L. R. James, *The Black Jacobins: Toussaint L'Ouverture and the San Domingo Revolution,* 2nd ed. (New York: Vintage, 1989 [1938]); Dessens, *From Saint Domingue to New Orleans,* 12 and notes there cited; Gary B. Nash, "Reverberations of Haiti in the American North: Black Saint Dominguans in Philadelphia," *Pennsylvania History* 65 (1998): 44–73.

20. Jeremy D. Popkin, *You Are All Free: The Haitian Revolution and the Abolition of Slavery* (Cambridge: Cambridge University Press, 2010).

21. C. L. R. James, *Black Jacobins*, 42–44.

22. Ibid., 11–15.

23. "Wim Klooster": Inter-Imperial Smuggling in the Americas," in Bernard Bailyn and Patricia L. Denault, *Soundings in Atlantic History: Latent Structures and Intellectual Currents* (Cambridge: Harvard University Press), 141–180.

24. Jeremy Popkin, *A Concise History of the Haitian Revolution* (West Sussex, England: Wiley Blackwell Publishers), 107–108.

25. 1930 U.S. Census. Francois V, age 67, said he was born in 1803 at Montecristi. Louis Antoine filed his death certificate November 20, 1880, saying that Francois V was born in St. Domingo. Record of Births and Marriages, Orleans Parish, Louisiana Division, New Orleans Public Library.

26. Commander Ferrand used privateers against American, English, and any non-French merchants trading with Haiti. They stopped merchant ships, took goods, and falsely promised they could be paid in Cap-Français; James Fichter, *So Great a Proffit: How the East Indian Trade Transformed American Capitalism* (Cambridge, MA: Harvard University Press, 2010), 100–101. Deborah Jenson, *Beyond the Slave Narrative: Politics, Sex and Manuscripts in the Haitian Revolution* (Liverpool: Liverpool University Press, 2011), 105–110, 150–165; Rene Chartrand, *Napoleon's Overseas Army* (London: Reed International Books, 1989), 20–21.

27. Dessens, *From Saint Domingue to New Orleans*, 16–20; Paul LaChance, "The 1809 Immigration of Saint Domingue Refugees to New Orleans: Reception, Integration and Impact," in Carl A. Brasseaux and Glenn R. Conrad, eds., *The Road to Louisiana: The Saint Domingue Refugees 1792–1809* (Lafayette, LA: University of Southwestern Center for Louisiana Studies, 1992), 245–284.

28. Jose Ortega, "The Cuban Sugar Complex in the Age of Revolution, 1789–1844" (Ph.D. dissertation, University of California Los Angeles, 2007), 237; Emily Clark, *Strange History of the American Quadroon: Free Women of Color in the Revolutionary Atlantic World* (Chapel Hill: University of North Carolina Press, 2013); Michele Reid-Vasquez, *The Year of the Lash: Free People of Color in Cuba and the Nineteenth-Century Atlantic World* (Athens: University of Georgia Press, 2011); See generally, Kenneth Kiple, *Blacks in Colonial Cuba, 1774–1891* (Gainesville: University Press of Florida, 1976).

29. Orleans Parish Recorder of Births, Marriages and Deaths, Death Certificates, Francois and Jean Baptiste Snaer, Death Register, Louisiana Division, New Orleans Public Library, vol. 6, colored vol., May 5, 1838, 244.

30. Dessens, *From Saint Domingue to New Orleans*, 16–20; Jacqueline C. Grant, "Public Performance: Free People of Color Fashioning Identities in Mid-Nineteenth-Century Cuba" (Ph.D. dissertation, University of Miami, 2012), 172: "Those settlers who could find a passing boat went to New Orleans," wrote Cuban novelist Alejo Carpentier. "But, for those who only had a schooner at their disposal, the Cuban coast offered surer and closer refuge."

31. Ibid., Paul LaChance, "The 1809 Immigration," 245–284.

32. Alejo Carpentier, *Music in Cuba* (Minneapolis: University of Minnesota Press, 2001), 146. Bryan Edwards, *A Historical Survey of the French Colony in the Island of St. Domingo* (Cambridge: Cambridge University Press, 2010 [1797]), preface, 413. Laurent Dubois, *Avengers of the New World: The Story of the Haitian Revolution* (Cambridge, MA: The Belknap Press of Harvard University, 2004), 94; Grant, "Public Performance," 173–174.

33. Grant, *Public Performance*, 182; Reid-Vasquez, *Year of the Lash*, 22–24 and notes there cited; Dessens, *From Saint Domingue to New Orleans*, 15, 18–22; Gabriel Debien, "The Saint Domingue Refugees in Cuba, 1793–1815," in Carl Brasseaux and Glenn R. Conrad, eds., *The Road to Louisiana: The Saint-Domingue Refugees, 1792–1809* (Center for Louisiana Studies, University of Southwestern Louisiana, 1992), 31.

34. Grant, *Public Performance*, 175–176. Someruelos held office from 1799 through 1812.

35. Ibid., 178–180.

36. Franklin Knight, *Slave Society in Cuba During the Nineteenth Century* (Madison: University of Wisconsin Press, 1970), 12–13, 23–24.

37. José Millet and Rafael Brea, *Grupos folklóricos de Santiago de Cuba* (Santiago de Cuba: Editorial Oriente), 1989.

38. Herbert S. Klein, "The Colored Militia of Cuba," *Caribbean Studies* (July 1966), vol. 6, 17–27; Guadelupe Garcia, "Nuestra Patria La Habana: Reading the 1762 British Occupation of the City," http:// nuevomundo.revues.org/61119

39. Rebecca Scott and Jean Hebrard, *Freedom Papers, An Atlantic Odyssey in the Age of Emancipation* (Cambridge, MA: Harvard University Press, 2012), Chapter 3.

40. Hugh Thomas, *Cuba, or, The Pursuit of Freedom* (New York: Da Capo Press, 1998 [1971]), 129.
41. Grete Viddal, "Cuba's Tumba Francesa, Diaspora Dance, Cuban legacy," *Revista Harvard Review of Latin America* (Fall 2007).
42. Ned Sublette, *Cuba and Its Music From the First Drums to the Mambo* (Chicago, IL: Chicago Review Press, 2004), 120, 133.
43. Ibid.
44. Arthur Jones, in *Pierre Toussaint* (New York: Doubleday, 2003), 58, describes how Toussaint was received in New York with his owners: "It was as an entertaining and capable 'Frenchman' in New York that Toussaint would gain acceptance in the parlors and boudoirs of the important families. Quite simply, his slave status was secondary among educated New York whites; it was his French refinement combined with his skills as a coiffeur that provided his entrée." Quoted in Grant, "Public Performance," 188.
45. Grant, "Public Performance," 178–200.
46. LaChance, "The 1809 Immigration," 109–141.
47. Debin, "Saint Domingue Refugees in Cuba," 89–91.

Chapter 2: Becoming Americans
1. LaChance, "The 1809 Immigration," 247–248. There were 9,059 arrivals between May 1809 and January 1810, including 2,731 whites, 3,102 free people of color, and 3,226 slaves. A majority of the whites were males and the slaves and free people of color women and children. Additional arrivals in the first part of 1810 brought the total to about 10,000.
2. LaChance, "The 1809 Immigration," 251.
3. Scott and Hebrard, *Freedom Papers*, 65–67.
4. Dunbar Rowland ed., *Official Letter Books of W. C. C. Claiborne* (Jackson, MS: State Department of Archives and History), IV, 388.
5. Rowland, *Letter Books*, IV, 407.
6. Beluche was born in 1780 in "Madame John's Legacy" on Dumaine Street. The house, rebuilt after the fire of 1788, still stands today. Madame John's Legacy is a National Historic Landmark owned by the Louisiana State Museum. The history of pirates has been greatly romanticized, see, for example, William C. Davis, *The Pirates Laffite: The Treacherous World of the Corsairs of the Gulf* (Orlando, FL: Harcourt, Inc., 2005), 56–57, 73–74; Jane Lucas De Grummond, *Renato Beluche, Smuggler, Privateer, and Patriot, 1780–1860* (Baton Rouge: LSU Press, 1999); John S. Kendall, "Shadow Over the City."

Louisiana Historical Quarterly 22 (January 1939), 142–165; Grace King, *Creole Families of New Orleans* (New York: Macmillan Company, 1921).

7. Kendall, "Shadow Over the City," 144–146; Caryn Cosse Bell, *Revolution, Romanticism and the African American Protest Tradition in Louisiana, 1718–1868* (Baton Rouge: LSU Press, 2004), 42–49; Sybil Kein, ed., *Creole: The History and Legacy of New Orleans Free People of Color* (Baton Rouge: LSU Press, 2000), 84–85. Davis, *The Pirates Laffite*; De Grummond, *Renato Beluche*. Thereafter, Lafitte reestablished his pirate base further west on the Gulf in Galveston, Texas. Beluche and some other Baratarians aided Simón Bolivar in Venezuela and other insurgents attempting to establish independent republics in Latin America.

8. Kein, *Creole*, 85 and note 27, cites Everard's findings on Snaer's father. The Cathedral, Presbytere, and the Cabildo are all Spanish. After the great fires in the late eighteenth century, the Spanish rebuilt much of the French Quarter. But the multistoried buildings centered around inner courtyards were common to all European settlements of the period. Other characteristics, such as large arched doorways and the use of decorative wrought iron, were also present in French and English buildings.

9. See, generally, Judith Kelleher Schaefer, *Brothels, Depravity, and Abandoned Women: Illegal Sex in Antebellum New Orleans* (Baton Rouge: LSU Press, 2009).

10. Thomas J. Davis, *Plessy v. Ferguson* (Santa Barbara, CA: Greenwood, an Imprint of ABC-Clio, LLC, 2012), 3, 50; *Plessy v. Ferguson* 163 U.S. 537 (1896).

11. John Churchill Chase, *Frenchmen, Desire, Good Children and Other Streets of New Orleans*, 3rd ed. (Touchstone, 1997 [1949]), 98–101.

12. Certificate of Apprenticeship, Jean Baptiste Snaer, October 19, 1818, Louisiana Division, New Orleans Public Library, Mayor's Office Indenture Book no. 3; Kein, *Creole*, 85 and footnote 27.

13. Margo Moscou, *New Orleans' Free men of Color Cabinet Makers in the New Orleans Furniture Trade, 1800–1850* (New Orleans: Xavier Review Press, 2008); Marcus Christian, Negro Ironworkers of Louisiana, 1718–1900 (New Orleans, Pelican Publishing, 1972); John Ethan Hankins and Steven Taklansky, *Raised to the Trade; Creole Building Arts of NOLA* (New Orleans Museum of Art exhibit catalogue, 2002); John Michael Vlach, "The Shotgun House: An African Architectural Legacy," in William Ferris, ed. *Afro-American Folk Art and*

Crafts (Boston: G.K. Hall, 1983), 275–296; Roulhac, Toledano and Samuel Wilson, *New Orleans Architecture 4, The Creole Faubourgs a history* (Gretna, La.: Pelican Publishing. Co., 1974).

14. The property bought by Francois Snaer for a grocery store and adjoining residence was Lot No. 16, in square No. 113, bounded by St. Claude, Rampart, St. Philip, and Dumaine streets, in the Second district of New Orleans on *Robinson's Atlas*, District 2, plate 7, Notarial Archives.

15. Shirley Thompson, *Exiles at Home: The Struggle to Become American in Creole New Orleans* (Cambridge, MA: Harvard University Press, 2009), 92–210; *Badillio et al. v. Francisco Tio*, 6 La. Ann. 129 (1851); *Macarty v. Mandeville*, F.W.C, 3 La. Ann. 239 (1848).

16. "The Passing of a People: Creoles of Color in Mid-Nineteenth Century New Orleans" (Ph.D. dissertation, Harvard University, 2001), 75–76 and notes there cited; Thompson, *Exiles at Home*, 139.

17. This amount, $2,150, was 80 percent of the national average of total individual wealth in 1860 and between 1790–1880 considered wealthy, www.measuringworth.com calculates the dollar amounts actually and comparatively; John W. Blassingame, *Black New Orleans 1860–1880* (Chicago: University of Chicago Press, 1973), 10–11. Theodore Hershberg, "Free Blacks in Antebellum Philadelphia: A Study of Ex-slaves, Freeborn, and Economic Decline," *Journal of Social History* (1971–72), vol. 5, 183–209.

18. Laura Foner, "Free People of Color in Louisiana and Saint Domingue: A Comparative Portrait of Two Three-Caste Societies," *Journal of Social History* (1970), vol. 3, 406–430; Judith Schaefer, *Becoming Free, Remaining Free: Manumission and Enslavement in New Orleans, 1846–1862* (Baton Rouge: LSU Press, 2003), 97,

19. List, Mayor's Office. Register of Free Colored Persons 1840–1863, Louisiana Division New Orleans Public Library; Thomas N. Ingersoll, "Free Blacks in a Slave Society: New Orleans, 1718–1812," *William and Mary Quarterly* (1991), vol. 48, 197–198.

20. Roger A. Fischer, "Racial Segregation in Ante Bellum New Orleans," *American Historical Review* (1969), vol. 74, 931–936; Thompson, "Passing," 74; Bell, *Revolution, Romanticism*, 77.

21. Kein, *Creole*, 27; Dennis Rousey, "Black Policemen in New Orleans During Reconstruction," in Ernestine Jenkins and Darlene Hine, eds., *A Question of Manhood: A Reader in U.S. Black Men's History and Masculinity* (Bloomington: Indiana University Press, 1999), vol. II, 85–88.

22. Blassingame, *Black New Orleans*, Chapter 1; Doris Lynch, "Justice Denied: The Treatment of Free Negroes and Slaves in the Courts of South Louisiana Prior to the Civil War, 1810–1860" (Ph.D. dissertation, Howard University, 1987), 202–207, 240–241; see the court definition of difference between slaves and free Negroes in the state in *State v. Harrison (a slave)*, Supreme Court of Louisiana, 11 La. Ann. 722 (1856).

23. H. E. Sterx. *The Free Negro in Ante-Bellum Louisiana* (Rutherford, NJ: Fairleigh Dickinson University Press, 1972). An insular settlement of free people of color on Ten Mile Creek, descendants of a group that had migrated there in 1804, became an issue because of Know-Nothing Party complaints about the votes of about fifty from their group, most of whom had the same last names. The newspapers published greatly excited complaints and countercharges but, apparently, they continued to vote.

24. Blassingame, *Black New Orleans*, 14; Emily Clark, "Atlantic Alliances: Marriage among People of African Descent in New Orleans, 1759–1830" (unpublished paper presented at a workshop at the Center for North-American Studies, École des Hautes Études en Sciences Sociales: Louisiana and the Atlantic World in the Eighteenth and Nineteenth Centuries, Paris, November 9–10, 2007), 22–23; see also Emily Clark, *Strange History*, esp. Chapters 3 and 4.

25. Paul F. LaChance, "The 1809 Immigration," 109–141; Lawrence Powell, *The Accidental City: Improvising New Orleans* (Cambridge, MA: Harvard University Press, 2012), 320.

26. The amount was 11,050 Haitian *gourdes*. Numa Lanusse was a brother of Armand Lanusse, who in 1845 edited *Les Cenelles*, the first anthology of poetry by Americans of African descent. *Le Télégraphe*, Gazette Officielle, Port-au-Prince, Haiti. Jean-Marc Allard Duplantier, "Creole Louisiana's Haitian Exiles." *Southern Quarterly* (Spring 2007), vol. 44, 68.

27. Mary Niall Mitchell, "'A Good and Delicious Country': Free Children of Color and How They Learned to Imagine the Atlantic World in Nineteenth-Century Louisiana." *History of Education Quarterly* (2000), vol. 40, 123–144; Letterbooks and Board Minutes, Institute des Orphelins, 1846–1869. Office of Archives and Records, Archdiocese of New Orleans.

28. Bell, *Revolution, Romanticism*, 145–221; Thompson, "Passing," 80; Joseph Tregle and Caryn Cosse Bell, "The Americanization of Black

New Orleans," in Arnold Hirsch, ed., *Creole New Orleans: Race and Americanization* (Baton Rouge: LSU Press), 259.

29. Jeanne Aliquot died in 1863 of pneumonia after traveling in a storm one night to aid a child in distress, Bell, *Revolution, Romanticism*, 129 and notes there cited. She had briefly, in 1846, lived with the Visitation Sisters in Mobile; Stephen Ochs, *A Black Patriot and a White Priest: Andre Cailloux and Claude Paschal Maistre in Civil War New Orleans* (Baton Rouge, LSU, 2006), 52; history on church website, www.staugustinecatholicchurch-neworleans.org; Thompson, "Passing," 86 and note 7 on the male-dominated versions of Colored Creole history.

30. Jean Baptiste's death was recorded on October 21, 1838. In 1841, Josephine, a widow, lived at 808 Burgundy St. along with four of their children in the 1841 city directory; Francois' wife was the sister of a woman who married a Pascal, either Eugenie or a second wife of Francois the elder. Jean Baptiste and Josephine had at least four children, including probably Auguste, who served in the Confederacy; L.A., who served in the Union colored troops as an enlisted man; and Vincent, who died in 1858 and was described in the *New Orleans Bee*, October 30, 1858, as a nephew of Francois Snaer. The Catholic Colored Creoles had two or three names, which were sometimes used alternatively.

Chapter 3: Family Troubles

1. Samuel was recorded as a professional music teacher in the 1870 Census, p. 259. Among his compositions was a Mass for three voices, James M. Trotter, *Music and Some Highly Musical People* (Boston and New York: Shepard and Lee, 1878). The Snaer descendants thought that Jonathan, born in 1830, trained to become a lithographer but died at age 20; however, this was not the same person. Sosthene Jonathan, the eldest of Marie Rochefort and Francois' children, was still alive in his early twenties when the estate was settled and the property was distributed to the children in 1855. Second District Court of New Orleans, Succession of Marie Rochefort, wife of Francois Snaer, Louisiana Division New Orleans Public Library, New Orleans Archives, September 25, 1855. "Free Negro Owners of Slaves in the US in 1830," *Journal of Negro History* (1924), vol. 9, 41, reports that according to the 1830 Census there was an "Ambroise" or "Amboise" Snaer with seven family members, one of whom was a slave. The name is probably a misreading of Francois. Francois purchased Rachel, who arrived from

Pensacola on the *Amelia* on December 4, 1826, New Orleans Louisiana Slave Manifests 1807–1860, Ancestry.com.

2. Parish Court Files, Louisiana Division, New Orleans Public Library, Index No.5769.

3. Succession of Marie Rochefort, Parish Court Records, Louisiana Division, New Orleans Public Library, 1855, 27.

4. Parish Court Records, Louisiana Division, New Orleans Public Library, Index No.7660; Francois claimed that Frederick Pascal owed $16 and Leonard Pascal owed $167. There were also miscellaneous bad debts of $197.62. Robert Reinders, "The Free Negro in the New Orleans Economy 1850–1860," *Louisiana History* (Summer 1965), vol. 6, 273–285, 282–284.

5. The three lots were in a square bounded by Prieur, Johnson, Lapeyrouse, and Onzaga streets.

6. Marie's remains lie in a burial plot in St. Louis Cemetery No. 2, Square Three, Aisle Three, west. Kein, *Creole*, 84, footnote 27, reports Francois the elder's death certificate on May 5, 1838, in the New Orleans Public Library, Death Register, Orleans Parish, vol. 6, No. 244. Although Marie Rochefort's death went unrecorded until October 30, 1838, that may not have been unusual for the recordkeeping at the time; Louis Anthony's birth in 1842 was not recorded until over three years later. In 1841, the General Council of New Orleans passed an ordinance establishing a Board of Health for the city. One of the provisions of this ordinance stipulated that the sextons of the various cemeteries should record death certificates presented to them and send the information recorded to the mayor at the end of the year for retention in the archives of the city. The book provided to the mayor by the sexton of the Catholic cemeteries (i.e., St. Louis Cemeteries Nos. 1 and 2) includes names, origin, address, cause of death, race or color, age, and the name of doctor who either attended the decedent or other person giving the information about the decedent. The abbreviation C.1. (*couleur libre*) is used to identify free people of color. In the St. Louis Cemetery No. 1, opened in 1789, whites and free people of color are often buried side by side and sometimes in the same tomb; in St. Louis Cemetery No. 2, opened in 1823, the square closest to Canal Street was set aside for free people of color and slaves.

7. 1840 Census, Schedule of the Whole Number of Persons Within the Division, Heads of Families, Free Colored Persons, 208; Succession of Marie Rochefort, Parish Court Records, Louisiana Division, New Orleans Public Library, 1855, 27–35; testimony of Francois Pascal.

8. 1850 U. S. Census; Succession of Marie Rochefort, Louisiana Division, New Orleans Public Library, New Orleans Archives, September 25, 1855.

9. It's not clear what happened to Francois' tin factory on Toulouse between Chartres and Levee (Decatur Street), valued at $2,000.

10. Succession of Marie Rochefort, Louisiana Division, New Orleans Public Library, New Orleans Archives, September 25, 1855. Testimony of Josephine Romaine for father-tutor: "the daughter and the second son, who is crippled always resided with the father"; Volmar was the youngest and Sosthene the oldest. Testimony of Frederic Callicot: Sosthene is 23 or 24; "Francois Michel or Samuel" also lived with his father.

11. Rodolphe Desdunes, *Our People and Our History* (Translation) (Baton Rouge: LSU Press, 1973 [1911]), 85.

12. Lester Sullivan, "Composers of Color of Nineteenth-Century New Orleans: The History Behind the Music," *Black Music Research Journal* (1988), vol. 8, 64, 68–69, 1880 U.S. Census.

13. Based on unpublished research by Wayne Everard; Kein, *Creole*, 85 and note 27. The children were Louis Antoine (b. 1842), Seymour R. (b. 1844), Pierre Anatole (b. 1843), Maria Francoise (b. 1846), J. Alexamore [Alexander] (b. 1848), Victor Joseph (b. 1850), Victoria Rose (b. 1853), Omer Joseph (b. 1856), George Pierre (b. 1858), and Emilio (b. 1862).

14. Father Etienne Rousellon from Lyons became the first pastor. When church officials gave official approval to a segregated nuns' order in 1842 they wanted the name Sisters of Presentation, as they had originally proposed for an interracial order. However, Father Rousellon renamed them the Sisters of the Holy Family. In 1852, at his urging, Henriette DeLille and Juliette Gaudin announced their vows publicly in the church. Bell, *Revolution, Romanticism*, 133–134 and notes there cited; Thompson, "Passing," 85–88. Ochs, *Black Patriot*, 52. History on church website (www.staugustinecatholicchurch-neworleans.org/). Father Jerome LeDoux, *The War of the Pews: A Personal Account of St. Augustine Church in New Orleans* (Donaldsville, LA: Margaret Media, 2011), Numerous stories in *New Orleans Times Picayune* from after Katrina; I have attended the church occasionally before and since 2005; see history on church website for official history of these events. St. Augustine suffered flood damage after Katrina when the levees broke, like much of New Orleans. The diocese reassigned the pastor and closed its doors in 2005 after so many members fled the ravages of

the flooding. But the church was pried open by those who returned to the city, from Uptown, the French Quarter, Bywater, and all around town. The church reopened and ultimately a repentant diocese appointed a priest as the public insisted.

15. John Duffy, *Sword of Pestilence: the New Orleans Yellow Fever Epidemic of 1853* (Baton Rouge: LSU Press, 1966), 105; Thompson, "Passing," 135–144, gives a cultural explanation of the epidemic.

16. Thompson, "Passing," 143.

17. Frank Joseph Lovato, "Households and Neighborhoods Among Free People of Color in New Orleans: A View From the Census 1850–1860" (M.A. thesis, University of New Orleans, 2010). There were 9,985 free people of color in New Orleans in 1860 (p. 40).

18. Blassingame, *Black New Orleans*, 10. Most of the free Negro males listed in the 1850 Census were engaged in fifty-four different occupations; only 9.9 percent of them were unskilled laborers.

19. Reinders, "The Free Negro in the New Orleans Economy, 1850–1860."

20. Thompson, "Passing," 145–147.

21. Lovato, "Households and Neighborhoods." See discussion in Chapter VII.

22. New Orleans was divided into three municipalities in 1836 until 1852.

23. Ellen Holmes Pearson, "Imperfect Equality: The Legal Status of Free People of Color in New Orleans, 1803–1860," in Warren Billings and Mark Fernandez, eds., *A Law Unto Itself: Essays in the New Louisiana Legal History* (Baton Rouge: LSU Press, 2001), 191–227.

24. Davis, *Plessy v. Ferguson*, 65–70, *Adele v. Beauregard* 1 Mart (o.s.) 183 (La. 1810), *Berard v. Berard* 9 La. 156 (E. D. La. 1836).

25. Bell, *Revolution, Romanticism*, 84; Robert C. Reinders, "The Churches and the Negro in New Orleans," *Phylon* (1961), vol. 22, 246.

26. Desdunes, *Our People and Our History*, 65; Mary Gehman, "The Mexico-Louisiana Connection," *Louisiana Cultural Vistas* (Winter 2001–2002); www.margaretmedia.com; Thompson, "Passing," 226.

27. This was an unreported case, *Anastasie Desarzant v. Pierre le Blanc and Eglantine Le Maizzilier, his wife*, no. 5868 14 La. Ann. xii, unreported December 1859; identified by Thompson, "Passing," 215 and note 67; see also Shirley Thompson, "Ah Toucoutou, ye conin vous: History and Memory in Creole New Orleans," *American Quarterly* (June 2001), vol. 53, 232–266.

28. Blassingame, *Black New Orleans*, 74; 1870 Census recorded Francois' birthplace as "Monti Christo."

29. Loren Schweninger, "Antebellum Free People of Color in Postbellum Louisiana," *Louisiana History* (Fall 1989), vol. 30, 345–364.

30. Bell, *Revolution, Romanticism*, 120–128; Blassingame, *Black New Orleans*, 108; Desdunes, *Our People and Our History*, 4–34, 133–146; *New Orleans Republican*, May 10, 1867; many of the officers who served during the Civil War were graduates of this school. Ochs, *Black Patriot*, 54.

Chapter 4: Fighting for Democracy

1. See generally, Mary Frances Berry, *Military Necessity and Civil Rights Policy: Black Citizenship and the Constitution 1861–68* (Port Washington, NY: Kennikat Press, 1977).

2. Mary F. Berry, "Negro Troops in Blue and Gray: The Louisiana Native Guards, 1861–1863," *Louisiana History* 8 (1967), 165–190.

3. *New York Times*, August 9, 1863; *Harper's Weekly*, August, 29, 1863.

4. Ochs, *Black Patriot*, 1–5.

5. Marion Southwood, *Bounty and Booty, The Watchword of New Orleans* (New York: published for the author by M. Doolady, 1867), 210–211.

6. *New York Times*, August 9, 1863; *Harper's Weekly*, August 29, 1863.

7. Roland McConnell, *Negro Troops of Antebellum Louisiana* (Baton Rouge: LSU Press, 1968).

8. Ochs, *Black Patriot*, 30–40.

9. James G. Hollandsworth, *The Louisiana Native Guards: The Black Military Experience During the Civil War* (Baton Rouge: LSU Press, 1998), 6; Ochs, *Black Patriot*, 83; on Rey, Bell, *Revolution, Romanticism*, 232.

10. Jean Baptiste and his wife, Josephine, had at least four children, including probably Auguste, who served in the Confederacy, and Vincent, who died in 1858 and was described in the *New Orleans Bee*, death notice, October 30, 1858, as a nephew of Francois Snaer. Colored Creoles, as Catholics, usually had two or three names and were alternatively called by them on occasion. Auguste married Marie Josephine Romain in St. Augustine Church on January 13, 1863, with a license issued on January 6.

11. Berry, "Negro Troops," 167; Hollandsworth, *Louisiana Native Guards*, 7–11.

12. Berry, "Negro Troops," 176; Letterbooks and Compositions, Institute des Orphelins, 1846–1869, Office of Archives and Records, Archdiocese of New Orleans.

13. John N. Ingham and Lynne Feldman, *African American Business Leaders* (Westport, CT: Greenwood Press, 1993), 411 and notes there cited.
14. Hollandsworth, *Louisiana Native Guards*, 10–11.
15. General Order No. 28, Department of the Gulf, May 15, 1862, *The War of the Rebellion, A Compilation of the Official Records of the Union and Confederate Armies* (70 vols. Washington, DC, 1880–1901), Ser. I, vol. 15, p. 42.
16. Berry, "Negro Troops," 176.
17. Shirley Thompson, "The Passing of a People: Creoles of Color in Mid-Nineteenth Century New Orleans" (Ph.D. dissertation, Harvard University, 2001), 239–241; Blassingame, *Black New Orleans*, 131–132, 152–153.
18. Berry, "Negro Troops," 167–168.
19. Joseph T. Glatthaar, "The Civil War Through the Eyes of a Sixteen-Year-Old Black Officer: The Letters of Lieutenant John H. Crowder of the 1st Louisiana Native Guard," *Louisiana History* (1994), vol. 35, 201–216.
20. Berry, "Negro Troops," 168.
21. Ibid., 175–176; Hollandsworth, *Louisiana Native Guards*, 24.
22. Hollandsworth, *Louisiana Native Guards*, 29.
23. Blassingame, *Black New Orleans*, 189–190; Hollandsworth, *Louisiana Native Guards*, 32–34; C. P. Weaver, ed., *Thank God My Regiment Is an African One: The Diary of Colonel Nathan Daniels* (Baton Rouge: LSU Press, 1998), 159.
24. Peter C. Ripley, "The Black Family In Transition; Louisiana 1860–1865," *Journal of Southern History* (1975), vol. 41, 369–380, 376–377; Blassingame, *Black New Orleans*, 45; Hollandsworth, *Louisiana Native Guards*, 24, 30.
25. Berry, "Negro Troops," 180.
26. Hollandsworth, *Louisiana Native Guards*, 36–47.
27. Ibid.
28. Glatthaar, "The Civil War Through the Eyes of a Sixteen-Year-Old Black Officer," 201–216.
29. Charles Sauvinet, a translator, stayed in the Second Regiment serving as Assistant Quartermaster, a staff position not commanding troops; Hollandsworth, *Louisiana Native Guards*, 76.
30. Ochs, *Black Patriot*, 138; Hollandsworth, *Louisiana Native Guards*, 25.
31. Berry, "Negro Troops," 181; Hollandsworth, *Louisiana Native Guards*, 80.

32. Hollandsworth, *Louisiana Native Guards*, Chapter 6; Berry, "Negro Troops," 185–188.
33. Hollandsworth, *Louisiana Native Guards*, 25–27.
34. Ochs, *Black Patriot*, 146–152.
35. John W. Blassingame, "A Social and Economic Study of the Negro in New Orleans, 1860–1880" (Ph.D. dissertation, Yale University, 1970), 90–93.
36. Ibid.; Rachel L. Emanuel and Alexander P. Tureaud, Jr. *A More Noble Cause: A. P. Tureaud and the Struggle for Civil Rights in Louisiana*, (Baton Rouge: LSU Press, 2011), 7–8.
37. Carded Military Service Record Louis A. Snaer, First Corps d'Afrique, Record Group 94, National Archives. Pierre and the Pascals served in the Sixth Colored Regiment, Louisiana Infantry.
38. Ochs, *Black Patriot*, 159–163; Jinx Coleman Broussard and Skye Chance Cooley, "Henry H. Perry, Confederate Apologist and Reporter," in Patricia G. McNeely, Debra Reddin Van Tuyll, and Henry H. Schulte, eds., *Knights of the Quill: Confederate Correspondents and their Civil War Reporting* (Purdue University Press, 2010), 395–406.
39. Inspection Report of Colonel N. Dudley, Adjutant General, Department of the Gulf, September, 19, 1863; Regimental Return, 1863, First and Third Corps d'Afriques, Record Group 94, Adjutant General's Office, National Archives; Hollandsworth, *Louisiana Native Guards*, Chapter 9.
40. Hollandsworth, *Native Guards*, 75–82.
41. See, for example, *La Tribune*, April 18, 19, 1865.
42. Weaver, *Thank God My Regiment Is An African One*, 15. The Second Native Guards Regiment, which mainly guarded prisoners during the war, is the subject of Natasha Trethewey's poetry collection *Native Guard* (New York: Houghton Mifflin, 2006); http://www.nps.gov/history/history/online_books/civil_war_series/2/sec14.htm, accessed May 18, 2013.
43. 38th Congress 1st Session referred to the Select Committee on Slavery and Freedmen, Record Group 46; the records of the U.S. Senate Sen. 38A–H19, National Archives.
44. Photographs exchanged May 7, 1864. Halstead first served in the U.S. Navy on the flagship *Minnesota*. They captured Hatteras Inlet, with Forts Clark and Hatteras, on August 28, 1861. He was commissioned by New Jersey's governor as a first lieutenant of volunteers to serve as aide de camp to General Philip Kearney of the First New Jersey Brigade at Fairfax Seminary. He then served as an assistant adjutant

general to General Augur from April 1862. Attached to General McDowell's command, they took Falmouth and Fredericksburg in the spring of 1862, and later in the summer Augur commanded a division in Banks' corps that took part in the "bloody battle of Cedar Mountain" in August 1862. He was captured and imprisoned in "infamous Libby" prison. He was paroled in the fall and exchanged in time to rejoin General Augur, who went to the Department of the Gulf in December 1862 in command of a division in the Banks expedition. He stayed with General Augur as his assistant adjutant general until after the capture of Port Hudson on July 9, 1863. After the surrender of Port Hudson he went north on sick leave and then was transferred to the staff of General Andrews, who commanded the Corps d'Afrique, and continued in duty at Port Hudson until the spring of 1864. He then went to Memphis as staff to General Chatlin and then on duty organizing colored troops. Then he was sent back to the Army of the Potomac and was in several battles, including "White Oak Road" with the Fifth Corps. At White Oak he was wounded but refused to go to the hospital "as long as I could ride my horse." He was present at the McLean house as staff to General Griffin when Robert E. Lee surrendered to General Grant on April 9, 1965, at Appomattox Court House, Virginia. He was then ordered to Trenton and honorably discharged in the winter of 1866.

45. Halstead's great-grandnephew offered information about the origins of tales about them and Halstead Bay, *Excelsior Lake Minnetonka Historical Society Newsletter,* December 1989, vol 1, No. 1, "History of Minnestra" accessed July 20, 2014, from City Clerk website, http://www.ci.minnetrista.mn.us/.

46. Hollandsworth, *Louisiana Native Guards,* 79, 96.

47. Hollandsworth, *Louisiana Native Guards,* 88.

48. Ibid., Lieutenant Colonel Henry Merriam to Lieutenant O. A. Rice, Adjutant Seventy-Third United States Colored Infantry, February 9, 1865, Box No. 5514, Record Group 94, National Archives.

49. Hollandsworth, *Native Guards,* 101–103.

50. Carded Military Service Records, Captain Louis Snaer and Lieutenant Colonel Henry Merriam, Seventy-Third United States Colored Infantry, Record Group 94, National Archives.

51. Charles Isidore Nero, "To Develop Our Manhood: Free Black Leadership and the Rhetoric of the *New Orleans Tribune*" (Ph.D. dissertation, Indiana University, 1991), 90–94; Camille Corte, "History of 73rd U.S.C.T.: First Black Troop to be Mustered into the Union

Army," citing Henry Merriam, "The Capture of Mobile," http://www
.blakeleypark.com/73rdusct.htm; the date Snaer was brevetted officially was October 14, 1868; *La Tribune*, April 16, 18, 1865.

52. *La Tribune*, April 18, 1865.

53. Declaration for Original Invalid Pension, August 13, 1878.

54. He was mustered out of service at New Orleans, "having been ren-
dered supernumerary by the consolidation of his regiment with the
96th USCT." Muster Out rolls; Carded Military Service Record,
Louis Snaer, Seventy-Third United States Colored Infantry, Record
Group 94, National Archives. His letter requesting leave, June 28,
1865, gave the address "New Orleans care of the Dumas Brothers."
They ran a tailor shop and may have been related to Francis Dumas,
the planter who was a major in the Second Native Guards; Kein,
Creole, 53.

55. *La Tribune*, September 24, 1865, quoted in Hollandsworth, *Native
Guards*, 103; *La Tribune*, October 30, 1865; Ochs, *Black Patriot*,
232–234.

56. Bell, *Revolution, Romanticism*, 187–217; Melissa Daggett, "Henry
Louis Rey, Spiritualism and Creoles of Color in Nineteenth-Century
New Orleans" (M.A. Thesis, University of New Orleans, 2009),
14, 20.

57. Bell, *Revolution, Romanticism*, 222–275; Daggett, *Henry Louis Rey*,
15–16.

Chapter 5: Becoming "Negroes"

1. Congressional Hearing on the New Orleans Riot of 1866, 39th Congress, 2nd session, House Select Committee Report 16, pp. 351,
528–556. Unlike other "colored" witnesses, he and Seymour Snaer
were not designated "colored." Sauvinet in his testimony described
himself to the Committee mistakenly, as already an officer in the U.S.
Army who arrived in New Orleans with General Butler. Justin Nystrom,
New Orleans After the Civil War: Race Politics and a New Birth of Freedom
(Baltimore: Johns Hopkins University Press, 2009), 82–115.

2. Hollandsworth, *Louisiana Native Guards*, 107; Eric Foner, *Freedom's
Lawmakers: A Directory of Black Officeholders During Reconstruction*
(Baton Rouge: Louisiana State University Press, 1996), 263.

3. House Report 16 on the New Orleans Riot of 1866, 171–172.

4. John Blassingame, "A Social and Economic Study of the Negro in
New Orleans 1860–1880," 122–126.

5. Ibid.

6. Ibid.

7. Joseph Tregle, "Utopian Socialism and the Failure of Presidential Reconstruction in Louisiana," *Journal of Southern History*, vol. XLV, 485–512; Philip D. Uzee, " The Beginning of the Louisiana Republican Party," *Louisiana History* (1971), vol. 12, 197–211.

8. Uzee, "Beginning of the Louisiana Republican Party."

9. Ochs, *Black Patriot*, 186.

10. Ibid., 187.

11. Select Committee on Slavery and Freedmen, 38th Cong., 1st sess., Records of the U.S. Senate, RG 46, Sen 38A–H19.

12. John Hope Franklin, *Reconstruction After the Civil War* (Chicago: University of Chicago Press, 1961, 1994), 21.

13. Ibid., 24–25.

14. Charles Isidore Nero, "To Develop Our Manhood," 97–98.

15. Kein, *Creole*, 58.

16. Nero, "To Develop Our Manhood," 177–188.

17. Elsie M. Lewis, "The Political Mind of the Negro, 1865–1900," *Journal of Southern History* (1955), vol. 21, 189–202; Charles R. Vincent, *Black Legislators in Louisiana During Reconstruction* (Baton Rouge: Louisiana State University Press, 1976), 29–32 and notes there cited.

18. Vincent, *Black Legislators*.

19. Ibid., 31–34.

20. *La Tribune*, January 15, 1865; Nero, "To Develop Our Manhood," 177–188.

21. Blassingame, *Black New Orleans*, 154.

22. Vincent, *Black Legislators*, 34–38; Shirley Thompson, "The Passing of a People," 278.

23. Nero, "To Develop Our Manhood," 125–129; *La Tribune*, January 28, 29, 1865; William P. Conner, "Reconstruction Rebels: *The New Orleans Tribune* in Post-war Louisiana," *Louisiana History* (1980), vol. 21, 159–180; Thompson, "Passing," 276–280.

24. Blassingame, *Black New Orleans*, 64–66; Eric Arneson, *Waterfront Workers of New Orleans; Race Class and Politics, 1863–1923* (New York: Oxford University Press, 1991).

25. Blassingame, *Black New Orleans*, 131.

26. Blassingame, *Black New Orleans*, 140–142.

27. Blassingame, *Black New Orleans*, 64–66.

28. Though Straight Law School, located at Esplanade Avenue and Burgundy Street between 1874 and 1886, trained black lawyers at the time, Snaer instead apprenticed with former Attorney General Belden

and then practiced with Belden and E. K. Washington, *Weekly Louisiana*, May 1, 1875.

29. *Rooney v. Succession of Marie Noel Snaer*, August 25, 1868. Rooney successful claimed that the property bounded by Levee, Rosseau, Jackson, and Josephine streets should be sold to pay a mortgage of $3,000 taken out in 1867, which was in arrears. Death Notice of Angelina Snaer, April 17, 1865, *La Tribune*.

30. 1870 Census, New Orleans; Louis Harlan, "Desegregation in New Orleans Schools During Reconstruction," *American Historical Review* (1962), vol. 67, 663–675. The Redemption government abolished desegregation, and eventually mandatory segregation was imposed.

31. Ochs, *Black Patriot*, 217.

32. Freedman's Bank Records, 1865–1871, National Archives; Walter Fleming, *The Freedmen's Savings Bank: A Chapter in the Economic History of the Negro Race* (Chapel Hill: UNC Press, 1927), 144–145.

33. Blassingame, *Black New Orleans*, 67. A number of churches and philanthropic societies also closed as a result of the crash.

34. Ibid., 68.

35. Ibid., 68–66, 147.

36. Ibid., 151, 158–159.

37. Ibid., 62.

38. *La Tribune*, September 24, October 30, 1865; James Hollandsworth, *Louisiana Native Guards*, 103; Uzee, "Beginning of the Republican Party," 205–206.

39. Steven Hahn, *A Nation Under Our Feet: Black Political Struggles in the Rural South From Slavery to the Great Migration* (Cambridge, MA: Harvard University Press, 2005), 178, 233.

40. Acklen vs. Darrall contest, 45th Congress, 1st session (1877). House Misc. Docs 5, pp. 217, 243, 323. Testimony of Seymour Snaer. E. Franklin Frazier, *The Negro Family in the United States* (Chicago, IL: University of Chicago Press, 1939), 125–145.

41. Bell, *Revolution, Romanticism*, 1–24, and notes there cited.

42. Vincent in *Black Legislators* describes the events discussed in the next paragraphs concerning Reconstruction.

43. Nero, "To Develop Our Manhood."

44. Foner, *Freedom's Lawmakers*, 200.

45. Some scholars, including historians David Rankin, Charles Vincent, and Eric Foner, characterize him as a wealthy Iberia sugar planter, but this is contradicted by the evidence.

Chapter 6: Opportunity and Tragedy in Iberia Parish

1. "Murder and Arson: The Murderers Lynched," *The Louisiana Sugar Bowl*, New Iberia, Iberia Parish, June 19, 1873. Ozome appeared to have been using an alias or nickname, but twenty-six-year-old Patterson and nineteen-year-old Frilot grew up in similar family situations, with farm laborer fathers and mothers who kept house. At the time of the incident, Patterson had a teenage sister and Frilot had two younger and three older siblings at home.
2. *New Orleans Picayune*, September 26, 1878.
3. "Murder and Arson," *Louisiana Sugar Bowl*, July 3, 1873, 2.
4. Ibid.; Gilles Vandal, "Property Offenses, Social Tension, and Racial Antagonism in Post Civil War Rural Louisiana," *Journal of Social History*, vol. 31.1 (Fall 1997), 127–153; see also *Lafayette Advertiser*, June 21, 1873.
5. 1870 Census, New Iberia, Louisiana. Some scholars, including historians David Rankin, Charles Vincent, and Eric Foner, characterize him as a wealthy Iberia sugar planter, but this is contradicted by the Census and district school reports on both Snaer and Wakefield.
6. Vincent, *Black Legislators*; Foner, *Freedom's Lawmakers*. Thirty-five other Negroes served in the House and dozens also served in the Senate before Reconstruction was over.
7. Journal of the Executive Proceedings of the Senate, Vol. 18, May 20, 1871; Charles DeCuir later occupied the post; Maurine Bergene, *They Tasted Bayou Water: A Brief History of Iberia Parish* (New Orleans: Pelican Publishing Co., 1962), 73.
8. U.S. Census 1870.
9. Glenn R. Conrad, "The History of New Iberia," City of New Iberia, Louisiana, http://www.cityofnewiberia.com/site403.php, accessed May 19, 2013.
10. Ibid.
11. The railroad finally reached New Iberia in 1879 (delayed some twenty years because of the war). The following year, passengers could take the train from New Orleans through New Iberia and to Houston. The railroad introduced lumbering to the area and the harvest of cypress trees began in earnest. Soon sawmills, shingle mills, and door factories popped up everywhere and the New Iberia economy picked itself up.
12. Vincent, *Black Legislators*, 130–142.
13. Charles Lane, *The Day Freedom Died: The Colfax Massacre the Supreme Court and the Betrayal of Reconstruction* (New York: Henry Holt, 2008).

14. 92 U.S. 542 (1876), 8–1 decision, Chief Justice Waite opinion, Clifford dissent.
15. *The Slaughterhouse Cases* 83 U.S. 36 (1873).
16. T. Harry Williams, "The Unification Movement of 1873," *Journal of Southern History* (1945) vol. 60, 349–369.
17. In the 1870s the German and Italian population increased substantially in the Creole neighborhoods of the French Quarter and Faubourg Marigny, while Eastern European, Jewish, Irish, and non-Creole African American populations were more likely to be concentrated in uptown working- and middle-class neighborhoods.
18. Lawrence N. Powell, "Reinventing Tradition: Liberty Place, Historical Memory, and Silk-Stocking Vigilantism in New Orleans Politics," *Slavery and Abolition* (1999) vol. 20, 127–149; Stuart Omer Landry, *The Battle of Liberty Place: The Overthrow of Carpetbag Rule in New Orleans, September 14, 1874* (New Orleans: Pelican Publishing Co., 1955).
19. Ibid.
20. Vincent, *Black Legislators*, 147, 153, 155, 165, 194, 198, 200; license issued on December 3, 1873.
21. Frank J. Wetta, "'Bulldozing the Scalawags': Some Examples of the Persecution of Southern White Republicans in Louisiana during Reconstruction," *Louisiana History* (Winter 1980), vol. 21, 43–58; *Daily Picayune*, Dec. 4, 1906, 6, 12; Dec. 9, 1906, 8.
22. Passport applications, 1795–1905, Roll 63, p. 829, renewed ten years later in 1867, Ancestry.com; National Park Service, "Civil War Soldiers and Sailors."
23. *Hall v. DeCuir* 95 U.S. 85 (1877); *DeCuir v. Benson* 27 La. Ann 1 (1877).
24. Loren Schweninger, "Antebellum Free Persons of Color in Post Bellum Louisiana." *Louisiana History* (1989) vol. 30, 345–364.
25. Transcript, U.S. Supreme Court, no. 17, *Benson vs. DeCuir*, October 6, 1875, 69; *DeCuir v. Benson* 27 La. Ann. 1 (1875).
26. Transcript, 69–71.
27. June 14, 1873, Counsel E. K. Washington and Snaer upheld by the state Supreme Court. Wyly dissented, saying it was commerce between the states and controlled by Congress.
28. Transcript of the Record, U.S. Supreme Court, no. 17, *Benson v. DeCuir*, October 6, 1875, 74.
29. Ibid., 55–60.

30. Ibid., 57–60.
31. Ibid., 67–68.
32. *C. S. Sauvinet v, J. A. Walker*, 27 La. Ann. 14 (1875).
33. *Hall v. DeCuir* 95 U.S. 85 (1877), Waite opinion; Barbara Welke, "When All the Women Were White, and All the Blacks Were Men: Gender, Class, Race, and the Road to *Plessy*, 1855–1914," *Law and History Review* (1995), vol. 13, 261–316, 294.
34. Census, 1880; Jack Beerman, February 20, 2013, e-mail to me.
35. *New Orleans Times*, November 5, 1874, election results: Seymour placed third, Roman won; *Weekly Louisianian*, May 1, 1875; Seymour's toast to Pinchback, *Weekly Louisianan*, March 27, 1875; *New Orleans Weekly*, October 22, 1879, and October 25, 1879.
36. Acklen vs. Darrall contest, 45th Congress 1 session (1877), House Misc. Docs 5, p. 242.
37. Ibid., 217, 243, 323; Rebecca Scott, *Degrees of Freedom: Louisiana and Cuba after Slavery* (Cambridge, MA: Harvard University Press, 2005), 66.
38. Acklen vs. Darrall contest, 182–184.
39. Ibid.
40. Ibid., 188–189.
41. Louisa's death was reported in the *New Orleans Bee* on December 27, 1876. Victor was still listed as a clerk in 1874, 1875, and 1876, living at 232 St. Claude Avenue. *Edward's Annual Directory*, published in 1870, has a Pierre Snaer, a cigar maker who worked at Perez between Dumaine and St. Ann Streets. Pierre is listed in 1873 as a cigarmaker residing at 253 Burgundy Street and in 1876 as a stripper residing on St. Philip Street between Claiborne Avenue and Derbigny Street; in 1877 he is again listed as a cigar maker at the same location on Perez Street.

Chapter 7: Mulattoes and Colored Creoles

1. Napoleon Joseph Perche, Pastoral Letter prescribing prayers in thanksgiving for the happy issue of our political troubles, 1 May 1877, Archives of the Archdiocese of New Orleans; Ochs, *Black Patriot*, 263–264.
2. John G. Van Deusen, "The Exodus of 1879," *Journal of Negro History* (April 1936), vol. 21, 111–129.
3. Blassingame, *Black New Orleans*, 151, 158–159.
4. Ibid., 62, 136–138.

5. Ibid., 140–142; Dorothy Sue Cobble, *Dishing It Out: Waitresses and Their Unions in the Twentieth Century* (Urbana: University of Illinois Press, 1991), 21–22.

6. C. Vann Woodward, *The Strange Career of Jim Crown* (New York: Oxford University Press, 1955); Blassingame, *Black New Orleans*.

7. Joy Jackson, *New Orleans in the Gilded Age: Politics and Urban Progress, 1880–1896* (Baton Rouge: Louisiana State University Press, 1969).

8. Some forms may result in injury across the spinal cord, causing diminished or absent sensation below the injury. This causes pain or other sensory problems, weakness or paralysis of muscles, or bladder and bowel dysfunction.

9. Their children were Louis Peter, b. 1879; Rose, b. 1881; Emma, b. 1882; Lily, b. 1888; Margaret, b. 1891; infant Snaer, b. 1879, d. 1879; Joseph, b. 1884 (?); Robert Felix, b. 1885.

10. In the 1850 city directory, Jean Presas lived at 125 Ursulines Street. At the time of his death they lived on Rue Street in St. Bernard Parish between Marais and Urquhart Street. In the 1870 Census, p. 118, Seventh Ward, they lived at number 1079, next to the Society of the Family of Saints at 1078. Joseph Presas and Joseph Gandolfi both worked as store clerks. Emma attended school, probably Catholic, Alzie kept house, and the other women stayed at home. Joseph died on February 27, 1923, in Chicago at age eighty-five; Alzie, who was also called Ann Zeliska and "Didi," died on July 8, 1914, in Oakland, California, at age eighty-two. In the 1870 Census she is recorded as possessing real estate worth $3,000 and personal property of $200.

11. Succession of Charles Boutte, 39 La. Ann. 128 (1878).

12. Emma Snaer's letter; *New Orleans Picayune*, July 28, 1890, June 22, 1895, and July 3, 1895.

13. Mary R. Dearing, *Veterans in Politics: The Story of the G.A.R.* (Baton Rouge: Louisiana State University Press, 1952), 411–418.

14. Badger used them to mobilize within Republican politics nationally and in rallying support for Kellogg's successful run for Congress from Plaquemines to Iberia Parish. When Cleveland came, they lost their jobs. Nystrom, *New Orleans After the Civil War*, 204 and notes there cited.

15. Colored Creoles also received help later from Walter Louis Cohen, who became head of customs, appointed by President McKinley. Cohen, a politician and businessman, born on January 22, 1860, was a free man of color in New Orleans. He was a page in the 1876

legislature and afterwards was active in Republican politics and business. Cohen was one of the few Colored Creoles or African Americans to hold political office after Reconstruction. Chairman of the Republican state central committee and Registrar of the land office in New Orleans, in 1905 President McKinley made him a customs inspector. Roosevelt named him registrar of the U.S. Land Office, and in one of the final appointments Republicans made as their racial politics changed, Harding named him to the office of comptroller of customs. A number of Colored Creoles were hired in the Customs Service.

16. Eric Arnesen, *Waterfront Workers of New Orleans: Race, Class and Politics, 1863–1923* (Urbana: University of Illinois, 1994), 34.

17. Ibid., 1, 106–114, 118. But see "Rick Halpern, Organized Labor Black Workers and the Twentieth-Century South: The Emerging Revision," in Melvyn Stokes and Richard Halpern, eds., *Race and Class in the American South Since 1890* (Oxford and Providence, R.I.: Berg Publishers, 1994), 44–77.

18. U.S. Census 1880, The ages are accurate for Seymour Rene's young son Seymour and Celeste Avet, his sister-in law: The Census records indicate Snaer, Rene. age 32, Lawyer [he was actually 35]; Snaer, Seymour, age 2; Avet, Celeste, age 36, sister-in-law [to Seymour senior]; Snaer, O. J., age 23, brother [to Seymour Avet]; Eulodie, age 16, niece; In the marriage record of Seymour and Marie Lalande 18 January 1877, Mary is listed as age 20. Marie Lalande's 1879 death certificate records her as 22.

19. *New Orleans Item*, December 3, 1880.

20. *New Orleans Item*, December 3, 1880, and March 25, 1881.

21. Ibid.

22. "Transcription," New Orleans (La.) City Insane Asylum Record of Patients, 1882–1884; 1888 (146–199), 140, 170, Louisiana Division, New Orleans Public Library.

23. Richard Lawrence Gordon, "The Development of Louisiana's Public Mental Institutions" (Ph.D. dissertation, LSU, 1978), 78–85.

24. Kirby Randolph, "The Central Lunatic Asylum for the Colored Insane: A History of African Americans with Mental Disabilities" (Ph.D. dissertation, University of Pennsylvania, 2003), Chapter 2, explains that after slavery, free African Americans began to appear in asylums where before there were none. Proslavery physicians claimed that abolition had made blacks mentally ill because slavery was a more appropriate environment. On the general lack of medical treatment for freed people, see, for example, Jim Downs, *Sick from Freedom:*

African-American Illness and Suffering During the Civil War and Reconstruction (New York: Oxford University Press, 2012).

25. Arlin Turner, "George Washington Cable's Beginning As a Reformer," *Journal of Southern History* (1951), vol. 17, 135.
26. Gordon, "Development of Louisiana's Public Mental Institutions," 78–85.
27. Ibid.
28. Sworn to also by Elodie. His real estate meandered two arpents (an arpent is 0.99 acres). In the Census, his neighbors were three white women, two of whom were widows. His property had been determined to be worth $500 along with a personal estate of $100 in the 1870 Census, "together with the undivided half of all the buildings and improvements thereon and thereunto belonging they appraised it at $400.00."

Chapter 8: Just Americans

1. *Plessy v. Ferguson*, 163 U.S. 537 (1896).
2. The Census taker on June 8, 1880, recorded Samuel, a musician, age forty-eight (which exactly fits his age), married to Felecia, whose father was Italian and whose mother was from Louisiana, together with a son, Morris, age six; Felix, age four; and Raymond, age one. In the household also was a brother, Paul, age twenty-four; a sister-in-law (ostensibly Paul's wife), age twenty-four; and a niece, Marie, who had been there but died at only five months of age during the year they lived at 415 Ursulines Street.
3. The New Orleans Death Records Index reports March 27, 1895, as the date of death for "female Francois" [Mrs. Snaer] born in 1821. The records of a court that in 1900 considered claims arising from the sale and resale of the property details the transactions. See *Gowland v. City of New Orleans*, 52 La. Ann. 2042, 28 So. 358 (1900).
4. Michael James Pfeiffer, *Rough Justice: Lynching and American Society, 1874–1947* (Champaign: University of Illinois Press, 2006), 79; and Michael James Pfeiffer, "Lynching and Criminal Justice in South Louisiana 1878–1930," *Louisiana History*, 40 (1990): 155–177.
5. Bridget K. Smith, "Race as Fiction; How Film and Literary Fictions of 'Mulatto' Identity Have Both Fostered and Challenged Social and Legal Fictions Regarding Race in America," *Seton Hall Journal of Sports and Entertainment Law*, vol. 16, 44.
6. Van Deusen, "The Exodus of 1879".

7. Blassingame, "A Social and Economic Study of the Negro in New Orleans 1860–1880," 308; Notice in the *New Orleans Picayune*, May 16, 1880.

8. Nystrom, *New Orleans After the Civil War*, 186.

9. *Times-Picayune*, July 28, 1890; "Louisiana Governors Since 1877," www.sos.la.

10. In 1870, a seventy-year-old woman, Hortense Jeans, lived with them. Louis Martinet's father had $1,000 in real property and $500 in personal property. In the 1880 Census, Hortense listed as Benoits and widowed. She was probably Marie's mother and Martinet's grandmother.

11. The Notarial Acts of Louis Andre Martinet, 1888–1917, New Orleans Notarial Archives.

12. Davis, *Plessy v. Ferguson*, 151.

13. L. A. Snaer, Pension file.

14. Ibid. Forty-seven-year-old Albert Bertonneau, of 346 North Claiborne Avenue, and Aristide Duconge, age forty-eight, of 229 Royal Street, said they had known him since 1865.

15. Bliss Broyard, *One Drop: My Father's Hidden Life—A Story of Race and Family* (Boston: Little Brown and Co., 2007).

16. Davis, *Plessy v. Ferguson*, 151.

17. Smith, "Race as Fiction," 6–9 and notes there cited.

18. *Plessy v. Ferguson*, 163 U.S. 537 (1896); Davis, *Plessy v. Ferguson*; Guichard had married Victoria Rose and was in the Customs Service after the war; then he became a commission merchant. They eventually had seven children, all living in the San Francisco and San Jose areas in California as white: Lily, b. 1878; Robert Felix, b. 1879; Emma, b. 1880; Harry Rene, b. 1882; Victoria, b. 1886; and Mary and Reginald, b. 1887. Louis Antoine's son, Robert Felix, was reported as colored in the New Orleans Parish Birth Index in 1885. Louis Antoine had kept a grocery store for Guichard in Cincinnati and Plaquemines and come home for visits in the 1880s while they were all still in New Orleans. Robert Guichard was listed in the 1930 Census as age seventy-nine and living with his son and his family in Alameda, California.

19. Louis Antoine's death certificate described his occupation as retired and his employer as the U.S. Customs Service.

20. Robert Felix, according to Larry Niekamp, seemed to be mentally fragile. He attended St. Ignatius College in San Francisco but left before graduation. He then entered the Army and was

medically discharged and worked for a while for his brother, Louis Peter. Eventually he was hospitalized in Los Angeles, where he died in 1953. Emma and Lily attended Our Lady of Lourdes School. Letter from Emma and *San Francisco Call*, June 8, 1904.

21. Letter from Emma.
22. Original data: Tenth Census of the United States, 1880 (NARA microfilm publication T9, 1,454 rolls). Records of the Bureau of the Census, Record Group 29.
23. They were all living at 1209 Bell Street at Ursulines Street in the Seventh Ward. Violet was recorded as colored in her New Orleans birth records and Omer Joseph, then forty-one, was identified as her father, 1900 U.S. Census.
24. 1900 Census; New Orleans city directory 1902, 879.
25. Social Security Death index, 1985; U.S. Census, 1920; Biloxi Ward 4, Harrison, Mississippi.
26. Census records for years noted and city directories and Rootsweb death index for Joseph.
27. *Weekly Pelican*, June 18, 1887.
28. Death certificate, New York State Department of Health, November 20, 1916.
29. E-mail from Denise Snaer-Gauder, Seymour Rene's great-granddaughter, June 8, 2012.
30. Ibid.; 1940 Census.
31. In the 1870 City directory, Victor Snaer's address was 1088 Highway, Mandeville, LA 70448. George, Louis Antoine's brother, was listed as a conductor and Leopold the son of Francois Michael Samuel as a driver.
32. Louis Antoine's pension in the meantime increased to $30 starting on June 13, 1917. Victoria Margaret lived with her parents, Louis Antoine and Emma, until her father's death, and then she continued living with Emma, even after she married Joseph Moore in 1926. Joseph had a child, who was cared for by Victoria after his wife died. Pension file, Louis Snaer (Act of May 12, 1912).

Chapter 9: At Home or Away: We Are Who We Say We Are

1. Arthe A. Anthony, "'Lost Boundaries': Racial Passing and Poverty in Segregated New Orleans," *Louisiana History* 36 (1995) 3: 291–312.
2. John M. Barry, *Rising Tide: The Great Mississippi Flood of 1927 and How It Changed America* (New York: Simon and Schuster Touchstone, 1998), 213–215, 219.

3. Anthony, "Lost Boundaries," 291–312. Auguste Snaer, a cigarmaker at 232 St. Claude Avenue was probably Emilio whose middle name was Auguste; he was a cigar maker according to his death certificate, New York State Department of Health, November 20, 1916.

4. Anthony, "Lost Boundaries."

5. Ibid.

6. Ibid.

7. Tom Smith, *Crescent City Lynchings, the Murder of Chief Hennessey, the New Orleans "Mafia" Trials and the Parish Prison Mob* (Guilford, CT: The Lyons Press, 2007), 210, 223.

8. "The Separate Car Bill," *Daily Picayune* (New Orleans), July 3, 1900; quoted in Christopher Joseph Cook, "Agency, Consolidation and Consequence: Evaluating Social and Political Change in New Orleans, 1868–1900" (Master's thesis, Portland State University, 2012).

9. Blair L. M. Kelley, *Right to Ride: Streetcar Boycotts and African American Citizenship in the Era of Plessy v Ferguson* (Chapel Hill: UNC Press, 2010); August Meier and Eliott Rudwick, "The Boycott Movement against Jim Crow Streetcars in the South, 1900–1906," *Journal of American History* vol. 55 (1969), 756–775.

10. Three white descendants of Francois Snaer and six colored Snaers, and one white Snaer living in New Orleans appeared to come from a later-arriving German family. Ancestry.com draft registrations, World War I.

11. Reportedly the darkest was Curtis, b. 1927, the third son of David and Lillian Perossier.

12. The census taker on June 8, 1880, reported Samuel, a musician, age forty-eight (which exactly fits his age), married to Felicia, whose father was Italian and whose mother was from Louisiana, together with a son, Morris, age six; Felix, age four; and Raymond, age one. In the household also was a brother, Paul, age twenty-four (her brother or one of Samuel's half-brothers); a sister-in-law (ostensibly Paul's wife), age twenty-four; and a niece, Marie, who had been there but died at five months old.

13. Robinson Map, Vol. 2, plat 144, 671 Royal Street in 1893. Leopold died in 1933 at age seventy-seven in New Orleans. In the 1880 city Directory Leopold, a driver, resided at 411 Ursulines Street and in 1881, as a carpenter on 413 Ursulines Street. In the 1882 directory, Paul was listed as a driver on 415 Ursulines Street. There was also Theodule, a laborer, living at the same address. They appear again in 1883 but disappear in 1884.

14. Census, 1900, 1920, 1930. telephone conversations Aroline Miller and her father Arol "Glennie" Miller, son of Ruth Snaer, Kenneth Snaer's sister. In the 1930 Census, Joseph Snaer, a white widower, age 72, lived in New Orleans as a boarder . This Joseph was probably Samuel's son.

15. Arolon Miller, Feb. 6, 2014, collected from cousins Karen Cagnolatti-Raines, Cheryl Snaer-McMurray, and Yvonne Snaer-Smedley and from Kenneth Snaer.

16. Arolon Miller, Feb. 6, 2014.

17. *Times Picayune*, July 28, 1890; Louisiana Governors Since 1877, www .sos.la.

18. Phone interview with Yolanda Sears Snaer, May 6, 2013.

19. George Lipsitz, "Mardi Gras Indians: Carnival and Counter Culture Narrative in Black New Orleans," *Cultural Critique* (Autumn 1988) vol. 10, 104.

20. National Park Service, "A New Orleans Jazz History, 1895–1927." http://www.nps.gov/jazz/historyculture/jazz_history.htm.

21. Claude F. Jacobs, "Benevolent Societies of New Orleans Blacks during the Late Nineteenth and Early Twentieth Centuries," *Louisiana History* (Winter, 1988) vol. 29, 22, 23.

22. 1930 Census, New Orleans Marriage Index 1817–1920; 1940 U.S. Census, Ancestry.com

23. In *Uplifting the Race: Black, Leadership, Politics and Culture in the Twentieth Century*, Kevin Gaines argues that educated blacks, who made up the black elite, responded to the burdens of Jim Crow by focusing on uplifting themselves to white America's standards. Black elites, according to Gaines, claimed class distinctions because they were the "better class," whose very existence was evidence of race progress. See generally also, John Scott Holloway, ed., *A Brief and Tentative Analysis of Negro Leadership by Ralph Bunch* (New York: NYU Press, 2005), 1st ed. Howard University, 1940.

24. Lionel Snaer, one of Samuel's grandsons, became a vice president of Vidalia in 1948.

25. In 1935 Straight merged with New Orleans University, founded by the United Methodists, to become Dillard University, which has remained in existence since that time.

Epilogue: Becoming Black

1. Michele Grisby Coffey, "*The State of Louisiana v. Charles Guerand*: Interracial Sexual Mores, Rape Rhetoric, and Respectability in 1930's New Orleans," *Louisiana History* (Winter 2013), vol. 50, 47–93.

2. "Brief of the Schools and Playgrounds of the Federation of Civic League," Roll 10, Box 12, Folder 32, A. P. Tureaud Papers, The Amistad Research Center, Tulane University, New Orleans.

3. Sharlene Sinegal DeCuir, *Attacking Jim Crow: Black Activism in New Orleans, 1925–1941* (Ph.D. dissertation, Louisiana State University, 2009) 116; "Protect the Bathers at Seabrook," *Louisiana Weekly*, June 9, 1934.

4. DeCuir, *Attacking Jim Crow*, Chapter IV.

5. DeCuir, *Attacking Jim Crow*, Chapter 8. Dejoie published and financed the paper with an investment of $2,000 while Taylor worked as the paper's first editor. Dejoie was not actively involved in the Federation of Civic Leagues. He was a member of the NAACP, but not a board member, and sought to provide objective analysis of the actions of the existing leadership. Dejoie graduated from Southern University at the age of seventeen and then worked in his family's drugstore on the corner of Canal and Liberty Streets. Later he worked for the United States Rail Mail Service. Taylor was born in Tyler, Texas, and migrated to New Orleans in 1913 after graduating from Wiley College and serving in the military. Taylor served as managing editor of the paper until 1927. Peter R. Crutchfield then took over as editor and remained in the position throughout the 1930s. Before serving as editor of the *Weekly*, Crutchfield, who moved to New Orleans from McAlister, Oklahoma, also worked for Unity Life Insurance Company.

6. Rachel Emmanuel and Alexander P. Tureaud Jr., *A More Noble Cause: A. P. Tureaud and the Struggle for Civil Rights in Louisiana* (Baton Rouge: LSU Press, 2011), 54–65.

7. Ibid.

8. Ibid., 51–53.

9. Ibid., 101–109.

10. Leonard H. Moore, *Black Rage in New Orleans: Police Brutality and African American Activism From World War II to Katrina* (Baton Rouge: LSU Press, 2010), 11.

11. Adam Fairclough, in *Race and Democracy: The Civil Rights Struggle in Louisiana, 1915–1972* (Athens: University of Georgia Press, 1995), 152–153, interprets Morrison's building programs for blacks as a way of "shoring up segregation" by defusing dissatisfaction with inferior facilities. Many black leaders found him sympathetic but unwilling to take meaningful action to address their concerns. Morrison's approach to race relations was progressive compared to the past but increasingly

fell behind the times as the civil rights movement of the 1950s and 1960s gained momentum.

12. Moore, *Black Rage* 30–36; Edward F. Haas, *DeLesseps S. Morrison and the Image of Reform* (Baton Rouge: LSU Press, 1974), 77–7813. Katy Reckdahl, "Fifty years later, students recall integrating New Orleans public schools," New Orleans *Times-Picayune* November 13, 2010, http://www.nola.com/politics/index.ssf/2010/11/fifty_years_later_students_rec.html.

14. Barbara A. Worthy, *Blacks in New Orleans from the Great Depression to the Civil Rights Movement, 1930 to 1950* (New Orleans: Southern University at New Orleans, Center for African and African American Studies, 1994), 11. This description was from 1840 but it basically remained the same in New Orleans in the era of Jim Crow and all over the South except for the number of artisans.

15. Emanuel and Tureaud, *A More Noble Cause*, 245.

16. Arnold Hirsch, "Dutch Morial, Old Creole in the New South," Working Paper No. 4, October 1990, Division of Urban Research and Policy Studies College of Urban and Public Affairs, University of New Orleans.

17. Audiotape, Kim Rogers interview of Morial, Amistad Research Center, Tulane University; conversation with Sybil Morial, March 4, 2013.

18. Conversation with Yolanda Snaer, May 6, 2013.

CREDITS

....

Cover Images
[Cover Image 1 / Photo 4.2]: Used by permission of Lawrence Niekamp;
[Cover Image 2 / Photo 6.2]: Used by permission of Arolon Miller

Chapter 3
[Photo 3.1]: Used by permission of Lawrence Niekamp

Chapter 4
[Cover Image / Photo 4.2]: Used by permission of Lawrence Niekamp

Chapter 6
[Photo 6.1]: Used by permission of Arolon Miller; [Cover Image 2 / Photo 6.2]:
Used by permission of Arolon Miller; [Photo 6.3]: Used by permission
of Lawrence Niekamp

Chapter 7
[Photo 7.1]: Used by permission of Denise Snaer-Gauder; [Photo 7.2]: Used
by permission of Denise Snaer-Gauder; [Photo 7.3]: Used by permission
of Lawrence Niekamp; [Photo 7.4]: Used by permission of Lawrence
Niekamp

Chapter 8
[Photo 8.1]: Used by permission of Lawrence Niekamp; [Photo 8.2]: Used
by permission of Lawrence Niekamp; [Photo 8.3]: Used by permission
of Denise Snaer-Gauder; [Photo 8.4]: Used by permission of Denise

Snaer-Gauder; [Photo 8.5]: Used by permission of Denise Snaer-Gauder; [Photo 8.6]: Used by permission of Lawrence Niekamp; [Photo 8.7]: Used by permission of Lawrence Niekamp

Chapter 9

[Photo 9.1]: Photo used by permission of Yvonne Snaer-Smedley; [Photo 9.2]: Photo used by permission of Yvonne Snaer-Smedley; [Photo 9.3]: Used by permission of Arolon Miller; [Photo 9.4]: Photo used by permission of Yvonne Snaer-Smedley; [Photo 9.5]: Photo used by permission of Yvonne Snaer-Smedley; [Photo 9.6]: Used by permission of Arolon Miller; [Photo 9.7]: Used by permission of Arolon Miller; [Photo 9.8]: Used by permission of Arolon Miller; [Photo 9.9]: Photo used by permission of Yvonne Snaer-Smedley; [Photo 9.10]: Used by permission of Arolon Miller; [Photo 9.11]: Used by permission of Arolon Miller; [Photo 9.12]: Used by permission of Arolon Miller; [Photo 9.13]: Used by permission of Arolon Miller; [Photo 9.14]: Used by permission of Arolon Miller

Epilogue

[Photo E.1]: Used by permission of Arolon Miller; [Photo E.2]: Used by permission of Arolon Miller

INDEX

....